Endorsements

Nita's love for the Lord comes through in her beautiful and heartfelt prayers. Reading her petitions to God and praying along with her as you read will enrich and deepen your own personal prayer life. As a daily devotional, her book of prayers will open the door to a more personal and ever-increasing love for our Lord and Savior. God answers prayers and desires to fellowship with us. Nita shows us how in the following pages.

Curt Currie, Captain
United Airlines Chappell Hill, Texas

After serving with Nita for many years now while involved in several ministries and watching her serve and grow, as well as pray and lead women as well as men in an intense setting, I can say that I have so enjoyed Nita's heart and knowledge of God's Word. She is more than capable of taking scriptural principles and applying them to people's lives and thus directing their thought process in their relationship with the Savior. Nita's love for Jesus Christ is so full and close that she is able to touch the heart of God as she prays. A mighty prayer warrior as well as an excellent teacher of the Bible, Nita has shown her expertise in taking verses from the Bible and making them into intelligent, thoughtful, and very spiritual oriented conversations with God. I trust that many will not only read these prayers, but also begin praying them and utilizing them for their own spirituality. As I have witnessed Nita's growth in her walk with God, I can unequivocally say that her prayers accurately display her very person and personality.

Jack Faulkner, Pastor
Greenvine Baptist Church, Burton, Texas

Probably one of the hardest disciplines for Christians is spending extended time before the throne of God, yet it is necessary if we want to get to know God. Through prayer, we learn God's heart not just for ourselves, but for others.

In this book, Nita shares with us the times she has spent before God's throne worshiping and praising Him along with the times she has spent searching and seeking. We pray along with someone who, like all of us, needs those times of baring her soul before the infinite, holy, loving God. You will not find in this book a woman who thinks she has reached the pinnacle of commitment; you will find a woman who is daily trusting God to bring her deeper into fellowship with Him.

This is a book for every Christian who wants to learn to pray and who needs the example of someone who is embarking on a lifetime of prayer. Thank you for sharing these personal moments with us, Nita. I look forward to reading the completed book.

Sandy Montgomery, Retired Teacher
Bellville, Texas

When we are busy with everyday life and challenges, it is easy to forget how much we need to have a personal and close relationship with God. We need time to stop and contemplate the Grace that we receive every day from God through His Love and Mercy, and recognize that He is always with us. Nita opened her heart and shared her deep love of God so I could experience God's presence every day. Reading Nita's daily prayers and reflections gave me that moment to open my heart to God, accept his Grace, and thank Him for everything through Nita's words. I know that this book will do the same for you.

Miguel A. Quinones, Attorney at Law
Spring, Texas

My wife Marty and I have witnessed Nita's love for the Lord for some time now. Her relationship with Him is a lifestyle for her, and it is amazing to see that love relationship work both ways between her and the Lord. Her desire is for everyone she meets to not only know His love for them, but for each one to love the Lord also and for them to develop their own love relationship with Him. This agape love is revealed throughout the pages of this book.

Coy Reese
Volunteer Chaplain (CVCA)
Pastor of Victorious Living Church B-side
Polunsky Prison unit TDCJ
Livingston, Texas

Before His Throne

Before His Throne

365 Days of Inspirational Prayers
to Bring You Closer to
Christ Our Lord

Nita Schnitzer

XULON PRESS

Xulon Press
2301 Lucien Way #415
Maitland, FL 32751
407.339.4217
www.xulonpress.com

© 2019 by Nita Schnitzer

Edited by Xulon Press

All rights reserved solely by the author. The author guarantees all contents are original and do not infringe upon the legal rights of any other person or work. No part of this book may be reproduced in any form without the permission of the author. The views expressed in this book are not necessarily those of the publisher.

249 scriptures were taken from the Messianic Jewish Family Tree of Life (TLV) Translation of the Bible. Copyright © 2015 by The Messianic Jewish Family Bible Society.

116 Scripture quotations taken from the World Messianic Bible (WMB) – public domain.

Printed in the United States of America.

ISBN-13: 978-1-5456-7537-3

Dedication

This book is dedicated to my parents James and Bobbie, my children Stephen and Krystal along with my grandchildren Domanic and Brielle. Thank you for supporting me and believing in me, as I share the message of the love of Christ.

Introduction

Over the past thirty-four years, my walk with Christ has not been as consistent as it should have been. There were times when I could wake to feel His presence to times when I wondered where He was.

In 2008, I attended a three-day renewal weekend. Since that time, my walk began to strengthen day by day. I then started watching Rabbi Schneider with Discovering the Jewish Jesus on TV. He did a teaching on the Shulamite Bride out of the book; Songs of Songs. This teaching made me fall in love with the Jewish side of Jesus. This is why I found the (TLV) Bible and the Hebrew language so incredibly beautiful. For me, it creates a feeling of closeness. A more intimate relationship between Him and me as I speak the words He would have spoken as He walked upon this earth.

I love journaling my prayers, and I spend time each morning before the Lord. A sweet sister in the Lord would send out verses on instant messaging to our Bible study group. God spoke to me to start sending out my prayers in the same way. It started just with this group and ended up being a ministry of its own. Eventually I was sending them out to over 250 people a day. I compiled some of these prayers to create this book.

My prayer is that each day as you read a prayer for it to bring you into a closer walk with Him. For them to inspire you and ignite a prayer life, a conversation with the One true God. Who loves you enough to collect all your tears, put them in a bottle and record each one, spoken of in Psalms 56:8.

Yes, He is a God who will judge us for all of our transgressions, but He is also so in love with you that He cares for every need, every detail of your life. How amazing and awesome is the mighty God, Yeshua, Christ our Lord.

May God, bless you on your journey. And if you find yourself in the desert, may His living water quench your thirst. May Adonai's face shine on you, be gracious to you and give you peace. Shalom!

Hebrew Words and Definitions

- *Abba*—Hebrew for Father
- *Adonai*—Hebrew for Lord and Master
- *Adonai Elohei Tzva'ot*—Hebrew for the Lord God of hosts
- *Adonai Elohim*—Hebrew for The Lord God
- *Adonai Nissi (Jehovah Nissi)* Hebrew for the Lord our banner
- *Adonai Tzva'ot*—Hebrew for Lord of hosts
- *Adonai Yireh (Jehovah Jireh)*—Hebrew for the Lord my provider
- *Baruch ha-ba b'shem*—Hebrew for blessed is He who comes in the name
- *Belial*—Hebrew for Satan
- *Ben-Elohim*—Hebrew for Son of God
- *Bnei Yisarel*—Hebrew for the children of Israel
- *Bracha*—Hebrew for blessings
- *Chazak*—Hebrew for be strong
- *Cheruvim*—Hebrew for glory beings
- *El malei Rachamim*—Hebrew for All merciful God
- *El Olam*—Hebrew for the everlasting God
- *Eloi Eloi*—Hebrew for my God, my God
- *El Roi*—Hebrew for the God who sees me
- *Elohim*—Hebrew for the all-powerful God
- *Elohim Yachal*—Hebrew for God of hope
- *Elyon*—Hebrew for God most High
- *Emunah*—Hebrew for faith
- *Halleluyah*—Hebrew for hallelujah
- *Hanukkah*—Hebrew for Feast of Dedication
- *Hey*—Hebrew for divine breath
- *Hineni*—Hebrew for "Here I am," to answer a call
- *Hoshia*-na—Hebrew meaning deliver us, or please save
- *Jehovah Jireh*—Hebrew for God our provider

- *Jehovah Nissi*—Hebrew for God our banner
- *Jehovah M'Kaddesh*—Hebrew for the Lord who sanctifies
- *Jehovah Machseh*—Hebrew for God my refuge
- *Jehovah Rapha*—Hebrew for the God who heals
- *Jehovah Rohi*—Hebrew for God my Shepherd
- *Jehovah Shammah*—Hebrew for the God who is there
- *Kedoshim*—Hebrew for brother and/or sister in Christ
- *Mashiach*—Hebrew for Messiah or Anointed One
- *Matzot/matzah*—Hebrew for unleavened bread
- *Mikveh*—Hebrew for a pool/bath used for ritual immersion
- *Mitzvot*—Hebrew for commandments
- *Moadim*—Hebrew for appointed time
- *Parokhet*—Hebrew for the" Veil" or curtain that separates the Holy place from the Holy of Holies
- *Rhema*—Hebrew for utterance or thing said
- *Ruach*—Hebrew for Spirit or breath
- *Ruach ha Kodesh*—Hebrew for Holy Spirit
- *Shabbat*—Hebrew for Sabbath/rest
- *Shaddai*—Hebrew for All Sufficient One
- *Shalom*—Hebrew for peace
- *Shavout*—Hebrew for Pentecost or 50 days
- *Shekinah*—Hebrew for settling of His divine presence
- *Sheol*—Hebrew for Hell
- *Tizrah*—Hebrew for she is my delight
- *Yahweh*—Hebrew for the great "I AM"
- *Yeshua*—Hebrew for Jesus
- *Yeshua ha Mashiach*—Hebrew for Jesus the Messiah
- *Yochanan*—Hebrew for John
- *Yom Shabbat*—Hebrew for the day of the Sabbath

January 1

All Things New

Behold, I will do a new thing. It springs out now. Don't you know it? I will even make a way in the wilderness, and rivers in the desert. The animals of the field, the jackals and the ostriches, shall honor me, because I give water in the wilderness and rivers in the desert, to give drink to my people, my chosen, the people which I formed for myself that they might declare my praise. — Isaiah 43:19-21 WMB

Abba, You make all things new every day; a new sunrise, a new breeze, new flowers in the fields. A new day of snow that glistens in the trees.

You make all things beautiful every day. I praise You, Lord, for the opportunities of making my life new in You this new year.

Take me on a journey. One I have not been on with You. Open up my eyes to new beginnings, of new, amazing ways of serving You.

Protect me in the wilderness. Bring me to the living water when I thirst. Remove the chains I have bound myself in because I can do all things in You.

For You are my rock and my salvation, the only one that I hope in. Give me today everything I need to sustain me. But most of all, let me feel Your peace, Your presence all the day through.

In *Yeshua's* name I pray. Amen.

January 2

You Have Searched Me

For You have created my conscience. You knit me together in my mother's womb. I praise You, for I am awesomely, wonderfully made! Wonderful are Your works—and my soul knows that very well. My frame was not hidden from You when I was made in the secret place, when I was woven together in the depths of the earth. Your eyes saw me when I was unformed, and in Your book were written the days that were formed—when not one of them had come to be. How precious are Your thoughts, O God! How great is the sum of them!
Psalms 139:13–17 TLV

You, my Lord, are more marvelous than words can say. You are more precious than all the gems in the world. You hold more knowledge than all of mankind put together.

For You are God, Creator of all things. Holy and Majestic is Your name. The angels bow down before You. The demons flee from You. Yet You have called me by name. You formed me to love You, to honor You and to please You. Continue to shape me, my Lord, in Your likeness.

I offer myself to You this day. May I be pleasing in Your sight.

In *Yeshua's* name I pray. Amen.

January 3

Believe And Not Doubt

But if any of you lacks wisdom, let him ask of God, who gives to all without hesitation and without reproach; and it will be given to him. But let him ask in faith, without any doubting—for the one who doubts is like a wave of the sea, blown and tossed by the wind.
James 1:5–6 TLV

Good morning, my Lord, be with me today and don't let me go. Forgive me of my sins and lead me in the way of righteousness. Help me to live my life as a bond servant to You. May I live my life blessing those who You put in my path.

Lord, King Solomon asked You for wisdom to lead Your people. You were pleased with his prayer and granted him more than he asked.

My King, I'm asking for wisdom, to lead my family, to lead those I work with and to lead Your people. I need direction, a clear understanding of Your will in everything. To be able to retain everything I am learning. That I don't fail You or those who are depending on me.

Increase my faith, *Adonai*. Not in the fact that You love me. For this, I truly do know. But increase my faith, that in my service You are right beside me, by giving me strength and wisdom. But may my heart always stay humble. For anything You give, You can take away if not used with the right heart and for the right purpose.

Let my whole heart be dedicated only to You. Be my husband, and I Your bride! Kiss me as the sun rises and hold me as the sun sets. Tell me, my King, of all Your wonders and majesty! Tell me of Your love for me!

In *Yeshua's* Holy name I pray. Amen.

January 4

Resist Satan

Stay alert! Watch out! Your adversary the devil prowls around like a roaring lion, searching for someone to devour. Stand up against him, firm in your faith, knowing that the same kinds of suffering are being laid upon your brothers and sisters throughout the world.
1 Peter 5:8–9 TLV

Adonai, just when I think I have trouble, I find someone who is having a much harder time in their life. So will You help us to share in our burdens. To lift each other up so we do not face them alone.

My Lord, I praise You that I am never alone. For the only ones who are truly alone, are those who are not saved. So help me to share my faith. That they find You and are never alone again!

Let this day be one where we look to save the lost, that we give food to the hungry and clothes to the poor. Let us get outside of ourselves and walk away from those wonderful pity parties we have designed, that others don't want to attend anyway.

May we to stand arm in arm, not letting our family or friends pass through into the darkness, where Satan would like to lead us all, so we fall into the pit of despair. But help our lives be such that others can't help but take notice and follow. Let us show Your *shekinah* glory to all who look our way!

I thank You, because with You all things are possible. And I know with You, I will make it to the other side, stronger and with such joy that nothing can take it from me.

For this is my prayer and I lay it at the feet of *Yeshua*. Amen.

January 5

Walk By The Spirit

*But I say, walk by the **Ruach**, and you will not carry out the desires of the flesh. For the flesh sets its desire against the **Ruach**, but the **Ruach** sets its desire against the flesh—for these are in opposition to one another, so that you cannot do what you want. But if you are led by the **Ruach**, you are not under law.*   *Ephesians 5:16–18 TLV*

My Lord, this is where the rubber meets the road. Do they still love themselves more than You, living a life of selfish desires? Or have they surrendered it all so that they can find You even in the stillness of the day.

Abba, take me up the mountain. Let it just be You and me, alone to commune. May You tell me of Your love for me. May You share with me Your heart.

Let me stand on top of this mountain, my King, and see all the beauty Thy hands have made. Let me see Your strength and your wounds. For You have given it all for me. Let me in turn give it all back to You!

This is my desire, not my flesh, not the things of this world. But I desire Your love and to feel Your breath upon my face.

For You are my King, my Lord, my Savior, my Redeemer. May I be Your child, Your servant, Your truth bearer, Your friend. May I be the one You look for, my King. For I need You to hold me right now and through the end of all time.

In *Yeshua's* name I pray. Amen.

January 6

Spirit Of Wisdom

*That the God of our Lord **Yeshua** the Messiah, the Father of glory, may give to you a spirit of wisdom and revelation in the knowledge of Him.*
Ephesians 1:17 WMB

Abba, I pray that each person who hears this prayer is given the *Ruach* of wisdom and revelation to know You more.

Increase in them their gifts that they are prominent in their lives. Increase their understanding of Your word so that they are able to share with others in ways they could not before. Increase in them the desire to serve You, honor You and glorify Your name.

I know *Abba,* that even the scholars who know much about Your character, Your word, Your truths, have only touched the tip of the iceberg of what will be revealed to us when we go home to You. Our minds have not developed enough to conceive the majesty of Your presence or the wonders of Your glory.

I can't wait to see You in all Your glory. To stand in awe of Your majesty, my King. For You are my Father, the Lover of my soul, every good thing and more that I could ever hope in or dream. It is to You alone I give everything.

To You, Christ my King! Amen.

January 7

Being Perfect

Therefore you shall be perfect, just as your Father in heaven is perfect.
Matthew 5:48 WMB

Abba, as I read this verse this morning, all I could think of is: how it is so far outside the realm of my ability to be perfect. But yet You call us to be.

Oh, my Lord, I can strive to do what I believe is right according to Your word, and I fail daily. For when I have had one family member that I have tried to help, another seems to get mad. I have given to others where it hurts, and they want even more.

But I do know that this walk is not easy, and I will never be perfect. For if I was even remotely close, I would think I could handle things on my own, which would be the biggest fault of all.

I thank You, my Lord, for Your gift of grace. For Your sacrifice of love that covers me. But do help me in my walk to have a clearer perspective of others. For to me, understanding the human heart is very hard—the selfishness, the greed, the hate. Help me find a way in Your perfection to remove any of this from me. And to show those around me Your perfect will in all situations.

I am stuck, my Lord. For I cannot do this without You. Fill me to the brim with Your *Rauch,* may He alone work in me and through me for all to see so that You, my King, will receive all the glory, honor, and praise!

In *Yeshua's* name I pray. Amen.

January 8

Nourish Me

Abide in Me, and I will abide in you. The branch cannot itself produce fruit, unless it abides on the vine. Likewise, you cannot produce fruit unless you abide in Me.   *John 15:4 TLV*

Abba, I need You this morning to replenish my soul. Fill me up with all the goodness of You. Nourish my roots that I do not wither and die. But allow me to grow ever strong in You!

My Lord, You have asked that I bear fruit, but in order for my fruit to be ripe and ready for others to partake. For it to be full of nourishment, so it provides health to those in need. I must partake of the living water to grow stronger every day.

So, my King, nourish me. Help me to give of myself to others. But Lord, when a drought comes, or all my fruit has been picked and my branches are bare, I will cry out to You to nourish me again, so I can be fruitful and give of myself once again.

Help me this day. Let me drink from Your cup. Let me grow big and strong so I can give all of myself to helping others grow and in glorifying Your name.

In *Yeshua's* name I pray. Amen.

JANUARY 9

Physical Battle

For our struggle is not against flesh and blood, but against the rulers, against the powers, against the worldly forces of this darkness, and against the spiritual forces of wickedness in the heavenly places.
Ephesians 6:12 TLV

Good morning, my *Adonai*. I love You so much! But it seems as if I am wrestling a lot with spiritual darkness. They seem to be coming in a swarm and are not letting go. Like Jacob wrestling with an angel. I, too, feel like it is a physical battle, and I am getting tired!

But there You are, my Lord, the King who sits on the throne most high, and who loves me and watches over me. Coach me, my Lord, that I can put them in a choke hold and bring them to their knees. Let them beg for mercy that my enemy is freed from them so they can see a light in this darkness and see You sitting there.

Lord, I pray salvation over my enemies. That they will have soft hearts, full of love and grace. Let the choices they make be based on Your word. Let their hearts be mended and devoted to no one but You.

I ask for covering over myself. That any wound I receive during this battle be one that can be mended. May any scar that remains be a good reminder that Your love never fails!

I give it all to You this day. May I be strong and courageous, ready to conquer any and all battles. For I have the greatest coach on my side.

It is in *Yeshua's* name I pray. Amen.

January 10

Give

Give, and it will be given to you—a good measure, pressed down, shaken together, running over, will be given to you. For with the same measure you measure it will be measured back to you.   Luke 6:38 WMB

Abba, many think that if we give money, time, or treasures, we will receive this in abundance back to us here on this earth. And yes, this can happen, but it does not always. It is about receiving Your love in abundance here on this earth and in the life to come. For the blessing in giving is not in the receiving, but of the joy in the face of the one you give it to. For when their face lights up, so does Christ's. Isn't that the greatest gift we could receive?

I know Lord, I have not always given as I should have. Other times I have given to where it hurts. But I get great joy out of watching those who are receiving. My prayer is that I am able to give that joy to You and someone else this day.

Please give me this opportunity, *Adonai,* even in the small things. Let my eyes, ears, and heart be open to others and to Your small voice.

For it is In *Yeshua's* name I pray. Amen.

January 11

Love Your Enemies

*But love your enemies, and do good, and lend, expecting nothing in return. Then your reward will be great and you will be sons of **Elyon**, for He is kind to the ungrateful and evil ones. Be compassionate, just as your Father is compassionate to you.*   Luke 6:35–36 TLV

Elyon, this verse has been such an influence on me. Because how bitter I would be if I did not believe in Your mercy, for I have given, and rarely have they given back. But when I give to someone, I am giving it actually to You in my heart. Then I sit and wait because I know that You will give back to me tenfold. And whether You give me anything in return does not really matter because You have given me eternal life. Something I don't deserve and something I could never repay.

Help me, *Adonai,* to always be grateful that I have the ability to give, that I have the spirit of wisdom and love. That You have taught me not to return evil for evil. But to be the likeness of You. And it is only through the power and indwelling of Your *Ruach* that I am able to do this.

I pray, my Lord, that Your mercy and grace is abundant for me, that I can give it freely. That Your name is glorified through me this day.

It is in the Holy name of *Yeshua* I pray. Amen.

JANUARY 12

Shadow Of Your Wings

*He who dwells in the shelter of **Elyon**, will abide in the shadow of **Shaddai**.* *Psalms 91:1 TLV*

Abba, take me to this secret place. Let me abide under the shadow of Your wings. Let me hear every word spoken through Your lips. Let me see Your splendor, my King!

Abba, I want to be so close to You that I can hear Your heart beat. I want to feel the warmth of Your hand in mine. I want to smell of this place that You live in. I want to sing with Your angels that are so divine.

Abba, please lead me this day into righteousness. Let me mend any of my broken ways. Help me mend any hurts that I have caused. Let Your will be what is seen and heard in me this day.

Let Your glory reign in all I do, my King. Let my enemy run in fear. Because what he sees is not that weak young child anymore, but a bride dressed in armor, complete in Your gear.

For I am Yours, my Lord, and You can do with me as You please. But keep me in Your protection. Keep me in the shadow of Your wings.

In *Yeshua's* name I pray. Amen.

January 13

Walk In Your Presence

*Sing praises to **Adonai**, who dwells in Zion. Declare His deeds among the peoples.*   *Psalms 9:11 TLV*

Adonai, You have given me a task of plenty! One that I pray will teach me how to handle life's circumstances with grace, how to show humility, agape love, wisdom, and discernment in my walk. One that I pray will lead me so close to You that I can feel Your breath upon my face.

Allow me to walk in Your presence so closely that others can read Your word upon my skin. Allow me to think upon all the good that You have provided. For even when times are hard, in all Your wonders You make all things new each day.

I praise You, my *Adonai,* for this day. I praise You for my family, their health and their goodness. I praise You, Lord for the hard times, because I grow stronger in them. I praise You for the good times, because in this, I can share the feast and the harvest. I praise You for Your word, because it teaches me how to live. I praise You for Your peace because it sustains me. I praise You for Your love, for it is life to me. For I shall sing praises to You always. For in everything, I am able to find You!

Adonai, may You cover those who are hurting today with peace. May You shelter them in Your wings. May they, even in their troubles, find within them all the reasons they should praise.

I love You with all that I am. It is to You alone I sing. Amen.

JANUARY 14

Take Up His Cross

Then He called the crowd, along with His disciples, and said to them, "If anyone wants to follow after Me, he must deny himself, take up his cross, and keep following Me. For whoever wants to save his life will lose it, but whoever loses his life for My sake and the sake of the Good News will save it."
Mark 8:34–35 TLV

Abba, please quench my heart today if I seek the pleasures of the flesh over the pleasure of Your word. Do not let me fail You in my anger and frustration. Do not let me gaze upon the things of this world and hunger for it.

For my place is at the feet of *Yeshua,* bathing them, praising Him. Giving unto Him all of my heart. My future is in the heavenly realms, singing of Your honor and glory.

I give You everything, my Lord. I beseech You for all of my desires. I don't want to make a decision unless I know You are in it. For I only want to please the Husband of my soul.

Take me in Your arms and put Your ring upon my hand. Let me seek to win Your love from now until the end of all times.

It is in *Yeshua's* name I pray. Amen.

January 15

If a man says, "I love God," and hates his brother, he is a liar; for he who doesn't love his brother whom he has seen, how can he love God whom he has not seen? **1 Yochanan** (John) 4:20 WMB

Oh, my Lord, how I struggle loving certain people. There are those who deliberately hurt others; some who need attention and will do anything for it. Some who don't care who they hurt as long as they get what they want in the end.

This is hard for me, my Lord! I am going to need Your strength in this. May Your grace flow through me that they may meet Christ and turn from these ways. May your grace speak through me as honey so they hear Your voice not mine. May Your grace flow through my actions as a river whose banks are overflowing in a flood. So they cannot stand in the current of sin, but are washed in blood of the Lamb.

Abba, may I be a vessel, a pot of clay, molded and shaped by You, filled with oil to be poured out on others. That by the end of my life, I may be empty, chipped and cracked, because I have poured out all I have on serving You. May the memory of my life be Your light shining through those cracks and of receiving the last drops of oil. So their lamp could stay lit as they wait for Your return.

I praise You, my Lord, for on the day I see Your face, You will take this old, broken pot and mend it and decorate it with brilliant jewels. So then I can then serve You in Your kingdom throughout eternity.

Oh, how I praise You. Oh, how I love You. Help this broken vessel love, because You love through me, now and forever more. Amen and amen.

January 16

Relying On You

We are therefore ambassadors on behalf of Messiah, as though God were entreating by us: we beg you on behalf of Messiah, be reconciled to God. For him who knew no sin he made to be sin he made to be sin on our behalf; so that in him we might become the righteousness of God.
2 Corinthians 5:20–21 WMB

How beautiful You are, my Lord. Your love consumes my soul. You have poured out blessings upon blessings upon me this season. For I have a home, food, health, and a family who loves me. But even if I was a beggar on the street, cold, hungry, and all alone, I would be blessed beyond words because You love me. You watch over me and hear my prayers.

Abba, may I rely on You daily, for what is seen is temporary, but what is unseen is forever. My life is just a speck of time. It is here one day and gone the next. But what I have done in that lifetime will be eternal.

For you will ask, "who have you brought with you to my kingdom?" My Lord, what shall I say? Have I been selfish and looked at only my life and the fulfillment of my pleasures? Or will I say, *Adonai* I gave and I have prayed and behold many have come with me. For I planted the seeds of Your love and others came behind me and watered them. May we enter into Your kingdom and serve You forever?

Abba, I pray for my family, my friends, the people who I work with, the families that I serve. I pray for my church and all who attend. Lord may we enter into Your kingdom. May we enter into Your courts of praise. May we see You sitting upon Your sapphire throne of grace. May we cry out with the elders: "Holy, Holy is the Lamb of God, for He alone is worthy of all praise!" Amen and amen.

January 17

One Path

Yeshua said to him, "I am the way, the truth, and the life! No one comes to the Father except through Me."   John 14:6 TLV

My Lord, My God, how beautiful You are to me. You hold me during the night and kiss me in the morning. Your love exceeds far more than rubies and gold. Far more than what man can understand.

There are so many churches teaching that there are many paths to You. That Your word can be picked apart to fit their lifestyle. That all we have to do is pray for something. No matter what, like a vending machine, You will give it to us.

Abba, their hearts are cold to their own desires. They enjoy the teachings that tickles the ear. They have no concept of the love of the Father. Why and what you choose to give and or withhold.

I pray for those lost souls, my Lord. For they seem to be the hardest to reach. Open the door of their hearts that they might come to truly know You. To see Your power and glory. But to know that You are a righteous God. And all will be judged according to Your word. For we must follow Your commands, for there is only one way. That way is through the blood of *Yeshua ha Mashiach.*

I pray for covering over my family and friends and their families. I pray for my work and all who enter in its door. May we all serve You and honor You. May we praise You for all the glory is Yours.

In *Yeshua's* name I pray. Amen.

January 18

Your Perfect Peace

*And the **shalom** of God, which surpasses all understanding, will guard your hearts and your minds in Messiah **Yeshua**.*
Philippians 4:7 TLV

Yeshua, You said Your *shalom,* Your peace You give to us. May we receive this peace and Your love this day. May we give this peace and love to all around us.

No matter what war, what illness, what hardship we are in or see, You are there fighting these battles for us. Your angels go before us making a way for us to serve You. To go into a deeper walk with You.

Abba, give us visions and dreams of things to come and Your desire for us. Let them be so powerful we cannot deny they are from You.

Abba, I thank You for Your peace, for Your protection and for the wisdom that only comes from You. May we put on the full armor of God and stand with the angels to war against the evil one. May he tremble in fear because the saints have grown in strength, in wisdom, and in number. May he flee and hide because he knows he cannot stand. For the battle has already been won!

May Your mark of the covenant rest on me and my household. May all who enter through the door post of my home be blessed because Your word covers them. To You, my Lord, I give my life. May I be submissive to You and worship You, my King, forever.

I ask all these things in Your Holy name. Amen.

January 19

Eyes Focused

*What you have learned and received and heard and seen in me—put these things into practice, and the God of **Shalom** will be with you.*
Philippians 4:9 TLV

Abba, I see how easily I can stray. How evil can sneak in through my weakness. How Your peace is immediately removed from me. Oh, my Lord, how I praise You. That You so quickly convict my heart. That You respond to me in a way that lets me know I am facing the wrong direction. This, my King, keeps my eyes focused on You and keeps me on the right path.

How blessed I am that I know Your peace and recognize its absence so quickly. How blessed I am that You love me this much!

May I seek You in the sanctuary. May I follow all your commands. May I study Your word. May I live each day to the glory of my God, my King. And may Your *shalom,* that passes all understanding, envelope and guide me this day.

I love you with all my heart, my Lord.

It is in Your majestic name that I pray. Amen and amen.

January 20

Merciful

*But love your enemies, and do good, and lend, expecting nothing in return. Then your reward will be great and you will be sons of **Elyon**, for He is kind to the ungrateful and evil ones. Be compassionate, just your Father is compassionate to you.*   Luke 6:35–36 TLV

Abba, You are a merciful God. The fact that You allow this country to stand is mercy unto itself. For this country is full of sin, looking more and more like Sodom every day. But Praise be unto You, O Lord. For You are not done with us yet! You are giving us a chance to spread the gospel, to show others Your love and mercy. So as many as possible can be saved.

God, let me not fail You in this. For I know I have many shortcomings. But You love me anyway. May the moment I get irritated with someone, the moment someone hurts me, may I stop and pray. Then I can see how You want me to love them. How I am to show mercy unto them. May I not fail in this, my Lord. Strengthen me, give me insight and wisdom. May I be hands of compassion and love for You, my *El malei Rachamim.*

Help me to forgive those who have hurt me, my Lord, for I will be forgiven in the manner in which I forgive others. Cover me with Your blood *Yeshua.* For I can only be saved by You. Let me share this gift, of Your mercy today with each person I meet. For You alone are God! You alone are worthy of all praise

May I and all my household be saved. May we worship You in Your kingdom forever and ever. Amen and Amen.

January 21

Testify Of You

*We know that we abide in Him and He in us by this—because He has given us of His Spirit. We have seen and testify that the Father has sent His Son as Savior of the world. If any acknowledges that Yeshua is **Ben-Elohim**, God abides in him and he abides in God.*
1 John 4:13–16 TLV

Abba, may we all stand at the judgement seat and testify of Your love. May we say that during our trials and troubles, during our times of temptation we cried out to You for mercy and grace. That Your blood has covered us and has set us free, for there is no god but our God, who lives and reigns forever and ever.

Abba, we know that Your time is at hand. But there is still much work to be done. May You find us in the streets of the poor. May You find us at the robber's house. May we be proclaiming Your love and of the sacrifice You made for all. For You are *Ben Elohim,* the Son of the Living God. Who gave His life to set the captives free!

Abba, I thank You for the breath of life today. May I use each breath to worship You, my King. May Your face shine upon me, Lord, and bless me. Build me up and make me strong in You. Give me a heart like Yours, my Lord. For this is my prayer.

For it is You, my Lord, whom I serve. It is You, my King, I worship. Please hear my cries and answer my prayer.

In *Yeshua's* name I pray. Amen.

January 22

Being Holy

*But sexual immorality and any impurity or greed—don't even let these be mentioned among you, as is proper for **kedoshim**. Obscene, coarse and stupid talk are also out of place, but instead let there be thanksgiving.*
Ephesians 5:3–4 TLV

Abba, how Your people have come to a place where sin is common place, where we are so numb to it, because it is a way of life. Convict us, O Lord; let not our hearts displease You. Let us be the salt and the light of the world. Let us be as John the Baptist, professing your word, Your ways to all we meet. Let us be so different than those who do not know You, that they can't help but take notice, so that their curiosity must find out why.

This is Your desire for us, O Lord. Fill us with your *Ruach ha Kodesh* to give us strength. Fill our minds with knowledge. Fill our eyes with love and our hands with mercy. Let us each and every day be deliberate in our actions as a witness. For our actions speak louder than words to others, even those we do not know are watching.

I pray, my Lord, for Your people. I pray for covering and protection of our households. I pray that anytime we are caught in a situation where sin is at hand, Your *Ruach* envelopes us, convicts us and gives us a way to witness rather than sin. I pray Lord that Your people stand united together proclaiming Your coming until the end.

How I thank You for my life and the lives for Your anointed ones. May we stand in the streets, on the rooftops and worship You forevermore. Amen.

JANUARY 23

Take The Wheel

*But I say, walk by the **Ruach**, and you will not carry out the desires of the flesh. For the flesh sets its desire against the **Ruach**, but the **Ruach** sets its desire against the flesh—for these are in opposition to one another, so that you cannot do what you want.*
Galatians 5:16–17 TLV

Abba, I am not nearly as strong as I want to be. I have desires of the flesh that hang over me. I rejoice when I am victorious over them and it tears my heart apart when I fail.

I want You to take complete control of the wheel. Take me to a place of restoration where we walk hand in hand; to a deeper more intimate walk with You.

May I rejoice when temptation comes, because I know You are there giving me Your hand to guide me away. May I rejoice when trials come, because this is the building of my faith. May I rejoice always because my eyes are fixed on You and You have already won the battle.

For You will bind Satan and his demons in hell for eternity. You will reign on Your throne forever. You spoke the world into existence and You chose to allow me the privilege of life and salvation that I may worship You forever.

What a mighty King I serve. May I show You this day and every day, just how much I love You! I thank You for hearing my prayer. I praise You for loving me!

In *Yeshua's* name I pray. Amen.

January 24

Making A Way

My children, I am writing these things to you so that you will not sin. But if anyone does sin, we have an Intercessor with the Father-the righteous Messiah **Yeshua***. He is the atonement for our sins, and not only for our sins but also for the whole world.*   *1 John 2:1–2 TLV*

How I praise You, my *Adonai,* maker of the universe. For You alone are Holy. You alone are worthy of all praise. No matter how hard I try, I fail You daily. Thank You for making a way for me. For when You knitted me in my mother's womb, You knew my faults, You knew my frailties. So this is why You came, that I might have eternal life. For I am lost both in this life and the next without You.

Protect all the ones on the roads today. Bring them home safe to their families. Protect the animals as they search for shelter. Keep the homeless warm and heal those who are sick.

I praise You, *Abba,* for this day and the wonders of Your love. Amen.

January 25

Diamond

Nevertheless, I am continually with you. You have held my right hand. You will guide me with your counsel, and afterward receive me to glory.
Psalms 73:23–24 WMB

Abba, how I praise You for Your faithfulness. How I treasure Your love. For You are like the brightest diamond, glistening on the top of a mountain. Showing me the way out of my troubles, as You wait for me there.

You are as gentle as a dove. Never forcing me, yet guiding me to a better life and a deeper walk with You.

Your words are a melody to my ears. Whispering the most beautiful love song I have ever heard.

How rich am I, my Lord, that You love me. How much more grandeur it will be when You take me home.

May I take each moment of my day and reflect on this love. May I give this agape love to those I know. For it is You, my Lord, who lives in me. May You, my Lord, flow through me to everyone I meet.

I thank You for this life and the people You have put in it. Bless us, cover us and lead us by Your hands until we go to paradise with you forever.

I praise You, my *Adonai,* and I ask all these things in Your Holy name. Amen.

January 26

My Soul Desires Thee

With my soul I have desired you in the night. Yes, with my spirit within me I will seek you earnestly; for when your judgments are in the earth, the inhabitants of the world learn righteousness.   Isaiah 26:9 WMB

O Lord, how I want You to inhabit this place. I want to be where Your presence is so strong, that I fall on my knees to worship You. I want to hear the elders saying Holy, Holy, Holy. I want to hear the angels' wings, singing praises to Your name.

To see the streets of gold shall be breathtaking. To see all the works of Your hands will be more than I could ever dream of. But to share in Your love.... To sit at the wedding supper of the lamb.... My Lord, I can't fathom how I will feel; the glory of it all, the honor of Your presence. And to know I, of all people, have a formal invitation written by Your mighty hand.

Adonai, as You prepare for Your bride to come home, may I prepare myself with jewels and splendor. May I put on Your righteousness today and be radiant in Your love. Then may You look down from heaven at me and be pleased with what You see. This is my desire, my King. May You always smile with gladness when You look upon me.

For it is in *Yeshua's* Holy name I pray. Amen.

JANUARY 27

Overwhelmed With Love

Turn your eyes away from me, for they overwhelm me! Your hair is like a flock of ewe goats descending down from Gilead.
Song of Songs 6:5 TLV

Abba, may I overwhelm You with my love each day. The way the Shulamite bride overwhelmed King Solomon. For I am blessed above all, for I am Yours and You are mine. That I can wake each day and ask, what can I do to please You? What can I do to make You smile?

May I spend every waking moment studying You and understanding Your desires. For You call me beautiful and lovely and I never want these words to leave Your mouth or Your heart.

My desire is that our love can grow deeper every day. That You will seek me out and find that I am at my Father's house. That I have favor in You. That one day You will say, "Arise, my darling, and come along." For You will show me that our love can be even deeper and stronger than it is today.

Let me be yielded to You and give up anything that is a barrier between us. Let me climb over any mountain, throw away any rock that is in my way as I cling to Your hand.

For in Your arms, in that place my soul craves to be. I will walk through this journey, we call life, seeking Your love each day.

In *Yeshua's* name I pray. Amen.

January 28

Committed

Whenever I sit down or stand up, You know it. You discern my thinking from afar. You observe my journeying and my resting and You are familiar with all my ways. Even before a word is on my tongue, behold, **Adonai**, *You know all about it.*   Psalms 139: 2–4 TLV

Abba, no one could ever know me the way that You do. No one could ever love me like You. How could I not give You all I am. How could I ever not follow Your commands? Yet still Lord, I fall into fleshly desires and selfish ways daily. Even so, You, my Lord, my King, come to rescue me.

Oh, my King, all I want is Your love. May I be so committed to You that I do not look into another's eyes. May I be so committed to You that others see the courtship between us. May they help me prepare for the day of our wedding. For on that day, I will be Your bride and understand the true meaning of love.

Cover me in Your righteousness. Make my gown as white as snow. May I take on a new name and receive the gift of salvations. For it is only You, Christ Jesus, that can deliver me from sin. It is only by Your grace I am saved.

Abba, cover the firefighters and police officers who have to work today in the cold wet weather, for they are here to protect us. May You wrap Your wings around them and keep them safe and warm. May You work in and through their lives as earthly angels. May blessings fall upon them for their sacrificial work they do daily.

I pray to You, my Lord, and all request I lay at Your feet. Amen.

January 29

Who Can Be Against Me

*Therefore I, a prisoner for the Lord, urge you to walk in a manner worthy of the calling to which you were called—with complete humility and gentleness, with patience, putting up with one another in love, making every effort to keep the unity of the **Ruach** in the bond of **Shalom**.*
Ephesians 4:1–3 TLV

Abba, You are the one I love. So if this is what pleases You, this is what I want to do. For in my ugliest moments, You offer grace. In moments when I thought I did something wonderful and started to boast, You showed me mercy. It is not easy to put away all selfish desires, but it is easy to love You. So how could I not want to please my Lord when He gives so freely to His bride?

Every day that goes by, it is one day closer to Your return. This means that Satan is on the prowl trying to devour everyone before he is bound forever. So may I study Your word so I cannot be deceived. May I pray, so I can stay strong in the *Ruach*. May I stay in unity with others, for where two or more are gathered, You are with them. May I stand guard over my home and my family and fight the evil that lurks outside. Keep me strong and courageous in this fight, my Lord, for he looks for a weakness to enable him to sneak in. But You, my Lord, are greater! You, my Lord, are King! If you are with me, who can be against me?

I praise You, Lord, for Your gentleness and kindness. I praise You, Lord, for Your power and strength. I praise You, Lord, for Your mercy and grace. I praise You most for loving someone like me! Hold me and mold me today into the image You want me to be.

I ask all these things in Your Holy name. Amen and amen!

JANUARY 30

Outpouring

*He is not afraid of bad news—his heart is steadfast, trusting in **Adonai.***
Psalms 112:7 TLV

Abba, how good You are to me! For You, my God hold my heart in Your hands. Whatever may come my way, You are there, teaching me, guiding me, and sometimes just holding me. How I need You this day. For I feel anxious about things happening all around. May I give these thoughts to You. May I be as Esther, my Lord, for things are not going according to my plans. May I fast and pray and may the outcome far exceed anything I could imagine. Because it is Your glory I seek and not my own.

Abba, I am desperate for Your outpouring of the *Ruach ha Kodesh.* For Your waterfall of grace to be poured out on this dry and thirsty land. There are so many souls that need to be saved! There are so many who do evil. For their hearts are cold and they work only for their own selfish desires. Father I beg You, that they turn and seek Your face. That they have come to have a heart like Yours.

I pray to Thee, my Lord. For You are amazing, ever giving, always loving and always covering and I am desperate and hungry for Your *Ruach* to be upon me. Change me, O Lord, that I may be changed. Save me O 'Lord that I am Yours for eternity.

On this day, may Your desire be done in this land, that all may see and praise Your Holy name forever.

For this is my prayer. Amen and Amen.

January 31

Temporary Dwelling Place

When I am afraid, I will put my trust in you. In God, I praise his word. In God, I put my trust. I will not be afraid. What can flesh do to me?
Psalms 56:3–5 WMB

You are a God of love. You are *El Roi,* the God whose eyes are never ceasing to watch over me, protecting me from both the seen and unseen dangers of this world. Oh, how I trust in You, my Lord. And when I take my last breath, may You tend to my soul forever.

Abba, do not let the problems of this world steal my joy. For it is You that I hunger and thirst for. It is the next life which I seek. For this is my temporary home, a temporary place to lay my head. Let me keep all my hope and trust in You.

Abba, there are those whose lives could have or should have been taken. But You, my Lord, chose for them to stay. For they have much work ahead of them, but their eyes have not been fixed on You. I pray, my Lord, that now they see the power in Your hand. That they feel Your unfailing love and know that You are King. May their days be counted for Your glory and may their rewards be given to them in full.

To You, my Lord, I give all I am and all I own forever and ever. Amen.

February 1

Contentment

Keep your lifestyle free from the love of money, and be content with what you have. For God Himself has said, "I will never leave you or forsake you," so that with confidence we say, "The Lord is my helper; I will not fear. What will man do to me?"
Hebrews 16:5–6 TLV

My Lord, no matter how rich we are in things, it is in our selfishness to want more. No matter how important our jobs say we are, we want to be the most important one.

Let me be satisfied in the little. For if we are paying attention, we can see You in the littlest things.

Just yesterday as I was driving to a meeting, I looked in my rear view mirror and saw one of the most beautiful sunrises I have seen in a very long time. I praised You for such a beautiful picture of Your love and for giving me a kiss to say good morning. It did not cost me anything but to pay attention to Your majesty to get one of the biggest joys of my day.

Let my eyes always stay open. My heart is ready to see anything You would like to show me of Your wonders this day. For Your fingers paint the skies and Your hand covers the fields with lilies. Your love flows in the waterfalls. Your grace is heard in the cries of a newborn.

I am watching, my Lord! May Your majesty be revealed to me and may my spirit be renewed to overflowing, to others this day!

In *Yeshua's* name I pray. Amen.

February 2

Your Children

For He remembered His holy word to Abraham His servant. So He brought forth His people with joy, His chosen ones with singing. He gave them the lands of the nations, so they inherited the labor of the peoples so that they might keep His statutes and observe His laws. **Halleluyah!**
Psalms 105:42–45 TLV

Abba, we are Your adopted children, joint heirs with Christ. Bring forth Your children with joy, Your chosen with gladness. May we follow Your statutes. May we tell others of Your goodness. May we sing of Your beauty. May we bask in Your love.

Abba, I am praying today for Your favor. For You to give us the lands of the heathens. May You increase our abilities to serve. Help us learn how to plow the land. Let us work and plant Your seeds.

For every seed that is planted, if we plant on fertile soil, will grow. For they will push forth from the ground to praise You. And its fruit will be full of the sweetest of juice. For it is only meant for You our King!

Increase in us Your knowledge. Increase in us Your truths. Increase the area in which we serve. But may we never lose sight of You, who so graciously gives to all who ask.

I love You, my King. May anything I have, my gifts, my love, increase so I can serve You more with each passing day.

In *Yeshua's* name I pray. Amen.

FEBRUARY 3

Your Favor

But let all who take refuge in You rejoice! Let them always shout for joy! You will shelter them and they will exult those who love Your Name. For you bless the righteous, **Adonai.** *You surround them with favor as a shield.*
Psalms 5:12–13 TLV

My King, I sing praises to Thee. I have woken this morning with a song in my heart. For I have heard Your voice calling my name.

Arise, O King of Jerusalem. Let all the people see Your glory. For You have shielded Your loved one from the fire. You have protected me and beheaded the serpent with Your sword!

Shower Your favor over me, my King, and adorn me with Thy jewels. Let others see Your favor and praise be given unto Thy name.

My King, may You find Your bride to be more radiant than diamonds, more beautiful than a rose. May she be sweeter than honey to Your lips and as gentle and soft as a dove.

For You are my King, and I am Your bride. On that day when You ride up on Your white horse, I shall be there with my lantern lit so You can find me. I shall be calling out Your name, saying, "Hosanna, Hosanna in the highest. How I will love Thee forever and ever!"

In *Yeshua's* name I pray. Amen.

FEBRUARY 4

My Every Need

Do not be anxious about anything—but in everything, by prayer and petition with thanksgiving, let your requests be made known to God. And the **shalom** *of God, which surpasses all understanding, will guard your hearts and your minds in Messiah* **Yeshua**.
Philippians 4:6–7 TLV

Abba, You know my thoughts. You know my desires. You created the heavens and the earth. You created the ladybugs and the bluebonnets. Every little detail is carefully placed. There is nothing You do that is not given great love and devotion.

Help me, my Lord. Bless me my Father with the desires of my heart. Cover the little details that I so easily overlook. Open up this path that You have set me on. Let me see the light before me for miles to come. Let the soil be fertile for planting seeds. Let the ground be a solid rock for building my home.

Let me use this place for Your glory in all I do. For you always tend to my every need. You even do more for me than I know how to ask. So I am laying this at Your feet.

In *Yeshua's* name I pray. Amen!

February 5

I Trust In Jesus

*In that day you will say: "Give thanks to **Adonai**. Proclaim His Name! Declare His works to the peoples, so they remember His exalted Name. Sing to **Adonai**, for He has done gloriously. Let this be known in all the earth. Cry out and shout, inhabitant of Zion! For great in your midst is the Holy One of Israel."*   Isaiah 12:4–6 TLV

Abba, Your name is great! It is above all names. For You hold heaven in one hand and earth in the other. All judgements are Yours alone!

Help us to think before each decision we make, what is wise, what would You have us do. Before we say a word, we need to think it through and let what is just, right and Holy be spoken.

For on that great day of judgement it will be too late to change things. It will be too late to make any wrong right. But I am grateful, my Lord, that on that day, there will only be one thing I can say: "I trust in *Yeshua,* for He is my great deliverer." Blessed redeemer, He is the Son of God! Who has washed me and took my sins away."

For *Yeshua* is my hope, my salvation, my blessed redeemer, my Lord and my God. Who was and is and is to come. There is nothing too grand or too small that is not in His plan for all to be saved. I praise You, my King, for showering me with Your love, even though I fail You time and time again.

You are the Holy One. My *Jehovah Jireh,* who provides everything I need. Provide a way for me this day to be who You desire me to be. Amen.

FEBRUARY 6

Create In Me

"So do not seek what you will eat and what you will drink, and do not keep worrying. For all the nations of the world strive after these things. But your Father knows that you need these things. Instead, seek His kingdom, and these things shall be added to you.
Luke 12:29–31 TLV

Adonai, You search my heart, You know my thoughts. You know every breath from first to last. You know my weaknesses and my strengths and You will be there helping me, to create in me, the person of Your desire.

For You are my cheerleader, my warrior, my provider, my friend. You are my Father, my love, my beginning and my end.

Everything I have in this life belongs to You. Everywhere I look, the earth cries Your name. From the worms in the ground that until the soil, so the seeds can burst forth to feed hungry souls. To the sun that shines down to light up our day, to the rain that pours over us, giving us life, refreshing our way.

Be with me this day, give me peace, give me strength. Let me take each thought captive. Let me focus only on Thee alone. Let me look for the good in each person I greet. Let my actions cry out *Yeshua,* even if a word is not spoken.

I am Yours! Captivate my heart today. For I am Yours every moment, of each and every day. Amen.

February 7

I Lift My Hands

Hear the voice of my petitions, when I cry to you, when I lift up my hand toward your Most Holy Place.   Psalms 28:2 WMB

My Lord, I lift up to you all those that are in my life. I cherish them, but not more than You do. For You know their comings and goings. You know the numbers of hairs on their heads. Be with them each and every moment. Do not let the enemy surprise them. Let them be fully armored before any attack so the enemy has no chance of winning. Let them be on the chase of him, that he is not able to attack anyone in their families. Let him be a defeated soul in all their lives and in all they do, may it glorify You.

Abba, I lift up to You my day. I do not know what lies ahead. But I know You will be there waiting for me. Let me not worry where I may go, or what I might eat, or how I will work. For You know all things and created this season in my life for my good. I give it all to You. I just ask that You show me the next step to take.

Last, my Lord, I pray for my family. You know the ones that hold my heart and even for the family members who have broken it. I pray for salvation for all of them. For a true revelation of You in their lives. That they seek You in the mornings and that they hold onto you at night. For as I went into my backyard and lifted up my hands in worship, I felt Your hand reach down and touch mine. This is what I want for each one of them, my Lord. For them to love You. To come to know You even more than I.

Open each door before me, let me see Your face on the other side. Then I will run towards You. For what awaits me in the not so distant future, is becoming Your precious bride.

In *Yeshua's* name I pray. Amen.

February 8

Every Thought Captive

For the word of God is living and active and sharper than any two-edged sword—piercing right through to a separation of soul and spirit, joints and marrow, and able to judge the thoughts and intentions of the heart.
Hebrews 4:12 TLV

Good morning, *Abba,* my love. I praise You for another day!

Just yesterday I heard a pastor who was speaking of how easily we can do things that we regret and not even an hour later I did that very thing.

Lord, forgive me and cleanse me of all unrighteousness. Create in me a pure heart, O Lord, a heart that does not judge and holds no records of wrong. Discern my heart, my thoughts, my actions and show me where I need to change.

For Your word is true and Holy. Piercing right through to my soul, and to all those when they fall short of honoring You.

May I take every thought captive and put everything before Your throne. So that when I speak or act, I will glorify You, my King!

For it is in *Yeshua's* name I pray. Amen.

February 9

Blessings From Adonai

*"What I am commanding you today is to love **ADONAI** your God, to walk in His ways, and to keep His **mitzvot**, statutes and ordinances. Then you will live and multiply, and **ADONAI** your God will bless you in the land you are going in to possess."* Deuteronomy 30:16 TLV

Adonai, even before I cried out to You. You poured out blessings upon me from Your hands. Even before I understood and knew Your statutes. You set in motion for me, all that You had planned.

For You knew that one day I would be Yours. One day I would want nothing or no one more. So You took a white rock and wrote my new name upon it. Then You wrote Your name, Your seal, upon my heart. Claiming that I'm Yours forever more.

All that I own is Yours, my Lord. Help it to increase, to bless and to multiply. Help me, my Lord, to teach, bless and most of all love others, for I am not very good at this, even though I try.

Help me to love others as if they were my child. Knowing they will do wrong, sometimes mild, sometimes severe. For this is how You have loved me. Even with all the times I have brought to Your eyes a tear.

For You never lost sight of me, You always kept me nearby. Putting road blocks in front of me. So I had no choice but to detour. Which was the best thing for me, because I saw You on the other side.

Thank You for this love, for it's so sweet, so pure and true. Help me pour this love out on others. That when they see me, they only see You! Amen and amen.

February 10

In Need Of The Holy Spirit

*"Now the One who prepared us for this very purpose is God, who gave us the **Ruach** as a pledge. Therefore we are always confident and know that while we are at home in the body, we are absent from the Lord. For we walk by faith, not by sight."* 2 Corinthians 5:5–7 TLV

My King how I praise You. For it was so confusing for Your disciples to understand "it was better if You left." For if I was in Your presence, I too would not understand, but only want to relish its beauty forever!

But then all who believed in You had to come see You. It would be impossible for all mankind to have a glance at You. Much less a relationship with You. But You, knowing our weaknesses. Knowing we can't walk by faith and not by sight on our own, gave us Your *Ruach* to live in us. To strengthen us and call us Your own!

I love how You teach me. How You talk to me throughout the day. That I don't have to go look for You. I can just stop, kneel, and pray. For You are with me all the time, no matter where I go. Let me be pleasing in Your sight. Let me take You where You want to go.

I praise You for this love so deep. For I feel it in my soul. That it's You in there giving me a kiss, telling me hello. You are the lover of my soul, my guide and in all that I hope. Hold me tight today, my Lord, and lead me closer to You than I ever thought I could.

In *Yeshua's* precious name I pray. Amen and amen.

FEBRUARY 11

May The Heavens Open

*"Rain down, O heavens, from above, and let the clouds pour down justice. Let the earth open up, let salvation sprout, and righteousness spring up with it. I, **ADONAI**, have created it."*   Isaiah 45:8 TLV

Adonai, this world is in thirst of Your love. They walk by the well and pretend it's dry, in fear that it's bitter and not sweet. They walk by the fields of wheat and claim it's all weeds. For they have been stuck by the thorns on the weeds before.

Abba, I have tasted the bitterness in others. I have found the weeds among the wheat. But I will not walk in fear of searching for You. I will not stop growing and learning Your word.

Because, here in Your presence, I find Your mercy. Here in Your presence, I find Your grace. Here in Your presence I find forgiveness. Here in Your presence, I see Your face. Here in Your presence I see Your glory. Here in Your presence, I find unsurpassable joy. Here in Your presence I find love and laughter. Here in Your presence You keep pouring out more and more.

So let the heavens open up, my Lord. Let justice rule this earth again. Let the waters be sweet to the thirsty once more. And pull the tares among the wheat, so new life can be won again.

So that they can find Your mercy, in Your presence, sweet Lord. Let them find in You justice. Let them find in You joy. Let them find in You glory. Let them find in You love. Let all the earth cry out for You. Let them search for You, my Lord.

For You are my Father, my Soul Barer, my Author. You are all I ever want or need and more. And forever I will praise You forever, *Adonai!* Amen!

FEBRUARY 12

Created In Love

"All those whom the Father gives me will come to me. He who comes to me I will in no way throw out." **Yochanan** *(John) 6:37 WMB*

Abba, I feel like dancing today. Dancing on Satan's grave! Because he hath no power over me! He has no authority in my life. He has to flee in the name of Jesus. And I belong only to Thee!

Hallelujah, *Yeshua* has set me free! I Praise Your name loudly in the streets. You are my God, the God who has created it all. And for some unknown reason, You have created me and called me by name.

Adonai, I'm so humbled that I have this love! I can't imagine anything I could do that would be good enough to please You.

But know this: that every day You give me breath and with every chance that I have. I will utter the name of *Yeshua* and proclaim His love. For no man comes to the Father, except through *Yeshua ha Mashiach,* His Son!

How I love You my mighty King. May I rest in Your arms forever more! Amen.

FEBRUARY 13

The Gift Of Love

If I have the gift of prophecy, and know all mysteries and all knowledge; and if I have all faith, so as to remove mountains, but don't have love, I am nothing.   *1 Corinthians 13:2 WMB*

    Abba, many of us are confused about which gifts You have given unto us. For others, Lord, it is so evident that there is no question.

    But Lord, You say the greatest gift is love. That perfect love that only comes through You. Teach me how to love this way. Let this kind of love ooze from every part of my being, for I love others, but not in the way I should.

    Build in me Your agape love, my Lord. For this is my desire from You. Let me be this example for my family, my Lord. Let them see Your heart in me.

    Let me see those on the streets through Your eyes each day. Let me carry the cross for a friend. When others are angry and fussing at me, bring to mind Your words that I have been taught in the Bible once again.

    I love You, my Lord, with all that I am. But I can't be this person on my own. Bless me with many gifts, my Lord. But let love be the greatest gift of all.

    In the Holy name of *Yeshua* I pray. Amen.

February 14

What Is Love

Love is patient, love is kind, it does not envy, it does not brag, it is not puffed up, it does not behave inappropriately, it does not seek its own way, it is not provoked, it keeps not account of wrong, it does not rejoice over injustice but rejoiced in the truth; it bears all things, it hopes all things, it endures all things. Love never fails.
1 Corinthians 13:4–8 TLV

My Lord, love is a word so many people say, without the knowledge or caring to what it really means. It is a word that people should use much more carefully, even I, before it is said.

But the truth is, if we abide in You, and You abide in us. Then we are to love everyone at all times! This world, my King, would look so different if we all would just honor this truth!

For the hurt and anger people harbor from being hurt by those they "love" should not be. But how lucky mankind is that You came and taught us how to be set free.

Help me to pour out Your love, so deeply, so true on those I am close to. Teach me to love others, even those I would not wish to be around. To love them in the way You want me to. I can only do his through the *Ruach ha Kodesh,* my King. So dwell within me, live through me. Let my life be Yours, now and through eternity. Let everything within me, about me, and around me proclaim the love of Christ!

Oh, how I thank You for Your love. For I so need it every day. Thank You for hearing this prayer. Thank You for answering it and showing me Your way.

For it is in Christ alone I have the faith to pray before Your throne. Amen.

FEBRUARY 15

A Gentle Kiss

*"Now to him who is able to do far beyond all that we ask or imagine, by means of His power that works in us, to Him be the glory in the community of believers and in Messiah **Yeshua** throughout all generations forever and ever! Amen.*
Ephesians 3:20–21 TLV

Oh, *Abba,* how sweet, how beautiful is Your love for me. For You have awakened me with a kiss from above. And I can't wait to see what all the gifts of love, those heavenly hugs that I will receive from You this day will be.

For Your love is softer than a gentle breeze, stronger than the ocean's tide, larger than the universe, with surprises all inside.

You know all of my hearts desires. For I have laid them at Your feet. Will I see an answer to any of them, my Lord? Or do You have something better for me?

For I think I know the direction I want to go. I think I know what I need to do. But then You come along and surprise me, my King. And make all my wishes come true.

For You know me better than I know myself, my Lord. So today I ask You this. Give to me what is YOUR desire, my King. For then it will be the best there is!

I love You alone, my King. You are my desire, my hope and my life. I'm content in You my darling. For You will always protect and cherish Your bride!

In *Yeshua's* name I pray. Amen.

February 16

No Greater Love

"Greater love has no one than this, that someone lay down his life for his friends." **Yochanan *(John) 15:13 WMB***

Abba, I see so many things within this verse. It is what heroes are made of. Like a firefighter who goes into a burning home to save someone he does not know. Like a missionary, going into a danger zone. Or a pastor who minister to others, so salvation can be their own.

I also see it as people using their time, talents, and money in a sacrificial way. That they are a true servant of Yours in every way. From not buying the dress they would love to wear, to buying shoes and socks and giving them to a homeless person instead. To not going out to dinner to that expensive, fancy restaurant. Instead going to an old folks' home and having dinner with a stranger so they are not lonely, but at that moment, they feel loved instead.

We need to not be so caught up in the pleasures of self, but to put others—strangers—first. Then we will learn the true meaning of love, in the manner You gave to all who thirst.

You were intentional and purposeful in every act that You did. Help me to look more like You, loving others with this agape love. Serving others as You did.

Thank You for living in and through me every day. Because it is in You, this and all things are possible in all ways. Amen.

February 17

Great Faith

*"Now when **Yeshua** came into Capernaum, a centurion came begging for help. "Master," he said, "my servant is lying at home paralyzed, horribly tormented." **Yeshua** said to him, "I'll come and heal him." But the centurion said, "Master, I'm not worthy to have You come under my roof. But just say the word and my servant will be healed. For I also am a man under authority, with soldiers under me. I say to this one, 'Go!' and he goes; and to another, 'Come!' and he comes; and to my servant, 'Do this!' and he does it." Now when **Yeshua** heard this, He marveled and said to those who were following, "Amen, I tell you, I have not found anyone in Israel with such great faith!"*   Matthew 8:5–10 TLV

Abba, what a gift this servant had. A Master with such great faith, that he sought You to heal his servant and so, it came to pass.

You also told Your disciples to go out into the world. To preach the gospel, cast out demons and heal the sick. And when they weren't able, it's because they had a lack of faith.

Abba, I want this *great* faith, that not only do I know You can do this. But for me and other believers to go into the world, ministering, casting out demons, and calling on You to heal the sick. For You are the same today, yesterday, and forever. What was done in the days of old, You are doing today through those who believe.

Let me be a strong servant for You and obey every command that You have told us to do. May I become a modern-day disciple, a servant of great faith. Knowing that when we ask of You anything, it will be done. Because this is a promise, a word spoken through Your lips and Your word cannot be broken.

Praise Your Holy name, *Yeshua ha Mashiach* for Your faithfulness. Amen and amen!

FEBRUARY 18

Trusting In Your Truths

"I give eternal life to them. They will never perish and no one will snatch them out of my hand. My Father who has given them to me is greater than all. No one is able to snatch them out of my Father's hand. I and the Father are one." **Yochanan (John) 10:28–30 WMB**

Abba, I am an heir to the promises of God! A child adopted by Your seed. You have not promised to give me all I want. But You will give me all I will ever need.

So I am moving forward in this race, looking forward to seeing mountains being moved and walls being torn down. For as You speak Your truths, You will make my walk level.

No matter how hard Satan may try to make me think I am alone in this life. The one thing You have promised and I know. You promised never to leave me or forsake me. You have promised never to let me go. So give me those tasks that are hard for me to reach. For the only way to accomplish them, is that it's Your face in which I seek.

As Satan starts raging a war against me in heavenly realm, You will send Your angels to fight for me as I plan a war against him. Then I am going to share the love of Christ with as many as I can. So we can all stand together praising You in Your throne room of grace.

I praise You *Yeshua* for giving me the strength and knowledge to live out each day in You. For You are more precious than gold to me. For I would not have a place in heaven, if not the sacrifice of You.

In *Yeshua's* name I pray. Amen and amen.

FEBRUARY 19

Reveal To Me Your Plans

*"Commit whatever you do to **ADONAI**, and your plans will succeed."*
Proverbs 16:3 TLV

My King, I am not sure why You have me planted where I am at. But I know I would not be there if not for You! I'm not sure what all I am to do in this place. But I know as time goes on, You will reveal it to me.

I'm not sure how I, someone without much skill. Without great talents or abilities can accomplish anything special for You! But I do know that You, *Adonai,* are at my right hand. You created the winds and the seas. You created the place in which I stand and You have put me here with a plan.

So I give it all to You: my work, my life, everything. Put me where I will serve You best! Teach me in a manner where I can learn to walk in Your footsteps.

For whether I'm poor or rich, sick or healthy, surrounded by others or all alone. I dedicate all of my life to You. And it does not matter whether or not I succeed in the ways of man, as long as I succeed in Your eyes. There is no greater plan!

Help me, my King, not to act like the world, but to earnestly pray over every decision, to know without question before I make a move. Then I know Your hands will cover me. I know You will see me through.

Praise You, my Holy Father. For I am truly blessed to be Your child! Amen.

FEBRUARY 20

Blessed are those who keep his statues, who seek him with a whole heart.
Psalms 119:2 WMB

My joy is found in You alone, even though things around me may be a mess. I do not have the wisdom to fix it, my King, and I feel I'm being put to the test.

But You, my Lord, give me joy in my trials. Because You will love me through it all. For if I was wise. If I knew I was able to keep my life in perfect order. I would not need You, for there would be no fear of a fall.

So I welcome the mess. And I stand in the midst of confusion. Because I trust in You, my Lord, alone. For You will hold me and protect me. You will show me the way. For only You, my King, sit upon the throne!

My heart belongs to You, O God. Oh, how I long to be in Your arms. So no matter the trials of the day, my joy is found in You. For You love me, not just today, but will all eternity long!

In *Yeshua's* name I pray. Amen.

FEBRUARY 21

Open The Eyes Of My Heart

"That the God of our Lord Yeshua the Messiah, our glorious Father, may give you spiritual wisdom and revelation in knowing Him. I pray that the eyes of your heart may be enlightened, so that you may know what is the hope of His calling, what is the richness of His glorious inheritance in the **kedoshim***, and what is His exceedingly great power toward us who keep trusting Him—in keeping with the working of His mighty strength."*
Ephesians 1:17–19 TLV

Yeshua, I know that I have been saved by grace. By the shedding of Your blood as forgiveness of my sins. I also know that You have created me with a specific purpose in mind. Yes, it is for worship. Yes, it is to testify of You, but You have a specific way in which I am to walk in which to honor You.

Open the eyes of my heart and give me spiritual wisdom and revelation. That I can do all things according to the plan which You have for me. Give me strength and understanding to win the battles that lie before me.

For Satan does not want Your children to succeed, my Lord. So he will do many things to try to extinguish this plan. But You are omnipotent and know all he has planned. So help me with my strategies, to win this war and move forward as You have planned.

I praise You that it is written "You will give spiritual wisdom to those who ask." So I will be still, my Lord, and wait on You, until You reveal to me this plan.

In *Yeshua's* Holy name I pray. Amen and amen!

FEBRUARY 22

Way Of The Righteous

*The way of the righteous is straight. Upright One, You make smooth the path of the righteous. Yes, in the way of Your judgments, **ADONAI,** we have waited for You. Your Name and Your remembrance is the desire of our soul. My soul longs for You at night, yes, my spirit within me seeks You. For when Your judgments are in the earth, the inhabitants of the world learn righteousness.* Isaiah 26:7–9 TLV

My love is for You alone, O Righteousness of Israel! For You have made Yourself known among men, with patience, grace and kindness. Yet still others walk this earth in pride.

But the times of the nations are shortening, my King. For soon You will come to take Your bride!

Then Your Son, *Yeshua ha Mashiach* will be ruler of this earth, where peace and love will flow through the land.

How I dream of this time, my Lord. To be able to walk with You, amongst the lions and the lambs.

This type of peace is so foreign to me, Lord. For I turn the TV on, and all I hear are rumors of wars. But You told us all of this ahead of time and behold, all of it is coming true.

So I will keep waiting for the day, every day. I will continually be looking to the skies, waiting patiently for You!

Thank You for Your grace. For without it I would be lost and all alone. But You created me to love You. Oh, my King, I can't wait to see You in my new home. Amen and amen.

February 23

Heavenly Kiss

I know what it is to live with humble means, and I know what it is to live in prosperity. In any and every circumstance I have learned the secret of contentment—both to be filled and to go hungry, to have abundance and to suffer need. I can do all things through Messiah who strengthens me.
Philippians 4:12–13 TLV

Adonai, I have come to a place where things are not always what I want. I am not where I want to be and my finances are not as I had hoped. To be honest, my Lord, I have cried many a tear this past year over these things.

But these past few weeks, You have given me Your peace. For it has been in the struggles that I have seen Your hand moving over me. That I have heard Your voice calling out to me and You have performed miraculous things before me.

So I am content in my present struggles, Lord. For You are so near to me that I feel Your breath upon my neck. Let me stay in this time as long as You are there, no matter how hard the situation may be, for there is nothing on this earth more valuable than this, and nothing more lovely than to feel a heavenly kiss upon my face.

Thank You, my King, for being with me in my past. Thank You for holding me in my present situation. No matter what the future holds, I can do all things because You will be there too. To hold and mold me to be like You.

I love You, *Adonai.* Hold me now and forever more. Amen.

FEBRUARY 24

How Sweet Your Love Is For Me

But let all those who take refuge in you rejoice. Let them always shout for joy, because you defend them. Let them also who love your name be joyful in you. For you will bless the righteous, Lord, you will surround him with favor as with a shield.   Psalms 5:11–12 WMB

Blessed am I, my *Adonai*. For I am covered by Your righteousness. Surely Your goodness will follow me all the days of my life. Every day I see Your favor, my King. How I praise You for providing ways for me to give others a portion of what You have given unto me.

For there is no greater joy, than to know You have used me. For then I know You will give me another job to do. I thank You, my Lord, for even when it has been the hardest for me to give, it turned out to be the most meaningful thing to do.

So help me, my King, to be humble and obey, even at times when it's hard. For then Your righteousness can cover me like the lilies cover the fields, and I can be covered in the cloak of Your protection.

How great and mighty a Warrior are You, my King. How sweet Your love is for me as a Father. For You know every detail of my longings and desires. And they are all wrapped up, in the pleasing of You!

In *Yeshua's* name I pray. Amen.

FEBRUARY 25

##

A wicked man hardens his face; but as for the upright, he establishes his ways.   Proverbs 21:29 WMB

Abba, how true this verse is. For I have seen the wicked be bold and foolish. I am seeing lawlessness rule our land.

These people are double minded. For when they see a police officer they say profanity against him. But when in trouble, they want and cry for their help.

Help me, my Lord, to not be double-minded. For You read my thoughts. You know the longings of my heart. Help me speak with boldness Your truths. Help me see the truths in what others have to say. Help me to balance situations that are out in front of me. Help me take what is wrong and make it right. Help me to be a better person each day. And may You hold me through the night.

For only You can change the hearts of man. Only You can make us see. Open the eyes of my heart this day. Let me see clearly and do all You need of me!

Thank You, Abba, for Your love never fails! Amen.

February 26

Live By The Spirit

*"If we live by the **Ruach**, let us also walk by the **Ruach**."* Galatians 5:25 TLV

But I know Your *Ruach* lives in me. And I wage war with my flesh all the time over certain things! For I try hard not to be a hypocrite. I try hard to speak of You. To learn more about You. To pray to You for all my needs. Yet I fail time and time again. Why then am I so weak? Why is it that I allow Satan a foothold?

Well no more Satan! You have had too much control over my past! You have caused havoc and dissension and it's not going to be tolerated anymore!

For *Yeshua* has already defeated You. You have been condemned to an eternal grave with fire and brimstone. And neither I, nor my family, will allow your presence through our doors.

For you are not welcome. You are not wanted. You only want to harm, and I will use the sword of the Spirit against you the moment you try to open the door.

So flee back to hell where you belong, because God's angels are surrounding me. His *Ruach* lives in me and *Yeshua's* blood covers me, and will forever more.

Thank You, Abba, for Your love and protection. Thank You for making me one of Your own. Thank You that since You live in me, I am able to do all things through Christ Jesus alone!

Praise Your Holy name forever and ever! Amen and amen!

FEBRUARY 27

Being Fair

"It's no good, it's no good," says the buyer; but when he is gone his way, then he boasts.   *Proverbs 20:14 WMB*

Adonai, why are people this way? They are so self-absorbed. They want only what they want. Can't they see their acts are hurting not only others, but also themselves in the end?

People will say and do anything to make more money. They will beg, borrow, and steal what is not rightfully theirs. Then they will brag about what they have done, never thinking twice about what will happen to others in the end.

I'm tired of dealing with people of this thought. It's hard for me to understand this sort of man.

Give me wisdom in all my financial dealings. For I only want to be fair. But I have so many people to take care of. I have to look at the whole, not just one man. Give me discernment when others speak the truth. Give me the boldness to confront when they are not. Give me the ability to be a blessing. Not just to one, but the whole lot!

In *Yeshua's* name I pray. Amen.

February 28

Compare Myself To Others
➤ ✝ ⬅

*"And not only that, but we also boast in suffering—knowing that suffering produces perseverance; and perseverance, character; and character, hope. And hope does not disappoint, because God's love has been poured into our hearts through the **Ruach ha-Kodesh** who was given to us."*
Romans 5:3–5 TLV

Abba, how blessed am I among the multitudes! For I was created in Your image, formed by Your hands, unique and different than others, to do a specific plan.

I have been judged because I am different. This hurts and has caused me pain. But when I know that I know I am in Your will, it does not matter what they say. For Satan is only speaking through their tongues, trying desperately to thwart all You have planned. But because You have given me each breath, I put my life into Your hands.

I will not compare myself to someone who is great and teaches the multitudes. For they have influence that is great and wonderful, it's true. But if I work hard to influence a few, I will have a bigger impact. Possibly this effect will have the "butterfly effect," to touch the multitudes.

For I will not be like Peter, comparing myself to John, worried that You love them more than I. For You made me to be unique and gifted, to do a job touching lives differently than others. In a way that only some will let You inside.

Thank You for the trials and tribulations I have gone through. For others who have judged me and all I have gone through. For it has only caused me to grow closer and stronger in You, making sure I am walking hand in hand with You alone.

Oh, how I love You, *Yeshua,* for You suffered greatly that I might have life and have it abundantly. So let me live this life, not to please others, but to please You alone! Amen and amen.

MARCH 1

Nothing Can Separate Us

"Who shall separate us from the love of Messiah? Could oppression, or anguish, or persecution, or famine, or nakedness, or peril, or sword?"
Romans 8:35 WMB

Abba, how thankful I am, that You, O Lord, are always there. You promised never to leave me nor forsake and Your promises are bound and can never be broken.

Abba, You keep me from losing my mind in this crazy world. It is no wonder there is so much chaos. For those who do not know You have no future or hope. So they grasp at anything and all they can for survival, unable to see the better plan.

But You, my Lord, are faithful. You are my rock on which I built my foundation. And even when hurricane force winds may blow, my house my look tattered, but it shall stand because it is built on the Rock!

Thank You for teaching me Your words of wisdom in Proverbs. The love You have for us in Song of Songs. In Psalms, You show us that no matter how hard or many times we fail like King David, if we have a heart that seeks You. We will always prevail.

Thank You, my King, for Your word. That we live in a country where we are allowed to have it, study it and proclaim it out loud.

Help us all learn to memorize Your word, so if one day it is removed from this land, no one can separate Your word for our hearts and our souls. Let us love You this much, because Your love never fails! Amen and amen.

March 2

My Focus On You

***Adonai** is my rock, my fortress and my deliverer. My God is my rock, in Him I take refuge, my shield, my horn of salvation, my stronghold. I called upon **Adonai**, worthy of praise, and I was rescued from my enemies. Cords of death entangled me. Torrents of **Belial** overwhelmed me. Cords of **Sheol** coiled around me. Snares of death came before me. In my distress I called on **Adonai**, and cried to my God for help. From His Temple He heard my voice, my cry before Him came into His ears.*
Psalms 18:3–7 TLV

Adonai, my God, how sweet is the love You have for me. How great is Your strength and Your shield!

I cry out to You, Lord! I am in bondage in my finances. I have much debt to pay and yet things have happened that need repair. Lord You are the maker of heavens and earth, open the heavens and bless me. Give me wisdom on how to handle all that You have given me that it is easy to have freedom through You.

I cry out for health, my Lord. Take any and all pain from me. Take all illness from my body. Give me strength, energy and the ability to serve You and my family!

I cry out to You for peace! I am tired and weary. I need You to envelope me. The enemy has been knocking at my door, taunting me with words of hate and evil. Cast them away, my Lord, as far as the east to the west and may peace reside with me once more.

My Lord, Satan is trying every tactic to get my focus from You, but he can't! Because You have called me by name! You have given me life and given it to me abundantly! You have given me prosperity, love, peace and a hope that never fails! For You are Lord of Lords and King of Kings and You have chosen me to be Your own. How beautiful You are to me and how I love serving a God like You! Amen!

March 3

Judgement Seat

Behold, he is coming with the clouds, and every eye shall see him, even those who pierced him. And all the tribes of the earth shall mourn over him. Even so, Amen.   *Revelation 1:7 WMB*

Yeshua, how I look to the day of Your return. For on that day the heavens will open, and You will call Your bride home. All those who remain will mourn and try to hide because they will see You and know their time has come. Judgement has come for them and their evil will be punished.

But Praise be to You, O Lord, for we have a God who is Holy, a God whose love is perfect and just. For we will miss this great judgement, because of You alone! For You loved me before I was born and took on my sins on Calvary. My life would be meaningless if I did not have You! How great and beautiful is Your love! How Holy and just is Your name!

I love You, my Lord, more than words can say. My voice is not capable in this human form to give You the praise worthy of Your Holiness.

So until that day, keep this child, hold me and mold me to be more like You. Give me visions and dreams that I may not turn in the wrong direction. May every day be all about You and the love You wish for me to share.

To You who sits on the great judgement seat, I lay my life before You! To You be all honor, glory and praise, forever and ever! Amen.

MARCH 4

Collecting My Tears

You count my wanderings. You put my tears into your container. Aren't they in your book?   *Psalms 56:9 WMB*

Adonai, You love me this much? That all, literally all of my wanderings are recorded? Every tear I have cried is in a bottle? How many books have been written? How big is this bottle for my tears?

Adonai, You would have to have spent just about every moment of my life doing this for me. That You would not have time for anything else!

Your love never ceases to amaze me! It never fails! It never stops! For there is not a season or a situation that You are not there with me. Teaching me with all You've got.

For I love the fact that my life is recorded in a book and I will have a chance in heaven to look back at it. For then I will see how You always led me through.

Since I have been forgiven, those recordings of my sins, I will not fret. Because Your blood will cover them and this book will show how Your love is far greater than all of that!

Oh, my Lord, when I see this bottle of tears You have collected just for me. It's going to be large enough to fill up a lake. Maybe even the seas.

Thank You for this tender, loving expression of Your love, for there is nothing more beautiful. Than how You are in my every moment, taking notice, caring and giving unto me with EVERY good gift from above.

I love You *Yeshua.* Hold me this day! Amen and amen!

MARCH 5

Your Servant

As each one has received a gift, use it to serve one another, as good stewards of the many-sided grace of God.   *1 Peter 4:10 TLV*

What joy it is, my Lord, to serve You. To see in others faces and the blessings You pour out on them. Being Your servant is hard at times. Oh, it is definitely not always easy.... But the *joy*, the end result, is so worth it all!

You have given me the ability to serve many. My Lord, I pray that I serve You well. If ever I am not doing exactly what You want from me. Quench my heart, that I may always be walking in the path You are guiding me.

Your *Ruach* flows through Your children so sweetly. For when we all come together, blessing those in need. There is no doubt *Adonai,* Your hand is in it. There is no doubt, how much You take care of all our needs.

Let me live and die serving You, my King. In every way I can, with all You have given me. So that others may be blessed. And that I, the lowest of the low, am able to glorify the *one magnificent king*!

It is to glorify You that I breathe. Amen and amen.

MARCH 6

Nothing Is Impossible

*"And looking, **Yeshua** said to them, 'With men this is impossible, but with God all things are possible.'"*   *Matthew 19:26 TLV*

Abba, there are times I depend on people for many things. But when I totally depend on them, I am usually let down. *Abba,* I know there are times I let others down too. This is because I can't do all things. I have time constraints. I might not have the wisdom in a certain area. Or I might not have the means in which to do it.

But You are not bound by any of those things. Because, You are Almighty. You are Everlasting. You are Omnipresent. You are Omniscient. And everything created, both in the heavens and here on earth, were created by Your hands. So why on earth don't I start depending totally on You?

For I depend on You for the sun to shine. I depend on You for the rain. I depend on You for each breath I take and I depend on You to come take me home one day.

So help me depend on You for all the decisions that I make. Help me depend on Your laws of tithing and of prayer. For man does not understand these laws, because they are opposite to all we are taught down here.

But let my spirit be in one accord with You. Let me spend all my day in prayer. For it is in this realm where I see You the most. It is there You show me nothing is impossible in You and just how much You care!

Praise You, *Abba,* for allowing me to enter into the heavenly realm with You. To fight for what is right and to come to You for wisdom, peace and strength. Thank You for never letting me down and for that amazing love, I only get from You!

In *Yeshua's* name I pray. Amen.

MARCH 7

Shelter Me In The Storm

***Adonai** lives! And blessed be my Rock! Exalted be God my salvation! God—He gives me vengeance and subdues peoples under me. He delivers me from my enemies. Indeed You lift me up above those who rise up against me. You deliver me from the violent man. Therefore I praise You among the nations, **Adonai**, and sing praises to Your Name.*
Psalms 18:47–50 TLV

Cleanse me, my *Adonai*, that I can look in a mirror and see You! May I enter into Your Holy Place and light the menorah. May Your Spirit fill me and give me strength. May I take part of the table of show bread, that I am saved by Your grace. May I light the alter of incense that You hear my prayers and petitions. May I enter in to the Holy of Holies and lay myself at Your feet

For I come to You, my Lord, to beg for forgiveness of any anger or doubt that I might be holding onto. May You heal me of any illness or disease. May You strengthen my faith and allow me to honor You in service this day.

For You are Lord of lords and King of kings, and I am kneeling before Your throne, laying these requests at Your feet. May I hear You say, "Yes, my child, that which you have asked will be given unto you. Not because of anything you have done, but because of my Son, *Yeshua ha Mashiach*. For He has come in your place, that your request may be known by me."

Oh My beloved King, I lift up my hands in praise! I am in awe of Your love! For You shelter me in the storms, You keep evil ones under my feet. You make life new and beautiful every day.

May I worship You, my Lord, in Your kingdom. May all that is Holy and good be praised for all eternity. It is to You, O Lord, I pray. Amen.

MARCH 8

Satan, Get Out Of My Way

What then shall we say about these things? If God is for us, who can be against us?   *Romans 8:31 WMB*

Satan, you have tempted to bring me down, to make me weak and unable to do His work. But my God is a mighty God and His plans cannot be thwarted. No matter how you try, you can't hold victory for long. For victory is in the eyes of the Lord.

For when I am unable to speak, God will send another. When my hands are unable to move, another brother or sister will share His love.

So Satan, get out of my way for I have much work that I need to be doing. And in the process, your plans will come to ruin!

Abba, I thank You for taking care of me during this time. Thank You that no matter what, Your hand never lost its grip of me.

For You are my *Abba,* my Creator the Holy One. And I praise You for being *Jehovah Rapha* for me this day.

In *Yeshua's* name I pray. Amen.

MARCH 9

Everlasting King

*But the mercy of **Adonai** is from everlasting to everlasting on those who revere Him, His righteousness to children's children.*
Psalms 103:17 TLV

Abba, embrace me as I go through this day. Hold me and do not let me go. Whisper to me in the wind: I love you. Give to me my daily bread and may I never forget whose I am!

Protect those who are running away from Your truths. Bring them to their knees that they see Your glory and praise. Heal those who are sick and weak; give them strength to make it through another day. May You provide me opportunities to feed those who are hungry and may we all worship at Your feet.

To You, O Lord, I pray. Through You, all things are possible. I love You, my King! And I want nothing more than to have Your love cover me and my family this day. For You are *Adonai,* who is Lord of Lords and it is in Your hands that I will remain.

For You are *El Olam,* the God who is from everlasting to everlasting, the God of Abraham, Issac and Moses. And it's to You, my Father, the Holy One of Israel, and to *Yeshua ha Mashiach,* my Lord, I will lift my voice and pray. Amen and amen.

March 10

Consume Me Like A Fire

*I wait for **Adonai**, my soul waits, and in His word I hope.*
Psalms 130:5 TLV

Abba, my Father who art in heaven, hallowed be thy name! For You are Holy and just, nothing comes to us that does not first pass through Your hands.

I wait on You, my King! For in You, there is truth. In You, there is hope and it is through You all things are made new.

Abba, may I enter in to Your Holy place. May Your *Ruach* consume me like a fire and speak to me in my soul. May I understand the season that I am in and how to reveal You to others through it. If it takes all that I am, all that I have for You to work through me, that others might be saved, so be it! If it is in the giving to others and showering them with gifts of love, may I have the means to do so. Whatever it takes for my children, their children and for the stranger on the street to know You, do this through me!

I wait on You, my King, for You hold the truth in Your hand. You know what it is I need this day. In my troubles, do not let my enemy deceive me, but may Your army surround me and the *Ruach* of the Lord guide my way.

To You, the one true King, I lay down my life. Let it not be mine, but Yours. Let others not see me, but You. Let me fade into the background and let Your *Ruach* rise up in me, strong, powerful, mighty and pure. May my enemies run in fear, and may the children draw near because of Your love in me.

To You, my Lord, I lift my voice in song. May I pour my perfume upon Your feet and may Your hand touch my head. May I hear You whisper I love you this day. I ask all these things in Your Holy and precious name. Amen.

MARCH 11

Dwelling Place

"I give them eternal life to them. They will never perish, and no one will snatch them out of my hand." **Yochanan (John) 10:28 TLV**

Abba, I cannot tell You how comforting this is. How reassuring that no matter what happens in my life, that I am secure in the palm of Your hand. For You are here, holding me, protecting me from all the evil that is in this world. Just as you protected Shadrach, Meshach, and Abednego in the fiery furnace, You will protect me during my earthly trials and from the eternal fiery furnace in hell. For Satan has no power over me or my family, because my God is greater! For You are *Elohim,* the all-powerful God! For You are the one true God and no one and nothing can change the love my *Abba* has for me!

Abba, may I be a pure tabernacle, a dwelling place for You. Circumcise my heart, that You may make me pure. Cover me with the blood of *Yeshua,* that You may find pleasure in me. May I be an incense of praise; worshiping You and loving You, now and throughout eternity. For You are the everlasting King and all I want to do is worship and serve You this day.

Thank You for loving me, for coming down from heaven for me. For holding me, protecting me and reassuring me that no one and nothing can stand between us. For the love of my God is great and powerful, amazingly undefinable, yet approachable. You are *Yahweh,* all that I ever need or desire. For You, my King, are worthy of all praise! Amen.

MARCH 12

Intercede

Therefore he is also able to save to the uttermost those who draw near to God through him, seeing that he lives forever to make intercession for them.
Hebrews 7:25 WMB

My Lord, I am so sorry that I put so many marks upon Your back. That I had chosen a life that was destructive to me and those around me. How blessed I am Lord that You chose to forgive each and every sin I have committed. That You have interceded for me to our Holy Father so I may have life and have it abundantly.

Abba, help me with what life I have left on this earth to use it for Your glory. May I be as Esther, fasting and praying so that You will lend an ear. May I do this so that I can see all my family saved! May I see that the works of my hands have been pleasing to You. That they have benefited others and that I am worthy to serve You in Your Holy temple.

To see You, my *Adonai,* to hear Your voice, to feel Your breath upon my check and Your hand upon my head. There is nothing greater that anyone could hope for than this!

Abba, I praise You so for those You have put in my life! May You cover each one today. Intercede for them according to their needs. Surround them with Your army and may strength and love be their name. May today and every day we see Your hand move in our lives in ways that testify of Your love.

I praise You *Yeshua* for hearing this prayer. For touching our lives and for giving of Yourself for me. To You, my King, I will praise forever. Amen.

MARCH 13

Trials Of This Life

*These things I have spoken to you, so that in Me you may have **shalom**. In the world you will have trouble, but take heart! I have overcome the world!"*
John 16:33 TLV

Adonai, there is so much turmoil all around me. Even though I know You are in control. Others are acting in ways they know they should not, because emotions are taking the best of them.

For patience and waiting is not something people of our generation have had to learn. Everything is instantaneous, from talking to someone on the phone to information on the internet. How can we learn that anything good is worth the wait, especially in relationships. For people do not change overnight. The only one who can even help someone to change is You. We must just get out of the way and let You do what only You can do. The only thing we need to do is pray!

Adonai, some of the trials I see are for our growth. Help us to see Your perspective in our lives. How You desire for us to handle the situations at hand. How we can receive joy in all circumstances. How we can show others You in ALL things. For this is Your desire for us, but impossible for us to do on our own.

In-fill me with the *Ruach* so my heart is not my own. Infuse in my mind Your words so I may speak truth with boldness to those around me. Help me be the light in this darkness, a star twinkling, catching people's attention because of its brilliance.

So when the waters do not part that we need to walk through. When the mountains do not move that we don't wish to climb. Help us to trust in You and You alone.

In *Yeshua's* name I pray. Amen and amen.

MARCH 14

Good Shepherd

*So that Messiah may dwell in your hearts through faith. I pray that you, being rooted and grounded in love, may have strength to grasp with all the **kedoshim** what is the width and length and height and depth, and to know the love of Messiah which surpasses knowledge, so you may be filled up with all the fullness of God.* Ephesians 3:17–19 TLV

Good morning *Abba*. In the mornings Your love is so sweet. For I have a clear mind to see You, for the troubles of the day have not begun. Oh how I treasure this time with You!

Abba, I beg You to teach me Your love. I want to understand completely how wide and how deep You love me. I want to be filled to measure with Your goodness. I want to have the power through my faith that I can withstand any and all flaming arrows that are thrown my way.

Consume me, my Lord! Give me all that I need to withstand this day, but nothing more that could take my eyes from You. May I have the privilege of seeing all my family saved! May I complete the work You desire for me to do. May I not let the world in, but keep on the full armor of God to protect myself from the world and the devil's schemes. For he is trying to bring me down Lord, but I am looking up to You.

For You are the good Shepherd who tends His flock. If needed, my Lord, break my legs and carry me, so I will never wander away. May I never again get lost or away from Your love. May I stay with the flock, my loved ones, and worship You, my King. May my praises rise into the heavens like incense rises to the skies. May it enter into Your throne room and be pleasing to You.

You are the Alpha and Omega. You are the author of my life. May I dedicate it to the One who created me, for now and through eternity. Amen.

MARCH 15

Awaken My Soul

We know that all things work together for good for those who love God, for those who are called according to his purpose.   Romans 8:28 WMB

Awaken my soul O mighty King of Israel. Bring me into Your throne room of grace, that I may worship You! May I lay down frankincense and myrrh at Your feet. For You are the Anointed One, Mighty and Holy is Your name!

Abba, I lay my sins at the burnt offering, I wash my hands in the laver. Your Holy *Ruach* burns within me. As I partake of Your goodness, my soul rejoices in You and my praises rises to the heavens. I lay my life at Your mercy seat and beg for Your love, for Your grace to be poured out on me!

For in You, I take refuge. In You there is salvation. For You are *Yeshua ha Mashiach,* and you have conquered the grave! You hold the key to heaven's gates and no one shall enter except with You!

Abba, I know that all things work together for Your good. In this truth, I have hope! Work through me, that I may see Your smile, and have Your arms envelope me this day.

I will praise You, my King, forever. Amen.

MARCH 16

Cheerful Heart

A cheerful heart makes good medicine, but a crushed spirit dries up the bones.   Proverbs 17:22 WMB

Abba, thank you for speaking these words of truth to me this morning, how nothing is too hard that I can't make it without You! For not only have I seen miracles happen to those around me, but even those in their time of need are there helping me!

Oh, Lord, how I praise You for these that You have put in my life, for they are strength to me. I see Your hands directing my path through those around me. Lord, I am so honored and humbled to have this love, this knowledge, this strength with those I am surrounded by.

Teach me, my Lord, to be cheerful in all things. For in the fun times it is easy, but in the hard times, it is far greater! For that is when Your hand moves so mightily that no one can doubt Your love. All they have to do is look with their eyes wide open to see You are all around.

I will praise You, *Adonai,* with a cheerful heart. No matter what might come my way, You are there guiding me and loving me, and You will never ever let me go. My heart yearns to see Your face. And my hands ache to touch Your garment. And I know one day, whenever that may be, You will answer this prayer too.

I love You with all my heart, my soul and my mind. I give it all to You, my Lord. For forever shall You reign. Amen and amen.

MARCH 17

A Seal Of Ownership

*Now it is God who establishes us with you in Messiah. He anointed us, set His seal on us, and gave us the **Ruach** in our hearts as a pledge.*
2 Corinthians 1:21–22 TLV

Oh, my Lord, how confident I am in Your love. For You have sealed me with Your *Ruach*. You have inscribed my name on the palm of Your hand. You know every hair on my head. You created me in my mother's womb. My cup runneth over with joy, for there is no love like Yours.

You know when I lie down and when I rise. You know my thoughts from afar. You have anointed my head with oil and called me Yours. How blessed am I, my Lord; for the Creator of the universe, *Elohim,* has called me His own and put His seal of ownership upon my soul.

Abba, my life is a roller coaster of emotions right now, from very hard times to moments of complete joy and awe. You know exactly what I need this moment to get me through this day. But the one thing I am so grateful for, is that no matter what my emotions are, Your love is constant, never changing, always looking out for my best interests.

I am holding on to Your garment, my Lord. I am clinging to Your every word. For in You there is hope. In You, there is the promise of an everlasting life in Your arms. For that is where I want to be today and every day throughout eternity.

For You are *Elohim-Yachal,* the God of hope and all my hope is in You!

In *Yeshua's* name I pray. Amen and amen.

MARCH 18

The Mystery Of Christ

*"The mystery that was hidden for ages and generations, but now has been revealed to His **kedoshim**. God chose to make known to them this glorious mystery regarding the Gentiles—which is Messiah in you, the hope of glory! We proclaim Him, warning and teaching everyone in all wisdom, so that we may present every person complete in Messiah. To this end I labor, striving with all His strength which is powerfully at work in me."*
Colossians 1:26–29 TLV

Abba, thank You for making Yourself known to me. Thank You that I was born at this day and time, in this country with the family that I have. I thank You for giving me another chance. A chance to correct the wrongs I have done. To spend my life serving You and showing others the way.

You enable me each morning to awake, to walk, to speak Your truths! Why wouldn't I want to spend all of my energy giving it back to You! For I know a time is coming when You will take me home to glory. Where I can pour out my perfume and wash Your feet.

But until then help me to proclaim the mystery of *Yeshua* to all I meet. Help me to pray and see healings, to cast out demons, to love as Christ does, to everyone, everywhere.

I am but one, my Lord. But if I do as You please, others will want to mimic You and Your love will grow here and overseas.

I love You *Yeshua* and I give You everything. Amen.

MARCH 19

His Love Endures Forever

*Enter His gates with thanksgiving and His courts with praise! Praise Him, bless His Name. For **Adonai** is good. His lovingkindness endures forever, and His faithfulness to all generations.*   Psalms 100:4–5 TLV

Abba, how amazed I am at the power of Your love. For You set the stars in the sky and put the planets into motion just by the commands from Your lips. You have created all beings in the heavens and below. You could have chosen to only create that which is perfect and beautiful; but You created me, knowing my faults my frailties. Knowing that I love You, but in my daily walk I would fail You day after day. How I love You, my Lord, for this life and for those who surround me. I pray that from Your lips You will guide my steps.

Abba, You spoke to Moses and to Abraham; speak to me. Teach me the ways of old and how they apply to my life today. Teach me how to be stronger in You. If it is through a trial or test, may I endure it. If is through visions and dreams; may I have them. If it is through the love of a complete stranger, may I experience it. Whatever will bring me closer to You, my Lord, whatever will help me understand the truths of Your word, may it happen to me!

All I want it to be held in Your hands. All I want is to kiss Your feet. All I want is to experience Your presence; may I have it now, and may it last forever more.

To You, I sing hallelujah and amen. To You, I will lift my hands. May I see You this day and worship You forever and ever. It is only You who I love. Amen.

MARCH 20

First Loved Me

*"He guards the paths of justice, and protects the way of His **kedoshim**."*
Proverbs 2:8 TLV

My Lord, forgive me for my faults. Forgive me for the times I have given in to temptation. For I cannot do Your work and guard Your truths if I am not walking in it, moment by moment! For if I want people to believe the words I say about You. I must live Your truths out each day.

Abba, I am passionate about Your teachings. Because I have seen Your miracles. And I know Your truths. Help me to live in them in every way.

So build me up in strength in You. Imprint on my heart: Your justice, Your truths. Let me stand guard at the doorway. That nothing evil can ever pass through. Let me protect Your holy ones. Let justice always prevail. If we fall into temptation, knock us off our feet, my Lord. That we know to bow before You, to cry out for mercy, then and there.

You are the God of mercy, the God of justice and of love. Thank You for sending us *Yeshua.* For He is the only way to You, the One who shed His blood for our salvation.

How I praise You for this time alone with You. Thank You for Your forgiveness and Your truths. For I want to walk hand in hand with You, now and forever, my King. Looking into Your fiery eyes of love, seeing Your pierced hands, knowing that this is only possible, because You first loved me.

How I praise You for You calling my name to seek and love You! Amen and Amen.

MARCH 21

Called To Be Free

Brothers and sisters, you were called to freedom—only do not let your freedom become an opportunity for the flesh, but through love serve one another.   Galatians 5:13 TLV

Good morning my Love, how beautiful is this day. You have called us to be free, to make choices. So that if we choose to love You, it is because we want to, not because we have to.

I cannot imagine not wanting Your love. It is the most beautiful thing under heaven. You give it freely to anyone who calls on Your name. It is pure and Holy. You love without ceasing, never keeping records of wrong. You created us and formed us to desire this love. And all those who do not find this love do not understand why they are never satisfied, always looking to fill that void. How blessed am I that I know Your love.

How blessed are we, my Lord, that we live in a country that has been free to choose to worship You. These freedoms, my Lord, are slowly being taken away. May our president be a person who loves, honors and worships You. Not with idle words, but with his heart. May he lead us in righteousness and be a blessing to this country. May You rule this nation once again!

Abba, lead me today as I enter into this world. May I freely give to those in need. May I choose to speak Your words so that others can hear. May Your righteous be what rules my life and may Your love be before me. May I be in constant prayer so I can be that person You created me to be.

I praise You for the miracles of healing that You are doing in those lives around me. I pray for continual healing, for complete restoration of their bodies. I pray for salvation of my family and for all the lost souls that I see daily.

Abba, it is to You we give this day and all our needs. It is to You, my Lord, I pray. Amen.

MARCH 22

Your Breath

*"For sin's payment is death, but God's gracious gift is eternal life in Messiah **Yeshua** our Lord."*   Romans 6:23 TLV

Abba, I loved learning yesterday about what it meant when You changed Abrams' name to Abraham.

For You added the letter H, which in Hebrew, *H* or *"Hey,"* means divine breath. For You took him from being dead, full of sin and put Your life into him and made him a new creature in You!

Wow, to see the salvation process of old, is beautiful! I can't wait to see my rock and bear my new name. I can't even imagine what it might be.

For You have breathed life into me and set me free from my past. In You, I have a future and forever it shall last.

I am Yours now and for always. Do with me as You will. For I have read the stories of old and You did amazing things in their lives. When they trusted You, as You foretold.

I trust You, my Lord *Yeshua.* I trust in You alone. I will walk on this path of life hand in hand with You, my Lord, until this journey takes me home.

How I praise You for being my *"Hey,"* every moment of every day. Amen.

MARCH 23

Strong And Courageous

Finally, be strong in the Lord and in the strength of his might. Put on the whole armor of God, that you may be able to stand against the wiles of the devil.   *Ephesians 6:10–11 WMB*

Abba, You are my Lord, my Majesty, and I, Your humble servant, bow down before You and lay my sword at Your feet. For You are a mighty King and worthy of all honor and praise!

Adonai, as I have gone into battle with You, I have taken on many scars. May You heal each one so they do not get infected by the world. But may they be a testimony of faith for others. For each scar, every wound has brought me to a deeper understanding of how to shield myself from Satan's flaming arrows and a desire for a closer walk with You.

Adonai, may I always stand ready with my sword sheathed. For I know the battles are not over. May I put on the full armor of God, so I am prepared for whatever may come my way. May I stand with Your angels and alongside the multitudes of saints. May Satan see our forces standing on the hill and run defeated. For where You are, the enemy cannot stand.

You are my King! To You only, my Lord, do I bow. Anoint my head with oil, my Lord, so that I can stand strong and courageous. May I serve You in the King's army forever.

It is to You alone I pray! Amen.

MARCH 24

Golden Altar Of Incense

*Another angel came and stood at the altar, holding a golden incense burner. He was given much incense to offer up along with the prayers of all the **kedoshim** upon the golden altar before the throne*
The Revelation 8:3 TLV

Oh, my Lord, how beautiful that an angel would bring my prayers before You. That my prayers and praises rise into heaven before Your throne with an aroma that is pleasing to You.

Abba, I pray to You, that I completely understand who I am in You; my gifts, my talents, my destiny. For You have empowered me with Your *Ruach.* So may I go forth into this world with Your power to change my life and those around me.

May I be in constant fellowship with You! Praying for deliverance of those in bondage, praying for those who hunger and thirst. Praying for the saints, that they would rise up, unafraid and proclaim the gospel of *Yeshua ha Mashiach.*

Abba, I pray this moment for Your hand to reach down from heaven and touch me, that I am not shaken but strong. That no one can steal my joy because it is in You alone. For You are my Rock and my Fortress, You are *Jehovah Jireh;* my provider. You give me all that I need to be sustained by You each moment of each day. May I commune with You this day, in prayer and supplication. Let me feel You presence in me, may You work through me this day.

For it is with great love and honor, that I am able to lay these requests at Your feet. Amen and amen.

March 25

Light House In The Ocean

There is salvation in no one else, for there is no other name under heaven that is given among men, by which we must be saved!" Acts 4:12 WMB

Abba, this generation is a perverse generation! They seek the love of self and the flesh. Our nation and the world has taken on the days of old, for we now look like the time of Sodom. How long, my Lord, can You let this go on? How long, my Lord, before You destroy the inhabitants of the earth?

Abba, the true Christians who are left on this earth need to be the light house in the ocean. Set apart by ourselves, beckoning for them to come home, showing them the way through the storm. May our light be so bright that no matter how dark and rocky the way, they see that without You there is no way to heaven, no safety. That only death and destruction will come to those who do not follow You.

Abba, help us to be bold and courageous to proclaim that You are the only way. That there is no other path! For You are the One true Christ. For no one can enter into the Holy of Holies except through the one gate; through Your sacrifice on the cross.

Lord, we must be like Paul, like Peter and tell everyone we meet. For the time is coming soon for Your return. May we not be ashamed at Your coming but know that we acted on Your word and proclaimed Your name to all we meet. For without us spreading Your word, there will be one less soul, one less loved one to enter into Your gates.

Fill me with Your *Ruach!* May You speak through me. May Your power control my life, this day and forever more.

For it is in the blessed name of Christ I pray. Amen.

MARCH 26

A Single Grain Of Sand

*"I did not know Him; but the One who sent me to immerse in water said to me, 'The One on whom you see the **Ruach** coming down and remaining, this is the One who immerses in the **Ruach ha-Kodesh**.' And I have seen and testified that this is **Ben-Elohim**."*
John 1:33–34 TLV

Praise be to our Lord, *Yeshua*, for His mercies are new every day. For the same *Ruach* that lives in You, lives in me. So I can testify of the truths of God.

For without You, I am just a single grain of sand blowing in the wind, making no impact, helping no man. But with You, I stand firm on the rock and it is there I proclaim Your truths to all men.

Speak through me as You did with John. Show me visions of truth, justice and of Your ways. Give me an understanding of Your word that is beyond my capabilities. Give me an anointing to show others the way.

Let my life be like John's. Strong in the ways of You. Let my lips testify of Your goodness, testify that You are *Ben-Elohim!* Let Your *Ruach* resonate in me, through and through.

Thank You for the gift of the baptism of the *Ruach ha Kodesh,* for His strength, His comfort and His peace. Thank You for all the truths You are revealing to me. May I give back some of what You have given unto me.

In *Yeshua's* name I pray. Amen.

MARCH 27

Praying For Others

*"****Shalom*** *to the brothers and sisters, and trusting love from God the Father and the Lord* ***Yeshua*** *the Messiah. Grace be with all those who love our Lord Yeshua the Messiah with undying love."*
Ephesians 6:23–24 TLV

Adonai, Help me to be like Esther. Where I fast and pray for those I love and all the *kedoshim* in Christ Jesus. May I pray for Your *shalom* to be their guide. That where ever they may be, peace covers them as they walk in it throughout the day and any troubles they might find. That Your prosperity be found at their door step. That they never lack for food, or the closeness of You.

Abba, give strength to their souls and health to their bones, that they can stand strong against the schemes of the enemy. Let them be surrounded by love from those who are godly. Let us stand together united as one. Let us be there to lift each other up when we fall, never using our lips to condemn, but bless.

Let us give selflessly to each other, so we do not lack for housing, clothes or the necessities of this life. Let us pray with and for one another, that all we do is in accordance with You. Let us love one another as we love ourselves.

Adonai, if this was true. Think of all the wonders we could do for You!

Help me and all my brethren live and love more like You this day. Bless each one and may we all grow closer to You! Amen.

March 28

I Believe

*"**Yeshua** said to her, "I am the resurrection and the life! Whoever believes in Me, even if he dies, shall live. And whoever lives and believes in Me shall never die. Do you believe this?"*   John 11:25–26 TLV

Yes, my Lord, I believe in the resurrection just as the stories have foretold. For since You have called me by my name. I feel You deep inside of my soul.

For You have given me more in this life than I ever could deserve. I can't wait to see heaven and the splendors, spoken in Your word.

For there are colors we have not seen, things for heaven just to behold. But to see You in Your glory, sitting upon Your throne!

Will I fall to my knees, unable to stand in awe of You? Or will I cry out with joy. Singing and dancing with the multitudes?

Whatever it shall be, the one thing that holds true. I will be worshiping with the elders, crying Holy, Holy are You!

So I praise You for Your sacrifice, for the resurrection of Your Son. For it is only through *Yeshua ha Mashiach* we can enter heaven and behold You, my God. The One and only, Holy One! Amen and amen.

MARCH 29

In Your Will

*"For those who live according to the flesh set their minds on the things of the flesh, but those who live according to the **Ruach** set their minds on the things of the **Ruach**."* Romans 8:5 TLV

Abba, I have been praying for an understanding of what to do and of where to go. For I only want to be in one with the *Ruach*. And even though I knew that this path I was on was a Holy one. I was not sure it was for me.

But then this weekend, You opened up the words for me. You gave me a peace, an understanding that I did not have before. Oh how I praise You, my Lord, for showing me the way. For flesh and blood could not reveal this to me. But only the *Ruach ha Kodesh* that dwells within me. For everything good, everything that is pure and right comes from You alone.

I am willing to go on this journey with You. Please open the doors and show me the way. Help me to keep my feet from stumbling, but let me grow stronger in every way. Purify my heart, fill me full of love and forgiveness. Let my hands do Your work and my heart be devoted to no one but You!

For You are my God of hope. The everlasting King! I will do anything You wish. Now and until You take me home. Increase my territory. Strengthen the gifts You desire me to use. Let me seize every opportunity to bring others to Christ.

I love You, my King, and I give You all of me. Take me anywhere You wish, for You alone hold the key to my heart. Amen and amen.

MARCH 30

Awaken To Your Presence

"Wake up, and keep the things that remain, which you were about to throw away, for I have found no works of yours perfected before my God."
Revelation 3:2 WMB

Good morning my Love, how I thank You for this day and all the glory that is in it.

Adonai, I ask that You search my heart and remove anything that is not of You. Make me complete and whole in Your presence. That I may come before Your throne to worship You forever.

Give me the ability of prophecy, that I might edify the church. Give me the gift of healing, that others may see Your mercy. Give me the gift of teaching, that others hear and learn of You. Give me a heart that is pure, so I shall behold Your glory.

Give unto me wisdom and discernment, that no man can deceive me. Give unto me Your strength, so I won't grow tired in the battle against the enemy. Give me Your *shalom,* that peace and prosperity is my countenance.

Give unto me my daily bread. Help me to forgive those who have trespassed against me. Complete in me all that is good. So when I awake in the next life. I awake only to glorify You!

Praise You my *Abba,* my *Adonai,* my *Elyon.* Thank You for being my everything in this life and forever more! Amen.

MARCH 31

Perseverance

Happy is the one who endures testing, because when he has stood the test, he will receive the crown of life, which the Lord promised to those who love Him.   *Jacob (James) 1:12 TLV*

My beautiful *Adonai*, how sweet is the mention of Your name. You stand at a distance, watching with gladness as we worship You in *Ruach* and in truth. Then You come to us, and we are overwhelmed by Your *Ruach!* Power and might falls on us, then we come into one with You. How sweet is Your love, my Lord. How mighty is Your name.

Abba, I humbly come to You. I beg You for strength and peace. I cry out for wisdom and understanding. I need clarity of what You are trying to tell me. For I am just a pilgrim on a journey, traveling down a road with many road blocks, detours trying to get my eyes off of You. Help my feet not fail me, Lord. Let me persevere and stand the test. For my destination is ahead of me where You will crown me with the crown of life.

Let me enter into Your gates. Let me stand with Your heavenly angels. Let me worship You with the cherubim and cry out Holy, Holy is the God all mighty. Worthy is the Lamb who was slain.

May I kiss Your feet! May I be held in Your arms. May I see Your face shining down on me. May I stand in the wedding as Your bride, dressed in white, adorned in jewels; for You have cleansed me and called me Your own.

I am longing for You, my King! Even so come, Lord *Yeshua* come! I am waiting for You. For You are coming soon! Amen and amen.

APRIL 1

My Salvation

*Behold, God is my salvation! I will trust and will not be afraid. For the Lord **Adonai** is my strength and my song. He also has become my salvation."*   Isaiah 12:2 TLV

Abba, You are my strength and my song. You take me down roads of affliction to bring me to a place of dependence on You. And once we start this journey, You pour out Your delight, treasures from heaven on me, so I can continue. You are amazing, my Lord. You know how weak I am so You strengthen me from time to time. Refreshing my dry thirsty lips so I can take another step. How beautiful You are that You love me and bless me so.

Forgive me *Adonai* of any wrongs I have done. Help me to walk the straight and narrow. Help me, *Adonai, to* get through this day. I have so much I need to do, but I can't do it in my strength and knowledge. Feed me, teach me, show me Your will for today alone. For tomorrow is not a promise but a hope, and all my hope lies within You.

May I give of myself to those in need. May I offer up a sacrifice of praise. May I pray for my enemies that they may come to know You. May I do Your bidding throughout this day. Bring me so close to You that I feel Your breath upon my face.

I love You, my Lord, and I ask all these things in Your precious name. Amen.

April 2

Circumcise Our Hearts

*All the congregation of Israel must keep it. But if an outsider dwells with you, who would keep the Passover for **Adonai**, all his males must be circumcised. Then let him draw near and keep it. He will be like one who is native to the land. But no uncircumcised person may eat from it.*
Exodus 12:47–48 TLV

Abba, Passover is coming soon. May we celebrate it as You have commanded. May we remember how You saved your people from bondage and that one day soon You will return and save us from the troubles of this world.

Circumcise our hearts, O Lord. Let us be cleansed of our past. Toss our sins into the bottom of the ocean where they will never be seen again. Cleanse us Lord of all our iniquities that we may be able to serve You, offering others grace and love. Give us wisdom and the desire to follow Your every command.

Abba, I have been blessed to live a life of health, love and freedom. But there are those who have not had these blessings. I pray for those who have been persecuted for their faith. May they be strengthened, may angels surround them and help lead them in this battle. For those who have not been loved, Lord my heart breaks for them. Pour out Your *Ruach* upon them. Let them see Your face. Let Your *Ruach* swell within them and may they find the one pure love that only comes from You. For those who are ill, *Jehovah Rapha,* I beg You to heal their bodies. Give them strength, give them wholeness. Let them stand strong in the battle against Satan. Let nothing hold them down. Let your grace abound in them.

Abba, all things are possible to those who believe. *Abba,* do not let the troubles of this world allow us to grow bitter or harbor ill towards each other. For we have all fallen short and have sinned. Let us look to You only for answers. May we seek You, every moment of every day. Amen and Amen.

APRIL 3

Freedom

*So you are to observe the Feast of **Matzot**, for on this very same day have I brought your ranks out of the land of Egypt. Therefore you are to observe this day throughout your generations as an eternal ordinance.*
Exodus 12:17 TLV

Abba, I thank You for bringing us out of bondage to a place of rest. To a place where we may dwell with You.

May we celebrate Your covenant of love, Your covenant of protection as we celebrate this time of Passover. May we reflect on where we were, where You have brought us and to know how that without Your indwelling *Ruach,* this would have not been possible. How blessed is this generation that Your love is in us. How grateful we are, that You have given us Your *shalom,* Your peace.

Abba, as I reflect on this past year, You have brought me through many trials and yet I am still in the midst of some. Help me understand how to be like You through these trials. Help me to show others who You really are. I cannot stand without Your peace, Your love, Your strength. For I am weak, my Lord, and I need Your arms around me to hold me in the midst of them.

I know *Abba,* that all tests are to build me up in You. All things work together for Your good. I know some of this mess is a battle with Satan and some I have brought on myself. But Lord, I need You to show up as You did with Moses. Put a pillar of fire between me and my enemies and open the seas that I may pass through to the other side. Take me to the promised land, a place of milk and honey. Let me taste of Your goodness. Let me rest in You this day.

Adonai, may I lay my crown at Your feet. For all I want is to worship You forever. Amen.

APRIL 4

Your Truths

For whatever was written before was were written for our learning, that through perserverance and through encouragement of the Scriptures we might have hope.   Romans 15:4 WMB

Abba, how I love the *Rhema* of God! Your living word You have spoken to us that we may know Your love. For You know every hair on our heads and You know exactly what we need to build us up in You each day.

Abba, give us clarity of mind, that as we search through Your word, we have revelation of Your truths. Let us apply it to our lives and speak it to others. For Your word is our lifeline, Holy and true. Blessed be the name of *Adonai!*

How foolish we can be, my Lord, to think we can choose which parts of Your word to believe and which parts we wish to toss into the sea? For in this act of selfishness and pride, we will suffocate and drown in our own iniquities and sin. Causing others to go astray and leading them into the depths of hell. Forgive, O Lord, let us see Your truths! Brand them on the doors of our hearts!

Abba, may Your *Rauch* quench our souls today whenever lies are spoken. Open our eyes to when the enemy is in front of us, trying to deceive us with sweet words or gifts. Let us be strong in spirit because You live in us and we know Your truths.

Let us stand on the roof tops and proclaim Your coming. Let us keep our eyes fixed on the heavens, because the things You have spoken of before His return are happening before our very eyes. Because one day soon, every knee shall bow, every tongue confess that *Yeshua* is Lord!

To You, my Lord, I give my soul. To You, my King, I praise forever and ever more. Amen.

April 5

Walk Across The Seas

*Answering, Peter said to Him, "Master, if it's You, command me to come to did you doubt?" Mathew You on the water." And He said, "Come!" And Peter got out of the boat and walked on the water to go to **Yeshua**. But seeing the wind, he became terrified. And beginning to sink, he cried out, saying, "Master, save me!" immediately **Yeshua** reached out His hand and grabbed him. And He said to him, "O you of little faith, why do you doubt?*   Matthew 14:28–31 TLV

Abba, my soul rejoices in You. My heart cries to be close to You. My body aches to be held by You. So I praise You, my Lord, for sending me the *Ruach ha Kodesh,* the great Comforter, the true healer, my companion, my friend!

Abba, You use times of trouble to build me up and strengthen me. But it can be so hard Lord! For when my eyes are focused solely on You, I know no matter high the waves of turmoil come, I can rise above them all. But when I start to drown, it is in those moments, if I allow the waves to be my focus, that I allow them to be bigger than You. For nothing can be further from the truth! Praise Your Holy name!

Help me, Lord! Continue to speak to me. May my eyes see nothing but You. If my eyes turn Lord, carry me, do not let me sink, but may we walk across the raging seas together. May we get to the other side and rejoice! For all things are possible if You are holding my hand!

For You are a God of love, a God of hope, a God of truth. If You say it, it cannot change. So I know Lord, that I am covered by Your blood and my soul can rest in You alone.

Thank You, my Lord, for choosing me to be Your bride. I will keep my lamp lit and await Your return. It is for You alone I live. Amen.

April 6

The Good Shepherd

I am the good shepherd. The good shepherd lays down his life for the sheep.
Yochanan (John) 10:11 WMB

Abba, who am I that You would leave heaven for? Who am I that You would suffer and die the most cruel of deaths for? Who am I but a speck of dust, a moment in time, a person who fails You over and over again. But You, my Lord, knew all these things. You knew that without You, I would be lost forever and chose to come lay Your life down for me.

May I learn to love like You. May I learn to speak like You. May I find ways to witness to those that are not like me, whose ways I don't understand, people who agitate me and or put me off. For I tend to walk away from them, but Lord, You did not walk from me. So *Abba,* I am asking for Your *Ruach* to do this through me. So I can bear witness. That one more soul may enter the kingdom of heaven. For wide is the path but narrow is the gate, and I know many will not enter.

May I fix my eyes on You this day, for no one knows what it holds. But I will trust in You moment by moment, my Lord. I will stay in prayer with You throughout the day. For I know that all things are possible because You are here and You promised to never let me go.

Heal my friends and family, my Lord, of any illness, hurt, or pain. Lead them into the everlasting and may Your glory reign over them now and forever more. I ask all these things in Your Holy name. Amen.

APRIL 7

Atonement For My Sins

For what does it profit a man, to gain the whole world, and forfeit his life?   Mark 8:36 WMB

Abba, I thank you for the atonement of my sins. For I am far too weak to have been held righteous, but it is through Your sacrifice I'm considered a saint. How humbled and amazed I am at the length You went through to save my soul. How great is the love You lavish on me.

Abba, I am in search for answers. I'm in need of understanding. Remove this plank from my eyes that I might see clearly. Fill my mind with knowledge. Let me know without question the path You have for me and how I am to walk it.

Give me strength today to do what is right. Give me discernment where there may be confusion. Let me be the answer and not the problem as I lead others at work. Let those who see and hear me, only see You. For You are the answer to every prayer. You are the words to every song. All I could ever want is You.

Infuse me, my Lord, to live a supernatural life; showing Your strength in my weakness, showing Your love when I do not feel loved, to be the grace for someone else.

Abba, I give You my heart, my soul, my song, my praise. I give it all to You.

For it is in Your Holy name I pray. Amen.

April 8

A Heart Condition

Do not love the world or the things in the world. If anyone loves the world, the love of the Father is not in him. For everything in the world—the desire of the flesh, the desire of the eyes, and the boasting of life—is not from the Father but from the world.   1 John 2:15–16 TLV

Abba, there are times when I am so lonely that I long for someone to hold and comfort me, but I know that this desire is a desire of the flesh and that if I keep my eyes completely focused on You, you take away these feelings. You cover me and hold me with Your wings, and every desire and every feeling of loneliness, hurt, or pain is quickly diminished.

You, my *Adonai,* are building me a place, a home in the heavenly realms. You fulfill every one of my desires that are good and holy. For I am Your bride and You laid down Your life for me. What more could I ever dream of? For no one could ever love me the way You do.

I praise You, Lord, for my family, for they love me so. I praise You, my Lord, for my friends and the treasures they share. I praise You, my Lord, most for Your unfailing love. And I will dream and prepare for the day of our wedding, for on that day I will understand what agape love truly is.

To You, I lay my life down. To You, I praise. Amen.

APRIL 9

Hosanna In The Highest

"So they took palm branches and went out to meet Him, shouting, '" **Hoshia-na! Baruch ha-ba b'shem ADONAI!** *Blessed is He who comes in the name of the Lord!' The King of Israel!"* John 12:13 TLV

Oh, my *Adonai,* how beautiful is Thy name. For You gave it all for me. You are my everything.

I lay down my branches, my cloak, my crown just to Thee. You are the only God in this universe, the only God who I seek.

I will seek You in the morning, in the night and all throughout the day. Because You gently whisper in my ear and show me the way.

The way is not common to this world. My culture is a foreigner to this land. But if I act like others do, I would only be taking Satan's hand.

For this world is corrupt, people fighting all over the world. But I am a born again believer. I will always be my *Abba's* little girl.

So I will take my palm branches and raise them singing to Thee. For only You can save us. Only You are the One true King.

You took on my sufferings so I can live with You and sing. Hosanna, Hosanna in the Highest. You alone are my everything! Amen and amen.

April 10

In Remembrance Of You
⟶ ⁂ ⟵

*And when He had taken **matzah** and offered the **bracha**, He broke it and gave it to them, saying, "This is My body, given for you. Do this in memory of Me." In the same way, He took the cup after the meal, saying, "This cup is the new covenant in My blood, which is poured out for you.*
Luke 22:19–20 TLV

May I proclaim of Your love, day after day; week after week; year after year, until You return for me, my Lord.

Let me come to You in humble reverence. May I come to You as a broken vessel. May I come to You knowing You hold life and death, the key to the gates of heaven and hell. And that I am nothing, my Lord, without You!

You are Holy my God and have given me the privilege of partaking of Your sacrifice for me. May I always remember it is only by Your amazing grace; by the Fathers love and the Son's sacrifice that I can pray and You hear my voice.

How I praise You my most precious King.

For it is in *Yeshua's* name I pray. Amen.

APRIL 11

Remember Your Teachings

For I received from the Lord what I also passed on to you—that the Lord **Yeshua,** *on the night He was betrayed, took* **matzah** *; and when He had given thanks, He broke it and said, "This is My body, which is for you. Do this in memory of Me." In the same way, He also took the cup, after supper, saying, "This cup is the new covenant in My blood. Do this, as often as you drink it, in memory of Me." For as often as you eat this bread and drink this cup, you proclaim the Lord's death until He comes.*
1 Corinthians 11:23-26 TLV

Adonai, it is so sad that in the hustle and bustle of this world, we often forget to think of You. For when we get angry at someone, our mind immediately turns to them, versus on You. Responding in our flesh versus how You would want us to respond.

When a financial difficulty comes our way, our mind wanders in all sorts of ways trying to figure out how to solve the problem. Instead, we should be on our knees, being thankful. For in reality, You alone are in control of this situation.

Help me this day and every day, my King, to take communion and remember You. For in the scheme of things, I have control of nothing but my actions. Therefore, I need to give everything else in my life to You. I need to praise You for Your ultimate sacrifice. For in it, is the only way of salvation.

Let me consume Your body and Your blood this day. Let me remember all Your teachings, all the sacrifices You made just for me. Then when trouble comes, may You consume me and let me resemble what I have partaken. So others will want to partake in You too.

You are the God of hope, the God of love. No one comes before You that has not partaken You in their hearts. I praise You for the sacrifice You gave just for me. Amen.

APRIL 12

Goodness Of The Lord

*Surely I trust that I will see the goodness of **Adonai** in the land of the livings. Wait for **Adonai**. Be strong, let Your heart take courage, and wait for **Adonai**.* *Psalms 27:13–14 TLV*

Adonai, I believe I heard You speak to me just yesterday about holding onto and trusting in You. That out of this trust I will be blessed.

Adonai, there is nothing in this world but You that gives me this hope, this love, this trust. For You alone have delivered me from the pit. You alone have redesigned this broken pot to hold water so that I may never thirst again.

Abba, I trust You! I am just asking for a small blessing, just enough to get me by. I don't need the bells and whistles, or all that is grand. I just need to know I am on the right path, then I know You will see me through.

Abba, Please teach me new and wonderful things about You! Let me have visions and dreams of You. Let me smell Your presence. Let me feel Your touch. Let everything around me call out Your name.

Help me to be consistent in my walk with You. For I know there will be seasons of plenty and seasons of drought. But my walk should not vary due to these. I want to make a difference in this life with my friends, family and neighbors. Let me not sleep until I have done all that You desire for me to do. Let my words, my thoughts, my actions be consumed by the fire of Your love. May this love You have given me, flow freely from my heart to others, now and forever more. Amen.

April 13

Laying It All Down

Therefore do not worry about tomorrow, for tomorrow will worry about itself. Each day has enough trouble of its own.   Matthew 6:34 TLV

Adonai, My King, blessed be Your Holy name. For You are mighty and just. Righteousness is Your countenance. Love and grace is Your name. For we have not begun to understand Your strength. We are not able to understand Your Holiness. For our minds are full of sin and our bodies are weak, all the way down to the marrow.

May I not worry about what may and may not happen today. May I give You all of me each moment of this day. For it cannot be repeated. It cannot be reclaimed, so we need to make today the best we can and offer it all to You.

So may we lay down our palm branches, our lives before You, in offering all we have to You. May we run through the streets gathering all we know to come hear the words of our King! Oh Lord, my heart is ready to see Your face and my lips are ready to sing, "Holy, Holy is the Lord almighty, blessed be His Holy name."

I thank You, my King, that You have not forgotten your children. That one day soon You will come and take us home. May we be prepared, for no one knows the day or the hour, but we know this day is coming soon.

May we all worship and pray and dedicate our lives to You this day and give ourselves as an offering of praise, now and forever more. Amen.

APRIL 14

Fore Knowing

Now it was just before the feast of Passover. **Yeshua** *knew that His hour had come to depart from this would to the Father. Having loved His own who were in the world, He loved them until the end.*
John 13:1 TLV

Abba, as we come into the celebration of Passover, may we try to understand what *Yeshua* was going through. To be brought in as King one day, to eat and drink with the disciples, then a few days later for Judas to betray Him. Then for many who called Him kind, to stand with the Pharisees and to call out His name to be crucified. But to have the foreknowledge of what would come after He had risen. This had to be the only way He could make it through.

I know I will never suffer to the degree You had to suffer. Praise be to God! But I am holding on to the knowledge You have given me. That through all things,, You are there. That if I am persecuted for Your name's sake, I will reap rewards in heaven. It is through this knowledge I can bear the hard times. It is through this knowledge that I have peace.

Help me love those who persecute me, my Lord. To show them Your love and to pray for them. This is not easy for me! Please teach me how during this Passover season. For I know this is Your desire for me, that I might be more like You.

Worthy are You, *Yeshua,* worthy of all praise, honor and glory. How I praise You for foreknowing what You had to do for me, who is so unworthy. Coming down from heaven and going through torture and suffering, so I could spend eternity with You. I love You! I love you with all that I am. Amen and amen.

April 15

Communion

Therefore whoever eats this bread or drinks the Lord's cup in a way unworthy of the Lord will be guilty of the body and the blood of the Lord.
1 Corinthians 11:27 WMB

Abba, many don't heed this warning that You give. But, my King, You don't waste Your words on us.

For when we receive communion, we do this to remember the sacrifice You made for us. To receive healing in our bodies and soul and to commune with You as one.

My King, let me never receive without a clean heart and a clear mind. Let this time be the most reverent of times, a joyous time with You.

I pray for those who do not understand this meaning. I pray for those who judge others and won't allow them to partake. For no man knows the heart, but You. I pray for those who do not partake. That they come to a place in You, where they find forgiveness and become new in You.

I praise You for Your sacrifice. I Praise You for every opportunity to be reminded that You gave it all for me.

I love You, my King. Hold me now, my Lord, and all through eternity. Amen.

April 16

Keep Me Strong

Little children, I am with you only a little longer. You will search for Me; and just as I told the Judean leaders, so I say to you now, "Where I am going, you cannot come." I give you a new commandment, that you love one another. Just as I have loved you, so also you must love one another. By this all will know that you are My disciples, if you have love for one another.
John 13:33–34 TLV

Abba, how easy it is to follow You and serve You when all is going well. But when Satan sneaks in and causes turmoil and destruction in our lives, we have a tendency to do things that are not of You. There will be a day when I am confronted by others of where I stand. It may keep me from a new job, having certain friends, a loan, or even my life, but I know, my Lord, that my life is worth nothing if I don't have You.

Peter walked and talked with You. But when You were not with him, becoming weak was easy. I praise You, almighty God, that You sent us the indwelling of the *Ruach ha Kodesh,* because through Him we have strength. Because now we don't just walk with You, but it is You who lives in us. We are weak but with You in us, we are strong! How gracious You are, my Lord, that You gave us Your Son to atone for our sins and then the power through Your *Ruach* to live a life of love and truth.

Fill me, my Lord, from the tip of my hairs to the bottom of my feet with Your *Ruach.* Let every part of my being be on fire with Your love. May You use my arms to hold those who are hurting. My legs to walk the miles I need to go to serve You. My hands to knead the bread so the hungry will be filled. My words, may they speak the truth, no matter how desperate the situation may be. May Your words pierce the souls of the wicked that all might believe. I give You my life, my home, my work, my soul. Help me, *Adonai, to* make it all about You. No matter the circumstances help me to be that pure example of Your love. Amen and amen.

APRIL 17

Grateful

"Even as the Son of Man came not to be served, but to serve, and to give his life as a ransom for many."   Matthew 20:28 WMB

Every year, my Lord, I think of the beating, the slashing of Your skin, the piercing from the thorns, then the holes driven in Your wrist by the nails. I can't imagine suffering in this way. I can't imagine the pain. But what makes it hardest for me, is knowing that it is my sin, some of this suffering were put there. Knowing that I have been selfish and looking out for my own desires helped to break Your heart.

Oh, my Lord, I weep over the thought of hurting You in this way. I would never want to cause another person this pain, especially You. If I had lived back then, what would I have done? Would I have been like Mary and followed every word? Or would I have been like Barabbas, angry at the world, only following the sword and my own hate? Not understanding that Your sacrifice was what would save us.

I am grateful that You brought me here to this place and time. To a family who knows Your word. To friends who love and honor You. I am on my knees in worship of You, my King. For You love me enough to know every detail of my life and to have prepared this day that I could know You in this way.

I lift up my hands to You in service, my Lord. For I hunger to give You all that I am. For this is the purpose for which You created me. I lift up my voice in song. For I want all to know how much I love You. For without You, my life would be in ruins. But with You, I am rich, I am strong, I am loved, and I am pure. With You all things are made new. And I am a new creation! For this I praise You, my Lord. I thank You my sweet Jesus!

May I inhale Your words, Your truth, Your forgiveness and may I exhale You in every way, every day.

For its in *Yeshua's* name I pray. Amen.

APRIL 18

Your Heartbeat

"Teaching them to observe all things that I have commanded you. Behold, I am with you always, even to the end of the age."
Matthew 28:20 WMB

Abba, I lift up to You my petitions and my praise.

For every word that comes forth from my mouth I shall be judged for. So may I teach Your word. Showing all I meet Your unfathomable love. Touching others and having You heal them. To praise You in a way that causes others to worship. To be so compassionate that it could only be You working through me. This, my Lord, is my plea.

For I want You to be so close to me that Your heart beat is all I can hear. And knowing that You are with me, holding me, standing between me and my enemy.

To know that as time goes by I shall see You face to face. To really become intimate with You; knowing the very details of Your character. And to know You are there until the end of all times. Well, my King, this thought takes my breath away.

I could dream of nothing more majestic, more wonderful than to be Your bride!

My life is Yours for the taking, this day and forevermore. Amen and amen!

APRIL 19

Reality Of Your Favor

Don't be deceived. God is not mocked, for whatever a man sows, that he also shall reap.   Galatians 6:7 WMB

Abba, I cry out to You for forgiveness. I have worked all my life for the American dream, for what I have been shown that I deserve. But truly Lord, I am only deserving of death, because of the sins in my life. But *Abba,* I praise You with all my heart because You have found favor with me. You have given me a home, a job and people in my life that make a difference in this world.

Abba, help me to be more sensitive to Your *Ruach* that lives within me. Let me know You in the gentle wind. Let me hear You in that still small voice. May I have visions and dreams. Teach me *Adonai,* how to be so close to You; that my walk is pure and true. May I grow every day in intimacy with You, because I am Your bride, and You are preparing a place for me to spend eternity loving You, serving You and worshiping You, my King!

Cover me this day with Your wings. *Adonai* I praise You for the protection of my family. There have been times when we do not see the angels keeping us safe. Yet there have been obvious times of Your love; catching us in a fall, keeping us from a wreck and You standing next to us when evil is near. Please *Adonai,* bring these times to the front of our memory. Let us not forget the goodness, the favor that has come from You. For the reality of Your favor keeps the intimacy of Your love visible for my eyes to see.

Thank You for loving me the way I need to be loved.

For it is in Christ Holy name that I pray. Amen.

April 20

Dwell Within My Soul

*Now may the God of patience and encouragement grant you to be likeminded with one another in the manner of Messiah **Yeshua**, so that together with one voice you may glorify the God and Father of our Lord **Yeshua** the Messiah.*   Romans 15:5–6 TLV

Abba, please forgive me! I walked Yesterday in my own strength. I showed anger, disappointment and frustration in myself and in others. This is not of Christ. This is not how You want me to be!

O Lord, just as You dwelled as a pillar of fire in the Holy of Holies, You dwell within my soul. Make Your mighty *Ruach* within me be a strong tower. Let me lay in the shadows of Your glory.

Move through me *Adonai* and give me strength. May I not act without thought of You. May I not speak unless it is to edify. I don't want to move, my *Adonai,* unless You are in control. I don't want to exist unless You are with me.

May I be a pure example and leader at my work. Help me bring us to one mind in You. May I plant the seeds that You water. May they bloom to be beautiful lilies in the field, with an aroma that is sweet as it arises into the heavens.

I praise You *Abba,* for hearing my prayer. I praise You, *Adonai,* for answering!!

May this day be about You and the life You give us each day through the sacrifice of our Lord *Yeshua ha Mashiach.*

To You, my Lord, I bow in worship. To You, my *Adonai,* we sing "Hallelujah to our King," forever and ever. Amen.

APRIL 21

Endure Temptations
❧⊹❧

No temptation has taken hold of you except what is common to mankind. But God is faithful—He will not allow you to be tempted beyond what you can handle. But with the temptation He will also provide a way of escape, so you will be able to endure it.   1 Corinthians 10:13 TLV

    Abba, it is so good to be with You this morning, to share the first fruits of my day. For You are more beautiful than a sunset reflecting upon a lake in the mountains. Your love is sweeter than the purest of honeycomb upon my lips. Your fellowship, my Lord, warms my inner soul. And Your grace, my King, well there is nothing that can compare. For You are, my Lord, my Savior, my God. All I want is to press into You and hear Your voice whisper things of Your love in my ear.

    Speak to me today, my Lord! Tell me of Your wonders. Tell me what my future may hold. Not if will I live here or there. Not if I will be rich or poor. But tell me, Lord, about being Your bride and all that I can do to please You. Tell me, Lord, where You wish for me to go and how I should serve You. Tell me, Lord, of the truths that keep me upon that righteous path. Tell me how to escape those temptations that come my way, for I do not want to grieve the *Ruach ha Kodesh,* to which I am sealed, for He is my strength, my comforter, my rock, my guide. Let us commune with one another this day and forever more.

    Abba, if there is something I do that displeases You, tell me. If there is someplace I am to go, show me. For my heart is open and my spirit is willing. Keep me from being deceived and from filling up my plate so much that I don't have my quiet time with You. You are my Father, my husband, my Lord, You are my everything! For You, my Lord, are the only reason I live.

    To You, my God, I give all praise. To You, my Lord, I lay down my life. Save my family Lord. Let them see and understand the wonders of Your love. Heal them, O Lord, so they may serve You, honor You and teach of Your grace. May we lift up our voice and may the heavenly angels join us in song, forever more. Amen.

April 22

Choosing What Is Better

But answering her, the Lord said, "Martha, Martha, you are anxious and bothered about many things; but only one thing is necessary. For Miriam has chosen the good part, which will not be taken away from her."
John 10:41–42 TLV

Abba, there are so many days I fill my time up with meaningless work. Staying busy but realizing none of it meant anything to me or anyone else. Then I think if I put so much of Your work in my life that I will please You. But that is not right either. Help me, Lord, spend the first moments of my day focused on nothing but You. Learning Your precepts, getting to know You intimately. Then Lord may I spend the rest of the day in service to others, serving my family first then my neighbor. Lord, I am ashamed! I do not even know most of my neighbors names, so how can I possibly serve them?

Ok Lord, get me out of my box. You know how hard it is for me to start a conversation. So, O Lord, speak through me that I may get to know them. Help me, O Lord; this can only come from You. Help me be more like Martha and be hospitable. Let me use the home You gave me to serve others. But at the end of the day when all I want to do is close my eyes and rest. May I seek Your face once more. May I lay down at Your feet all that happened on that day so then, Lord, I can rest in You.

My Lord, this is a lot for me, but through You, all things are possible. I love You and I know You will help those whose heart is pure and whose thoughts are Yours. May I be like Mary and sit at Your feet today.

In *Yeshua's* name I pray. Amen.

April 23

Obedience

*Now therefore, fear **Adonai** and worship Him in sincerity and in truth. Get rid of the gods that your fathers had worshipped beyond the River and in Egypt, and worship **Adonai**. If it seems bad to you to worship **Adonai**, then choose for yourselves today whom you will serve—whether the gods that your fathers worshipped that were beyond the River or the gods of the Amorites in whose land you are living. But as for me and my household, we will worship **Adonai**!"*   Joshua 24:14–15 TLV

Adonai, I praise You for the wisdom and understanding that was imparted unto me this week. I only ask, my King, that this be the beginning of a new way of life for me.

That since I have been called, that I might rise to the level of Your expectations just as Joshua did. And even though I am unaware of all You might have for me. I will go in obedience in the direction You are leading.

Increase in me Your truths. Allow Your *Ruach* to arise in me and may the blessings of sound judgement, discipline, understanding, and truths be firm in my foundation, written upon the walls of my heart. May I have the mind of *Yeshua* to teach the nations of Your perfect love that You have for all.

For Just as Joshua followed You and led the Israelites into the promised land. May I lead others to put away other gods and to follow You into our promised land, our heavenly home.

As for me and my household, we shall worship You, my *Adonai* forever! Amen.

April 24

Suffering

*But **Adonai** has been my fortress and my God the rock of my refuge.*
Psalms 94:22 TLV

Adonai, You know all things and You allow all things to work for our good and Your glory. But *Abba,* I have a hard time understanding how when a little one suffers it is for our good. Why the Holocaust had to happen, or why people die from starvation.

But I know Your word is perfect and is Holy and just. So if salvation can come for them, or for those around the ones suffering. To God be all glory, honor, and praise!

Adonai, I will take my refuge in You alone! For I know that You have not only given me all that I have, but You give me each breath I take, and with each breath, there is a purpose under heaven. My Lord, give me strength as I take each step today to fulfill its purpose. Give me the ability to say the right things that will minister to someone else's heart. Give me a life full of wonder and hope in You!

For You are my rock and my shield, the one who protects, loves, and endures all things. You are my God and I will praise You forever! Amen.

April 25

Accepting Christ As Lord

*So the soldiers, when they executed **Yeshua**, took His outer garments and made four parts, a part for each soldier. They took His tunic also, but it was seamless, woven top to bottom in one piece. So they said to one another, "Let's not tear it, but cast lots for it to see whose it will be." This was so the Scripture would be fulfilled, "They divided My garments among them, and for My clothing they cast lots." So the soldiers did these things.*
John 19:23–24 TLV

Abba, even the smallest of details that were prophesied were fulfilled in order that all who read Your truth, the *Rhema* of God may know that *Yeshua* is Lord!

Abba, I know in my heart that You will give each person every opportunity to accept You as Lord before their last breath. I have family and friends, my Lord, who are not saved. I beg of You, Lord, that You send them people in their lives they will listen to. Put situations in their lives that can't be denied. Make it happen daily until they fall on their knees, beg for forgiveness, and cry out to You to be saved. This Lord is the most important thing I could ask for. They need You! I need You and want Your touch every day until my final breath and beyond the grave. For You are my Rock and my Salvation; in You alone I trust.

I thank You, my Lord, that You hear this prayer. I ask all who read this, pray it for their family and friends too. For one day soon, You will be coming in the clouds to take us all home. May we all be waiting and ready for Your return.

In *Yeshua's* name I pray. Amen.

APRIL 26

The Journey

*"The heart of man plans his course, but **ADONAI** directs his steps."*
Proverbs 16:9T LV

My King, You have taken me places and taught me things I never thought possible! You have put before me a path, a course, I thought could only be a dream. And I am not sure the full extent of where You are leading me.

But I know this: If I take one day at a time, completely trusting in You. Growing in my knowledge of You! Being willing to serve and honor You above all things. Wherever this path leads, You will not only direct it; You will be there, seeing me through!

Adonai, I have stepped out in obedience. Knowing that this path I am on, I cannot do unless You are there—unless You guide me through. For I am weak, but You, my King, are strong!

Since I have stepped forward in obedience, You have removed from me all un-forgiveness and all bitterness; all the hurts from my past are gone! Praise Your Holy name!

So I know without doubt this is the road You will have me travel. And I'm looking forward to this journey. This experience in and with You!

Thank You *Yeshua* for this truth, for Your unsurpassable love. For believing in me and giving me more than my hearts desires!

For its in *Yeshua's* name I pray. Amen and amen!

April 27

Written Law

"It is clear that you are a letter from Messiah delivered by us—written not with ink but with the **Ruach** *of the living God, not on tablets of stone but on tablets of human hearts."* 2 Corinthians 3:3 TLV

Abba, it has been evident in my life that people need the law written to understand what is right and what is wrong, due to our selfish hearts.

But when You come to live in our hearts, You rearrange the mess we created to live in and design a heart so beautiful that others want to take it in.

You throw out self and put others in its place. You trash anger and bought us grace, to light our way. You wrap it in love so that others feel warm and protected. You write Your truths upon our hearts so that we never are without them and never wonder whose we are.

The prophets of old knew that Your temple had to be rebuilt in the hearts of man, for we can never be good enough to follow all the laws. But all is possible with You living in us, instead.

For just as in a marriage, the men are to live as *Yeshua,* laying their life down for their wife. The women are to be like the *Ruach ha Kodesh,* the "helpers" to their husbands, serving and loving with all they have.

This is the law that is written upon our hearts, to live this way toward the church, the body of Christ. For if this was what we all strived for. What a different world this would be!

Let me strive for this every day. And I can only be this with You living through me each day. Amen and amen.

April 28

Various Gifts And Abilities

*"The purpose is that through Messiah's community the multi-faceted wisdom of God might be made known to the rulers and authorities in the heavenly places, which is in keeping with the eternal purpose that He carried out in Messiah **Yeshua** our Lord."*
Ephesians 3:10–11 TLV

Abba, Yeshua stated: that we are to love our neighbor as we love ourselves. And I have seen this during this past week in our community of believers, people helping people who have lost everything. Going out of their way, sacrificially, to give unto others as they would give unto You.

Because we are multi-faceted in our abilities and gifts, there have been many different ways in which others are able to bless. And I know that in the midst of troubles. I did not cry as much about the mess as I did about the blessings.

My Lord, how rich I feel in the favor of Christ Jesus. That He would surround me with love from others and how much in love with You I am.

It's good to see this in times of desperation, my Lord. I wish we could see it more in our day to day lives. For this is my prayer.

My King, I am Your daughter, a vessel open to do the will of Your choosing. Please show me anything You would have of me this day, anyone to bless or to serve. May I be the likeness of You!

In *Yeshua's* name I pray. Amen and amen!

APRIL 29

Disciple For Christ

"Therefore accept one another, even as Messiah also accepted you, to the glory of God."   Romans 15:7 WMB

Abba, may I always love others, even those who are very different from me. Even those who do evil before You that I can be the example of Christ.

For it was this kind of love and the many prayers from my grandmother, that took me out of a life of sin, into a life of worshipping You. For she never condemned me, but she showed me by example and always speaking Your truths: That Your agape love covers a life of sin. That in You, all things are made new. And I shall forever praise You for Your forgiveness and love.

Abba, as a disciple for the Lord Jesus Christ, I need to be the most tolerant of them all. For everyone was made in Your image. So when I look at others, I need to see them as You do, for they may be lost, but they are never forgotten. You are always seeking for them to come home.

Let any remembrance of me be that I loved You first, and then that I loved others and sought to bring all to the knowledge of You.

In *Yeshua's* name I pray. Amen.

April 30

A New Way Of Life

*"Happy is the man who finds wisdom and the man who gains understanding. For her trade-value is better than silver, and her yield better than fine gold. She is more precious than jewels and nothing you desire compares to her. Length of days is in her right hand. In her left hand are riches and honor. Her ways are pleasant ways, and all of her paths are **shalom**. She is a tree of life to those who embrace her, and blessed will be all who hold firmly to her. My son, hold on to sound wisdom and discernment, do not let them out of your sight."*
Proverbs 3:13–18, 21 TLV

Adonai, I praise You for the wisdom and understanding that was imparted unto me this week. I only ask, my King, that this will be the beginning of a new way of life for me.

That since I have been called, that I might rise to the level of Your expectations. And even though I am unaware of all You might have for me, I will go in obedience to proclaim the gospel of Christ.

Increase in me Your truths. Allow Your *Ruach* to arise in me and may the blessings of sound judgement, discipline, understanding and truths be firm in my foundation, written upon the walls of my heart. And may I have the mind of Christ to teach the nations of Your perfect love that You have for all.

For this is the perfect will of Christ, and it's in His name I pray. Amen.

May 1

Even a fool, when he keeps silent, is counted wise. When he shuts his lips, he is thought to be discerning.   Proverbs 17:28 WMB

Adonai, there are many test, many trials just ahead of me. Let me be as wise as a serpent and as gentle as the dove. Let me hold my tongue and speak only the words that You choose to give me. And even though I do not understand why these things must be, may I trust that You have a purpose under heaven for them in my life. That there is a reason for every season and that the end result will be, a closer walk with You.

Abba, I am so hungry for Your love, for your arms to be wrapped around me, for Your tender words to be spoken in my ears, for Your presence of strength and wisdom to go before me. For then I will know that I am safe and secure in Your arms forever.

For Your head is of pure gold, the strong and mighty head of my heart, my home my life. Your hair is as locks of dates; dedicated to the righteous, the One who tends to every detail of my life. I praise You, Lord Jesus, from the top of Your head to the bottom of Your feet that You will guide me in righteousness through every trial and test I might enter into.

Thank You for loving me this much. That You have chosen to forgive me and renew my spirit in You.

For it is in *Yeshua's* name I pray. Amen.

MAY 2

Find Your Heart

Call to Me, and I will answer you—I will tell you great and hidden things, which you do not know."   *Jeremiah 33:3 TLV*

Abba, I call to You, not for You to give me things of this world. But to find Your heart, Your desires for that which I might do this day, that will be pleasing to You!

For as I call upon Your name, I will see and hear new ways of pursuing You. And as I walk toward these pursuits, You will unfold more and more love for me.

Adonai, how majestic, how Holy is the Lord our God. Worthy are You of all praise!

My *Adonai,* please tell me more of You this day. That even though I may not understand how or why things are happening the way they are, I just need to act in obedience and to stay in prayer. For then, my Lord, as You control the oceans waves, You will pour out a new wave of revelation of things that are hidden to me. Your love will increase in me and the gifts You have given unto me will become defined and perfected, that I might become an apostle for Christ.

Thank You that I know that I know You will answer this prayer. For You hear the cries of the saints. And Your desire is that we grow to know You more every day.

In *Yeshua's* name I pray. Amen and amen.

MAY 3

The Eyes Of The Lord Are On the Righteous

*For the eyes of **Adonai** are on the righteous and His ears open to their prayer, but the face of **Adonai** is against those who do evil."*
1 Peter 3:12 TLV

My Lord, You are *El Roi,* for Your eyes are upon all the places that I go. You are *Jehovah Shammah,* always there and Your ear hears every word that I say. You are *Jehovah Jireh,* my provider, for Your hand moves the rocks that are my stumbling blocks. Your arms carry me during the times when I cannot take another step.

Who am I but a sinner, my Lord. One who should be hiding in the shadows. Running away from You as fast as I can.

But You took me from the pit and turned Your face towards me. You told me I was Your child and that *Yeshua's* blood has covered my sins.

So now I run into my *Abba's* lap, where all my fears go away. I can call upon Your name, and You are instantly there. If I have a need, You bless me in every way. If I have a want, You discern what is best for me.

You are the most incredible Father anyone could ask for. And I ask that You to hold me this day. My Lord, will You make this world go away for just a little while. For the only thing I need right now is You!

Thank You that there is not a moment I doubt You hear my prayers. For this is a promise, which is sealed and cannot be broken and I can take comfort in knowing You are there. Amen and amen!

MAY 4

Order For Everything

*Trust in **Adonai** with all your heart, lean not on your own understanding.*   *Proverbs 3:5 TLV*

    As I look upon the beauty of the world, I am in awe of Your majesty. You have placed an order for everything. The flowers produce seeds to start new life. The bees must pollinate for us to have food and fruit. The sun must shine down in order that they will grow and live.

    So it is with us! There is an order You have put into motion. We must accept *Yeshua* by faith in order for us to be saved. We must read the Word in order to bear fruit. We then must witness in order to lay seeds that there may be new life.

    Abba, it is easy to see the order in which You set things in motion so why is it so hard not to always lean on You? Help me today as I struggle to understand why things are going in the direction they are. To look at the flowers, the stars, the moon and remember: You have a reason for everything. If I will follow You, and trust You, the path before me will open and my life will be safe, secure and blessed. Maybe not according to what I am wanting at that moment. But in the end there will be such beauty, such love, my heart will be overwhelmed with joy

    Let me keep my eyes wide open, that I don't miss the smallest of blessing. For I love that You send little love notes throughout the day. Help me see them, to hear them, that I might be reminded of Your love throughout this day.

    I give to You all my love. For I am devoted to no one but You. Envelope me and hold me. For my trust is in You alone.

    In *Yeshua's* name I pray. Amen.

MAY 5

The Veil

Make a fine woven linen curtain of blue, purple and scarlet, with **cheruvim**. *It is to be the work of a skillful craftsman.*   Exodus 26:31 TLV

Abba, as I study about the Tabernacle and how each piece of furniture teaches us about having an intimate relationship with You. I now come to the veil. The one thing that separated You from the priest. That no one could pass through this curtain without being cleansed and sanctified.

How blessed are we among generations, my King, that we have been born after Yeshua's death on the cross. For now we have the privilege of entering into Your presence daily and not just once a year. Not just through priest, but each of us are able to meet You there.

Abba, I want to enter into this place of worship. Into one with You. For I am opening up the veil to my heart and my soul and I am asking for You to reside there. Let me kneel before You, my Lord, and breathe You in. Consume me with fire, with peace, and with the overwhelming joy of Your presence. For this is where I want to stay. May no one and nothing take this from me!

Abba, as I stand here before You, I beg for Your grace to be poured out on me for all the wrongs I have done. I pray for this generation, for the perversions they accept as normal. I cry out for Your mercy to heal my family, my friends and this country. For You alone can save us from ourselves and the evil that is all around us. Arise, my King, and take back this country and all that is Yours!

One day, You will open the heavens and I will come home. Until then, my Lord, I need You, I want You, I must have You all the time residing in me. Let this prayer rise before Your throne and be a sweet fragrance to Your soul.

It is to You alone, my King, I pray. Amen.

MAY 6

Fruit Of Righteousness

*The result of righteousness will be **shalom** and the effect of righteousness will be quietness and confidence forever.*   Isaiah 32:17 TLV

Abba, let me be still before Your throne this day. Let Your peace, that perfect *shalom* resonate through my soul. Let Your confidence be my guide. May the *Ruach ha Kodesh* speak for me and through me so what is spoken are words of wisdom and grace. Let me not be shaken, but strong because You are there holding me and leading the way. May all things work together for Your good and Your glory this day.

May You extend grace to those who will change their ways and turn to You. May You choose justice for those who will continue doing evil as their cause. Let Your righteousness be seen in all its strength and splendor this day.

May Your army of angels encamp around us with their swords sheathed so that the evil one shivers in fear and runs to hide. May we take hold of Your hem that we draw our strength from You. Let no one and nothing get in our way of doing what is right and just in Your eyes.

Let me be at Your feet this day. Anoint my head with oil. Help me to take the plank from my eyes so that I might see clearly and be the one who makes a difference in the lives around me, one soul at a time.

I ask all these things in the name of my Lord, *Yeshua ha Mashiach,* who lives and reigns forever. Amen.

MAY 7

Alpha And Omega

*I am the Alpha and the Omega," says **Adonai Elohim**, "Who is and who was and who is to come, the Almighty!"* The Revelation 1:8 TLV

Adonai, You are the Alpha and the Omega, the One who is, who was, who is to come. You are my rock, my fortress, my sword, my shield, my provider, my healer and the lover of my soul.

You know all things, You hear all cries. You see all hurts and feel all our pains. You knew me when I was in my mother's womb and You know when I will take my last breath. You will never leave me nor forsake me. In all of this I have faith. In all of this I trust. For no matter what I go through. No matter how easy or hard the road I travel might be, You foreknew all things and You are there with me.

Abba, You have moved mountains that I might see You. And You have calmed the seas that I would not drown. You have sent the dove to quiet my spirit in the storm. You have sent me the rain to refresh me in the drought.

I lack nothing, my Lord. Because everything I hope for, all I need, I can find in You. In this I shall rest today. In this I shall praise!

For You are God alone, and You love me!

It's in *Yeshua's* name I pray. Amen.

May 8

Passing Through The Veil

*You are to hang the curtain under the clasps, and bring the Ark within the curtain of the Testimony. The **parokhet** will divide for you between the Holy Place and the Holy of Holies.*   Exodus 26:33 TLV

Abba, as I learn about Your Tabernacle, I see myself and things that have happened in my life. I understand that now, being accepted and saved, I have come into a relationship with You and into the Holy place.

But I want to enter into the most Holy place, my Lord! I want to lay at Your feet. For You to stroke my hair and tell me everything will be OK. To feel Your breath upon my face and hear Your voice, audible to my soul. But the only way to enter into that type of fellowship is to pass through the veil, which had no opening. But the Jews believe the priest were spiritually transformed into this room.

Let me be a high priest today, let me be transformed in my spirit so I can pass through the *parokhet.* Forgive me of all my sins, my Lord. Let me wear the garment of righteousness that all can hear the bells of my robe, knowing I am in this place, yet that I am safe and secure with You.

Speak to me *Adonai,* as You spoke to them. And as You resided between the cherubim as a pillar of fire, may You reside between the walls of my heart. Consuming me, so I am radiant in Your power and love.

Abba, give me wisdom as I go through this day, so I may lead the people that surround me in righteousness and truth. Let me be as strong as the ox and as gentle as the dove. Seeing others the way You see them. Help me to keep my heart and eyes wide open in and through You this day.

My King, my Lord, all I want to do is to worship You forever.

In the name of the Most High God, I pray. Amen.

MAY 9

God's Workmanship

*For we are His workmanship—created in Messiah **Yeshua** for good deeds, which God prepared beforehand so we might walk in them.*
Ephesians 2:10 TLV

My King, never once did I imagine I would be here at this time and place, in this position of servanthood, in this position given by grace. For when I have tried to accomplish things on my own, I have failed time and time again.

But here and now, I see that this is Your design and not mine, for this is to grow and stretch me like I have never been before.

So mold this lump of clay into the vessel of Your desire. But if I may ask, let me be a water urn that Your living water flows through. That as I am pouring out You onto others, for this well to never run dry. For just as the miracle of the five loaves, You will continue to refill it with more and more of You, until we are all satisfied and are at rest in Your arms forever more.

Thank You for preparing my day. And I am choosing to make every minute to count for You. So help me to pour out grace upon grace on others this day.

In *Yeshua's* name. Amen and amen!

May 10

Sharing With Others

Direct them to do good, to be rich in good deeds, to be generous, sharing, storing up for themselves a good foundation for the future, so they might take hold of the true life.　　　1 Timothy 6:18–19 TLV

Abba, this command has it's easy ways for me and yet it's hard ways too. For I greatly enjoy giving, because it shows love to others. But for some, money is security or something they refuse to let go of. They feel as if it is something they must hold onto and can never let go of.

My problem in giving, my Lord, is that when I have helped someone, they have turned around and taken advantage of me. This hurts and at times I have grumbled because of this.

So help me, my Lord. That when I give to a friend or a stranger, let me give without thought. Because my gift is for You. Let me not expect people to repay kindness with kindness. For then I am giving for all the wrong reasons.

But allow me, Lord, to know in my heart, my soul, my mind. That with every good gift I give unto You, I am building up Your kingdom and my eternal treasures too!

For this is my joy. This is my song. Let me praise You each morning and all the day long! Amen and amen!

MAY 11

The Lord Does Not See

*They gush out, they speak arrogance—all the evildoers keep boasting. They crush Your people, **Adonai**, and afflict Your heritage. They slay the widow and the outsider, and murder the fatherless. So they say: "**Adonai** does not see—the God of Jacob pays no attention."*
Psalms 94:4–7 TLV

Adonai, this world is in denial of Your existence. They say I'm a fool to follow after one who's unseen. That You don't hear the cries of Your people. That You never help or give us one thing.

There is cruelty and illness in this life. We all know it is true. But Satan needs to get ready. Because soon he will be bound, for his reign is almost through!

I pray for justice for the oppressed, love for the widow and the orphan some food.

But my biggest prayer, my King, is for anyone who does not know the love of the Father. For them to have one night, a vision, an encounter with You.

My Lord, then they shall see You in the morning sunrise. For Your finger paints a picture of love for us all. They will hear You in the birds singing and see how they care for their young. Just as You take care of Your children and all!

My Lord, You have always shown Your love to us in Your creation. Let them see Your goodness, Your holiness all around them. In every way, this day! Amen and amen!

MAY 12

Do Not Sin In Anger

"Be angry, and do not sin." Don't let the sun go down on your wrath, and don't give place to the devil." Ephesians 4:26–27 WMB

Abba, there are situations in this life that truly make me angry. For I do not understand pure evil and I believe it's hard for any believer to understand. But Satan is cunning and slowly changes society, a word here, a thought there. until the world has taken Your Holy word and says; " I only believe this part." "I do not believe that a good God would send people to hell." "If there was such a God, he would not let bad things happen to good people." *Abba,* this makes me angry. The pure disregard of Your word. I expect that from unsaved people, but for those who claim to follow You, it's a shame!

I also get angry when people idly stand by and watch others get hurt, when there is something they could do to make it stop. Like the soldiers in Germany, who were told to kill the Jews. Many of those soldiers hung themselves instead of hurting others, but then there were those who just obeyed. Never giving a thought to what the outcome was to be.

Abba, as a young believer, I thought it was wrong to be angry. But now I understand. That if I am angry enough and do not sin in my anger, I can make a positive change. I can work to stop the evil in this land.

Help me, my Lord, not give the devil a foothold in my anger, because for me, this is easy to do. But let me seek answers and solutions from You. Then I can move forward with Your army of truth. May we all stand for justice and freedom. May we all take this stand. Let us show mercy and grace to one another. May our sisters and our brothers walk strong and united, with You as our Commander standing at our right hand. May we use Your weapons of warfare to fight the enemy. Let us learn to use each one and to remember; Satan is the real enemy, not our sisters and brothers who walk this land. Amen and amen.

May 13

Slow To Speak

So, then, my beloved brothers, let every man be swift to hear, slow to speak, and slow to anger.   Jacob 1:19 WMB

Adonai, just yesterday, as I went to work I got angry. Lord, I allowed this anger to take Your peace from me throughout the day. This is not of You. This is not how You want me to be!

Yeshua, I cry out to You for wisdom and for Your peace! Help me in times of frustration and hurt, not to allow it to steal my joy. But teach me, my Lord, to do what is right in You!

Help me to be slow to speak, quick to listen and slow to get angry! Help me learn how to let go, and let You take control of the wheel. For You, my Lord, have a righteous anger. So I know there is a way in and through You to handle these situations where righteousness prevails.

May I learn to walk away, to pray, then allow the *Ruach ha Kodesh,* the Holy Spirit to speak through me, that those who have hurt me may hear You, instead of me. Be *Jehovah Jireh* to me, the God who provides and provide for me Your peace, Your wisdom, Your words. Give me this day my daily bread, forgive me of my trespasses and those who have trespassed against me. Lead me not into temptation, but deliver me from evil. For Thine is the kingdom, the power and glory, forever and ever. Amen.

MAY 14

The Trinity

*Therefore You are great, my Lord **Adonai!** For there is none like You, and there is no other God besides You, as we all have heard with our ears.*
2 Samuel 7:23 TLV

Abba, how sweet the moment that You, Lord above all, have chosen to reveal a truth in such a simple way, that even I can understand.

How I have always tried to wrap my head around the trinity, three persons in one. Then one of my teachers at school taught it so eloquently and yet so simple to the children, that even they understood.

For I am Nita, yet I am a daughter, a mother and a boss, I am one person with three different jobs. Three different parts of who I am, and I do not operate the same with any of them. Yet I am still me.

For You are God, the creator of the universe. A Father to all, and the lover of our souls. Yet, You are *Yeshua,* the one who came to save and forgives us of our sins. You are the *Ruach ha Kodesh,* who lives in us, so that we can draw on Your strength, who gives us wisdom to get through this life and defeat the enemy. How it is all You, just in the three different ways in which You serve us.

How perfect and how beautiful You are. For You are the great I Am. And You are everything we need wrapped up in One mighty King!

Abba, how I want to stand in front of Your throne forever and cry out with the four living creatures and all the angels saying" Holy, Holy, Holy is The Lord God Almighty. Who was and is and is to come. It is to You, my God, I pray. Amen.

MAY 15

Speaking Against Another

Do not speak evil against one another, brethren. The one who speaks against a brother or judges his brother, speaks evil against the Torah and judges the Torah. But if you judge the Torah, you are not a doer of the Torah, but a judge.   *Jacob (James) 4:11 TLV*

Abba, who am I but a sinner. For I have sinned against You from afar. I have hurt myself and others. So who am I to cast judgement on others.

Help me not to hold onto the past. Help me to forgive and let go of all wrongs done to me. Let me stand before Your throne washed by the blood of the Lamb. Let me speak Your truth and let me honor You this day.

For You are a God of hope, a God of peace, a God who judges the sins of the wicked and forgives those who cry out to You.

Abba, take this plank from my eye that I might see clearly and help me to take the hands of the sinners and show them the way. May I take time to pray for them, to feed them and to clothe them. For if I turn a blind eye, I have sinned. But if I extend a helping hand, I have extended my love to You.

Pour out Your love on me this day. Fill me with Your peace and let me be so full that it overflows into all that surrounds me. Let me have eyes full of love and compassion for others, not just for those who are close to me, but for those on the streets and for those who agitate me.

Help me to be Your hands and feet this day and every day that I am here upon this earth.

It is in *Yeshua's* name that I pray. Amen.

May 16

Captivate My Soul

*Set me like a seal over your heart, like a seal on your arm. For love is as strong as death, jealousy as cruel as **Sheol**. Its flames are bolts of fire, the flame of **Adonai**.*   Song of Songs 8:6 TLV

Oh, my Lord, how You have captivated my soul! Your eyes gaze upon me with a fiery love. Your wings cover and protect me through the night. You open up the heavens and bless me with Your provisions. Your hands gently move me into a closer walk with You and You whisper in my ear and speak peace, truth and hope. Oh, my King, how my soul is drowning in Your love!

My King, I am forever Yours and You are mine! And for You, alone, I am preparing for our wedding day. May I be dressed all in white because I am cleansed by Your blood. May I be adorned with jewels, so that Your light reflects from all the brilliant stones. May You tell me I am beautiful to You and that You will love me forever more. For this is my hope and the only reason that I breathe.

Abba, I can feel Your presence, I can feel Your love, how I know that You are near! I praise You, my Lord, for allowing me to experience this moment, and how I pray that others can experience this peace, this joy, deep within their souls along side of me.

You say that anyone who ask, receives. So I am asking for my family and my friends to experience this encounter with You. For I know that this reality of Your love will sustain us for any trial that might be ahead.

For You, my King, are the author of everything good. And I have faith that all who will ask, will receive, and know the goodness that only comes from a life devoted to You.

For it is in *Yeshua's* name I pray. Amen.

MAY 17

Your Kiss Upon My Heart

Let him kiss me with the kisses of his mouth! For your love is better than wine. Your ointments have a pleasing fragrance. Your name is poured out like perfume. No wonder maidens love you! Draw me after you, let us run! The king has brought me into his chambers. Let us rejoice and be glad in you; let us extol your love more than wine. Rightly do they love you!
Song of Songs 1:2–4 TLV

Abba, Your fragrance fills my home with peace. Your kiss fills my heart with love. You are more beautiful than rubies, more precious than gold. For I delight in Your love, my King! How I can't wait until You take me home.

Let me go to the *mikveh* pool and be immersed in the waters, so I can come up cleansed and united with You.

Let me go to the Tabernacle to learn of Your ways. To grow in knowledge of You, that I might please You and make You smile.

As a bride studies her groom and works to please his heart. May I do all these things for You, my Lord, my King, my Love!

Thank You that You chose me to be Your bride! Thank You for every kiss You have placed upon my heart. For my love deepens for You daily. I look forward to the day I will be taken away with You.

In *Yeshua's* name I pray. Amen.

May 18

May I Sing To You

*Then Moses and **Bnei-Yisrael** sang this song to **Adonai**: I will sing to **Adonai**, for He is highly exalted! The horse and its rider He has thrown into the sea.*
Exodus 15:1 TLV

May I sing to You, O God of all nations! For You hear my voice, my plea. You have reached Your hands down from the heavens and have touched my life with beauty and grace. How blessed am I, O Lord my God, for You to lift me up on high.

May I sing to You how deep is my love. For You have rescued me from the pit of fire. You saw me in my darkest moments and chose to light my way. No matter how deep or rough the waters might be, You throw a lifeline to pull me out. How great are You, O God Almighty, for You are more than life to me.

May I sing to You, my God, my King, for one day You will come to take me home. May I keep my eyes focused on the heavens so not to be consumed with the ways of this world. May I sing of Your strength and Your beauty! May I sing of Your power and might. For when the shofar shall blow, all those You have chosen will come live with You in Your kingdom. How great are You, O King of Kings, that I might live with You in the heavens forever more.

To You, my King, I shall sing of praises. I shall serve You, my King, for You heard my cries and chose to save me. How beautiful You are to me. Amen.

MAY 19

A Gentle Answer

A gentle answer turns away wrath, but a harsh word stirs up anger.
Proverbs 15:1 WMB

My King, so many people want the last word. They feel they have to impress on others their opinions and their ways.

People are fighting and rioting over politics and religion. There are politicians trying to tell us what we are to believe in. What laws to accept and approve.

But these people have fallen so far away from You, my Lord. You can see their hearts are full of confusion and deceit.

My King, I know that even in the turmoil that I am seeing on TV every day. You are speaking to those who choose to hear. What they should say and how to win the lives of those souls who are lost.

When *Yeshua* came into the city, some thought He should take it by force if he was their king. But He came speaking peace and love and won so many hearts that day, and it is still this love that's winning souls today.

So when I hear foolishness, when I am angry at the evil which they do. Please, my King, let Your Spirit take control of me. Let others not see me, but see only You!

For if You speak through me, seeds of love will be planted. Then You can rain Your truths upon this land and the fruits of Your peace and love can rule our country once again.

In *Yeshua's* name I pray. Amen and amen.

MAY 20

Confessing My Sins

He himself bore our sins in his body on the tree, that we, having died to sins, might live to righteousness. You were healed by his wounds.
1 Peter 2:24 WMB

My Lord, how beautiful You are to me. For I am a woman of much sin, Yet You made a way for me to come to You that I may live eternally before Your throne, singing praises to the Almighty King!

Abba, as I lay here before You confessing my sins, may You cleanse me at the brass laver. As I look into the mirrors that this laver is made with, may it be Your reflection that I see. For then I will know that Satan will have no hold on me. For where You are, Satan will flee. Because he is a coward, a theft in the night. He cannot live in the light, so he prowls in the dark trying to devour his prey. Remove him as far as the east is to the west from my life, my family, and my friends, so Your plans for us will prevail.

Abba, You are ever present with those who love You, who seek You, who commune with You. May I commune with You this day. May I eat from the table of showbread. May Your everlasting presence change me from the inside out and give me the strength and the courage to do what You have planned for me. Help me not to waiver and look at my own iniquities, but to look at Your power and Your glory. For if You wish that I do a work, I know I can complete it, because it is by Your grace and Your might, that all You put into motion will prevail! Hallelujah, my Lord, and amen!

Thank You for this amazing love! For Your incomprehensible grace! For Your power and might that is leading my life. May there not be a moment of this day that I do not confess my sins, so nothing can stand between the love You have for me. To You, my Lord, I give each breath. To You, my Lord, I give all I have.

For it is in *Yeshua's* Holy name I pray. Amen.

May 21

I Cry To You In Prayer

Hear O Israel, the Lord our God, the Lord is one. Deuteronomy 6:4 TLV

Eloi, Eloi, I cry out to You in prayer! Hear my voice, O Lord. Hear my cry! For I need Your provisions, I need Your strength Your love! Pour out Your blessings upon me out of Your riches that are in heaven. Give me my manna for this day. May I have just what I need to get through this day, but give me nothing more. For my eyes only desire is to be focused on You alone!

You are the God of all! The One and only King! All who will come before Your throne will bow and worship You. All who have lived will acknowledge You are King! How majestic are You, O Lord. For I exist only for Your glory!

Abba, as I walk through this desert, this wilderness, take my hand. For I know that it is in this time You are disciplining me and training me for something better; a love that is deeper and more pure in You.

Abba, You are my life, my breath, my Alpha and my Omega, the Everlasting to Everlasting King of all Kings. I love You from the depths of my soul. I worship You with every word spoken from my lips. May I see You in Your kingdom! May I wash Your feet forever. Let me pour out my perfume upon You. Let me feed You grapes at night. My heart sings with love for You. My arms long to hold You tight.

For I am Yours and You are mine, and my destiny awaits in Your arms forever! To You, my Lord, I give all honor and praise. Amen.

May 22

Artist Who Designed My Soul

The king is captivated in its tresses! How beautiful and how pleasing you are, O Love, with your delights!   *Song of Songs 7:7 TLV*

Good morning my love, how I delight in Thee. For You are the artist who designed my soul, my flesh, and Your desire for me is good!

You created me to sing of Your beauty and love. You created me with Your desires in mind. Help me, my Lord, and heal me from any illness that is within me. Give me strength and clarity of mind. For You created this earthen vessel for Your glory and to honor You. Fill me with all that is good!

Bless me, O Lord, with provisions to cover my household. May these blessings pour over in abundance, that I may bless others with Your gifts. Give me wisdom, my King, that I may be a good steward of all that You give to me. Bless me with honor and glory in You.

For You offer life and You give love abundantly to those who seek You. My Lord, You know I seek You! You know I love You from the depths of my soul! And even now in the midst of the chaos, my soul has been anointed by Your *Ruach*. You have given me such peace, that it amazes me! I praise You for Your indwelling from within me, for You are life and love to me.

Without You, my Lord, I am just a grain of sand, lost in the millions, tossed with the winds. But with You, I am a strong tower, grounded on the rock, and there forever shall I stand!

May I stand here today shouting Your praise! Telling others of Your healing powers, of Your blessing. Of how a life in grace is worth more than rubies and pearls, it's worth more than anything this world might offer. Amen and amen.

MAY 23

The Message

Fear not, for I am with you, be not dismayed, for I am your God. I will strengthen you. Surely I will help you. I will uphold you with My righteous right hand.   Isaiah 41:10 TLV

Oh my beloved King, how I praise Thee this morning! For You have taken me, a person of great sin, a person who only deserves death and damnation. And yet You uphold me in Your righteous right hand!

Who am I, my Lord, that You would love me this way? Who am I, that You would hear my prayer. Yet it is not by my acts that I am called righteous. But it is only the blood of *Yeshua* that cleanses me.

My King, I owe You everything. There is nothing I have or do that You have not given unto me. How can I ever repay such a debt? How can I ever tell You just how much You mean to me?

All I know to do, my Lord, is to serve You with my hands. To give, and to love, as You have loved me. To be a message in a bottle, that even people I don't know can read of my love for You!

This, my Lord, is what I ask Your help in. To reach the distant shores with Your teachings. To touch lives in a way they will not forget, to show them the power and love of my mighty God. For the God of Abraham and Isaac is also mine!

How I love You with all of my heart, my soul and my might, my Lord. Let me be intentional in every word and act that I do. Let me be Your messenger this day. Let me live like this, my whole life through.

In *Yeshua's* name I pray. Amen.

MAY 24

Guarding My Lips

He who guards his mouth guards his soul. One who opens wide his lips come to ruin.
Proverbs 13:3 WMB

Oh, my *Adonai,* how at one time I was so careful about every word spoken from these lips. Because I knew that I will be judged by the words that I say. I need, Lord, to go back to that time. To keep my lips sealed and think very carefully before I speak. That my words are not careless and without thought of others, that they do not harm those I am around. And even when truth needs to be spoken, I am careful not to put in my emotions, but to use words from the gospel so that no man can rebuke them.

Adonai, this takes strength, wisdom, and most definitely the *Ruach ha Kodesh* dwelling within to uphold this task. My Lord, it seems like it would be so simple, but it is harder for me than to give my last dime.

Indwell in me, my Lord. Envelop me with goodness and grace. Let Your *Ruach* speak through me words of affirmation and love, but most of all grace. This is the one thing that is the hardest to give, and the one thing we all need the most!

Let me be a shower of blessings upon the earth. May the flowers bloom and fruit be produced because You rained upon this land. Let them see You in my eyes, hear Your words in my lips, feel Your presence in my song, and see Your works in my hands. Let me be that person in You this day!

For it is in *Yeshua's* Holy name I pray. Amen.

MAY 25

Blessed Am I

*Blessed is the one You discipline, **Adonai**, and teach him from Your Torah.* Psalms 94:12 TLV

Blessed am I, O God! For You have chosen to give me life full of love in You!

For You have given me the love of a family, and a friend to call from time to time. In the night when I am lonely, You wrap Your arms around me and hold me tight. What more could a person want? What more could I ever need, than to have my sweet and precious Lord love and take care of me?

May I seek You this morning as I arise to start my day. May I whisper that I love You, every moment and in every way.

May I look in the Bible to seek answers to my problems. May I pray for my family and friends so their love, too, may soon blossom.

May You search me and remove anything in me, that is not of You. Fill me up in goodness, and may You cover me in grace too.

For You are my God, my King, the author of my story. May I give You all my love, and honor. To You, O Lord, is all the glory, forever and ever. Amen.

MAY 26

Do Not Fear

A thousand may fall at your side, and ten thousand at your right hand; but it will not come near you.   Psalms 91:7 WMB

Abba, there are times in our lives when we allow Satan to come in and cause us fear. Fear of the unknown, of where our money will come from, of illness, of terrorism, and even of our own leaders in this country. But You told Isaiah we are not to fear them! We are to fear You, to dread You, for then You will be our sanctuary, our Lord, our God! For You are the Mighty One, the Holy One of Israel, and when You are with us, the chains of hell are broken and our enemies will flee. No power on earth or under heaven can move what God has begun. I praise You from the depths of my soul for hearing my cries and for doing a mighty work in me!

Continue to change me from the inside out, my Lord. Make me strong and courageous in You! Let no weapon that has formed against me prosper but only the goodness and blessings that come from You! Let me not boast of myself, but may others see this change in me and hunger for what I have.

Abba, may I be as Joshua and call out to You. Then may You make the earth quake and the rocks tremble and cause my enemies to fall beneath my feet. For You say a thousand may fall by my side, but no harm will come to me. Father in You shall I trust, in You only shall I believe!

May I be as Mark, someone full of sin, hated by many, to become the righteousness of You. Full of wisdom with the ability to lead others to the faith, for it is by faith that we cast out fear! And fear has no place in my heart but only the righteousness of God!

Abba, mold me this day into a vessel full of power and might; wearing the full armor of God, standing in the gap for others, living a life of faith, and holding onto the hem of Your garment. May I forever have this privilege of serving You in Your army, my Lord. Amen.

MAY 27

A Heart That's Open

Yeshua answered and said to him, "If anyone loves Me, he will keep My word. My Father will love him, and We will come to him and make Our dwelling with him.   John 14:23 TLV

Abba, make my heart Your dwelling place. Make it gentle, make it kind. Help me not to be self-seeking, but looking out with others' best interests at heart. Help me not to be boastful about myself, but may I boast about the love You pour out on me. Fill each crevice with grace so that I am able to pour grace upon grace on others. Knowing that they don't deserve it, but neither do I, and You have given it to me so freely. Help me to make my heart open so that others are invited in. May we all take part of the great wedding supper of the lamb.

My Lord, people in this world are fallen. Some will hurt you and not mean to, others will do so deliberately. How did You, my Lord, let go and love? Even unto death You asked Your Heavenly Father to forgive them. My Lord, I want to love like that. I need to love like this.

I praise You, my Lord, for the provisions You have provided. I praise You, my Lord, for healing me. I beg You, my Lord, to heal each one in my family of any illnesses, bitterness and greed. May we stand strong together. May we stand strong in You this day and every day.

Bless my friends, my family and those I work with. Give us just what we need to get us through this day. Cover us with Your wings of protection so that Satan and his schemes cannot come in. Anoint us with Your oil so that we may do the bidding of The Lord.

I serve You, my King, my Master, with all hope, honor, and love. It is to You all praise is given and I lay all these requests at Your feet. Amen.

May 28

Seeking God Wholeheartedly

Draw near to God, and He will draw near to you. Cleanse your hands, you sinners. Purify your hearts, you double-minded.   Jacob 4:8 WMB

Adonai, anoint me with Your presence. Come to me in a tangible way that I cannot deny Your love. Bring unto me Your *Ruach,* that I am filled and given gifts that are supernatural. Gifts I am unable to do in my flesh, but in You make them active and able to change lives around me.

Abba, as I press into You this day, make the words on the page of Your book come to life. Speaking to me as if You are in the room. Showing me that this life, while it may have beauty and joy, cannot compare to the splendor of Your majesty.

You are Immanuel, God who is with me. You make my life about me, when in reality, it's all about You. For without You my heart will not beat. The breath of my lungs can be gone in a second, at a time that is unknown to me. If I do not live this life about You, in the next life I would have wished I had.

Purify my heart, give me Your *Shalom.* Show me how I can make my day to be pleasing in Your sight and to Your heart.

I love You with all that I am and I will forever more. Amen and amen.

MAY 29

Worshiping In Spirit And In Truth

But the hour comes, and now is, when the true worshipers will worship the Father in spirit and truth, for the Father seeks such to be his worshipers.
Yochanan *(John) 4:23 WMB*

Adonai, You are the great I AM! You formed the seas and the mountains. All power is in the tip of Your finger.

Yet people mock You. They say there is no God, for He would not destroy the land or allow harm to our children.

But Your creation and this life is truly amazing! For those who trust in You may suffer. But the spirit rejoices with Your *Ruach.* For nothing in this world can remove You from communing with our souls.

For as a child looks to their father for help, I look to You for life. As a mother loves her newborn, Your love for us exceeds it all!

How can one so small, so insignificant as I, be loved by the mighty King of the universe?

This is what does not make sense! But You prove it to me every day as I worship You in spirit and truth.

I pray today for all who are suffering, for Your *Ruach* to rest on their souls. I pray for anyone who does not know You. That they seek You and find You this day.

For even though they think You are far, far away. You are knocking at their door. May they allow You to enter in. And may Your love consume them forever more! Amen and amen!

May 30

An Appointed Time

*"But you will receive power when the **Ruach ha-Kodesh** has come upon you; and you will be My witnesses in Jerusalem, and through all Judah, and Samaria, and to the end of the earth."*   Acts 1:8 TLV

My sweet *Adonai*, hallowed be Thy name! For You had a *moadim*, an appointed time, for Christ to be born and testify of Your goodness. For Him to die on the cross for our sins and for Him to rise from the grave that we might have eternal life.

And on the day of *Shavuot,* which the Christians call Pentecost, was another *moadim* with You! For You sent the *Ruach ha Kodesh* to fall upon the disciples, like a fire, so that they would be filled, speak in tongues, and be able to have all power to go into the world and profess the gospel of *Yeshua ha Mashiach.* And You have commanded that all Christians do the same.

I praise You that You have given me an appointed time with You. That You are showing me new and wondrous ways of professing in and of Your goodness. That until I have my appointed time to leave this earth, no matter how weak I am, or how poor I may be, Your power can rise up within me and my testimony can win souls to You.

For nothing I do is by my strength or ability. Nothing I have is because of something great that I have done. But in everything and in every way, I will give glory to You, my God!

And when that *moadim* comes for You to take me home. May I hear, well done! I love You, my precious one. Amen and amen.

MAY 31

Immersed In The Ruach

*Blessed be the God and Father of our Lord **Yeshua** the Messiah, the Father of compassion and God of all encouragement. He encourages us in every trouble, so that we may be able to encourage those who are in any trouble, through the very encouragement with which we ourselves are encouraged by God.*   2 Corinthians 1:3–4 TLV

Abba, You are truly amazing! You are God, creator of all things, yet You want to commune with us. You don't need humans, but You desired us, and You created us for this very reason.

You walked with Adam and Eve. You had Moses build the traveling Tabernacle for You to dwell in. And since *Yeshua* died on the cross, the *Ruach ha Kodesh* came to live within us. How this totally amazes me! How totally humbled I am!

I praise You, *Abba,* for the *Ruach ha Kodesh,* for He is what gives me strength and the courage to defend the faith in the face of Satan. He comforts me when I am sick or sad. He convicts me when I am not doing Your will in my life. He is the perfect companion. He is truly my best friend.

Completely immerse me in Your *Ruach* this day. Fill me from the tip of my hair to the bottom of my feet. Let me kneel in front of the Ark of the Covenant and may You reveal Yourself to me there, between the cherubim, so that I may draw nearer to You and know what I am to do this day.

To You, my Lord, I give all praise. For You are truly Lord of my life and the lover of my soul. Thank You for every breath I have! Amen.

JUNE 1

The Knowledge Of You

*Now when they saw the boldness of Peter and John and figured out they were laymen without training, they were amazed. They began to realize that these men had been with **Yeshua**.* Acts 4:13 TLV

Abba, it is said that the knowledge of the world is great, but the knowledge of *Adonai,* surpasses it all!

If we are rich in the ways of men but do not have God, we are poor. If we are geniuses in the eyes of man but do not know or understand Your truths, we are ignorant. If we believe that we have the answers because men of science say it is so, we are fools!

So teach me Your ways, O Lord. Let there not be a day in which I don't learn something about You. As I open up the Bible, may the power of the *Ruach ha Kodesh* imprint it upon my heart. Let me have dreams and see visions, things You would have me to do. Give me knowledge like unto Daniel, where I can interpret others' dreams. Teach me to be more like Peter and John, and may I help to change the world with one kind gesture, with one spoken truth, with one act of grace, one day at a time.

For without You, I am a mere wild flower, here for a moment, then soon forgotten. With You, I am a picture of a sunrise that will be imprinted upon the hearts of man, showing others how beautiful is the love of my Father in heaven.

For You are the One who knows all things and gives according to Your will, from Your riches which art in heaven. Give me this day the wisdom and love that only comes from You.

I praise You, my *Adonai*. Amen.

June 2

Our Shepherd

*Know therefore that **Adonai** your God, He is God—the faithful God who keeps covenant kindness for a thousand generations with those who love Him and keep His **mitzvot**,* Deuteronomy 7:9 TLV

Abba, You are a God above all. There is nothing Your hands have not made. There is nothing too big for You! Be our *Jehovah Rapha* and heal us, O Lord. Let us touch the hem of Your garment and take in Your healing power.

Be to us as You were with the woman at the well, may we never thirst again. Be to us as You were with Sarah, may we have our deepest desire. Be to us as You were to Esther, may we be wise in the blessing of our people. Be to us as You were with Peter may the *Ruach ha Kodesh* be so strong in us that we perform miracles in order that all may believe.

Yeshua, we are the sheep and You are our Shepherd. Break our legs and carry us if we go astray. Call out our names, because we know Your voice. Take us to the stream of living water so that we may never thirst. For as sheep trust only the shepherd, may we trust only in You.

Abba, may our eyes stay focused on the heavens every day. Because just like in the day of Moses when You opened up the water so the Hebrews could cross to the other side and enter into the promised land, so it will be at Your return. You will open up the heavens so that we may cross over into heaven, into our promised land forever.

We love You, O Lord. May You have mercy on our souls! May we seek You today and obey Your mitzvot, Your commands. Amen and amen.

June 3

Washed

So if I, your Master and Teacher, have washed your feet, you also ought to wash each other's feet. I have given you an example—you should do for each other what I have done for you. "Amen, amen I tell you, a servant isn't greater than his master, and the one who is sent isn't greater than the one who sent him. If you know these things, you are blessed if you do them!"
John 13:14–17 TLV

My Lord, my Love, how sweet is the morning with You. You show us many wonders in the heavens, for I have seen the moon turn to red. Now I am watching the skies turn beautiful colors as the sun rises. You think of every detail to show us Your love. Even unto the washing of our feet.

I think about Peter and what He said to You, "You could not wash his feet." I understand him, my Lord. How could a God, creator of all these beautiful things, wash my feet? It is hard for me to understand. But in this act of love, I know that I could never stand again, but only fall on my knees to worship You. The act of a Holy God cleansing me is so humbling and more than I think I could bear.

Lord, may I wash Your feet when I get to heaven. May I kiss the ground that You walk upon. Let me be Your humble servant. Let me be Your bond slave. For I want to be completely Yours, devoted to no one else. Consume me this day, my Lord. Consume me forever more.

Thank You for washing away my sins and giving me a white robe to wear, one the saints will be wearing before Your throne. For this is the home I am longing for. This is the place where love resides.

In *Yeshua's* name I pray. Amen and amen.

June 4

Blameless

*Now this I pray, that your love might overflow still more and more in knowledge and depth of discernment, in order to approve what is excellent—so that in the Day of Messiah you may be sincere and blameless, filled with the fruit of righteousness that comes through **Yeshua** the Messiah, to the glory and praise of God.* Philippians 1:9–11 TLV

Abba, How gracious You are to me that I have life in You. That I can seek Your face and You hear me. That I can call out for Your help and Your angels protect me. That I do not have to fear the things of this world because You are walking with me every step of the way. I praise You, Lord, for loving me so. May I give all I am to You.

Adonai, help me to be more like Paul. Help me to be strong and courageous. Let the words I speak be praises to You and teaching to others. Let my heart be like David, pure and true never looking to please myself. Knowing all I could ever want, I will receive in pleasing You. Let me have the eyes of Esther, able to see the needs of my people, and able to bless them in Your power and love. I praise You, my King, for listening and blessing me with these gifts every day that I live here on earth.

My Lord, I pray for my family, my friends and my fellow believers in You. That the *Ruach ha Kodesh* will make Himself known to them today. That He may build them in strength and unity. That He may give them powers to do mighty things through You, for each other and people they do not know. That Your love, Your discernment, Your knowledge may abound in them and guide them. That they may be blameless on the day of Your return.

May each one of us look for opportunities to serve, honor and bless our fellow believers first, but may we also serve, honor and bless those who curse us, that they too may see the glory of our King in all we do. Thank You, my King, for allowing us the privilege to enter into Your throne room with prayer and praise. Amen.

June 5

Write Your Story

> *But this is the covenant I will make with the house of Israel after those days"—it is a declaration of **Adonai**—"I will put My Torah within them. Yes, I will write it on their heart. I will be their God and they will be My people.*
>
> Jeremiah 31:33 TLV

Abba, I call upon Thy name to: "write Your story upon my heart!" I don't want to be who I am or who I was. I only want to be Yours, a new person in my soul. And, my King, the only way this can be true is if You write Your love, Your laws upon my heart.

I wait for You this day with expectation of Your presence, for Your love reaches beyond the skies, beyond the seas. My heart is trembling inside for You. For You chose me from the beginning to be Your bride, Your best friend.

But how can that be? For You are the Creator, not human, but so much more! You are every aspect of my life and I want to be the story that shows others Your love.

When I look into the eyes of a babe I see Your love, Your strength, Your infinite wisdom. This is how I want to be; all new, and only learn of You, not anything of this world.

Abba, I am an open book, with blank pages from this date forward. So I am asking You to fill each page with the desires of Your heart for me.

I love You, my Lord, for You are the author of my soul. Amen.

Hallelujah

Then I heard something like the voice of a great multitude—like the roar of rushing waters or like the rumbling of powerful thunder—saying, **"Halleluyah!** *For* **Adonai Elohei-Tzva'ot** *reigns!*
The Revelation 19:6 TLV

Holy are You, *Adonai,* the Lord my God. For You alone are worthy of all praise. You are the Lamb who was slain. You *are Yeshua ha Mashiach,* Jesus Christ, my Lord! And You are coming in the clouds, coming to judge the unclean and take home the saints.

My King, the only cleanliness within my body is the *Ruach ha Kodesh* who resides within me. For without You, I am as lowly as the dust. Without You, I deserve judgement, hell and damnation forever.

But with You, I am as white as snow, cleansed by Your blood, the only reason I can see Your heavenly home, singing before Your throne alongside the saints.

Yeshua, I await this day. When You will roll back the heavens like a scroll. Then all eyes shall see Your glory. May I fall to my knees in worship, not in fear. Because You chose me before the laying of the foundation of the world. You chose me and knit me in my mother's womb. You chose to love me in spite of myself, and You have chosen to make me Your bride.

My heart sings, "Hallelujah, for you are Holy. You are Lord God almighty. Worthy is the Lamb who was slain. Hallelujah, for You, my God, are worthy of all praise and honor, forever and ever. Amen and amen.

June 7

Reflection

Behold, I will do a new thing. It springs out now. Don't you know it? I will even make a way in the wilderness, and rivers in the desert.
Isaiah 43:19 WMB

Abba, as I enter into this new season, I cry to You to make all things new. Take me out of the dryness of the desert. And lead me to the land of milk and honey, a land where I can grow deeper in my walk with you.

I want to learn all this mind can absorb about Your word. I want to experience Your love in new ways that I can share.

I am happiest when I am doing Your bidding. So give me opportunities this day to serve You well!

I praise You for the life You have given me. For all the trials and test that I have gone through, for they are just refining me each and every day. Bringing me a little closer to You.

Make me a diamond, my Lord: one of rare beauty, so people want to know more about its reflection. I reflect only You and Your glory, that which lights up the room.

In *Yeshua's* Holy name I pray. Amen.

June 8

Delight In My Offerings

For You would not delight in sacrifice, or I would give it, nor be pleased by burnt offerings.⁹ The sacrifices of God are a broken spirit. A broken and a contrite heart, O God, You will not despise.
Psalms 51:18–19 TLV

Abba, I come to You broken in my heart. For I have not done the works of my hands in the manner in which You would desire of me. I have been selfish, doing what I want, going where I want to go. Doing things to please me, versus pleasing You. Please forgive me, my King. For I want You to delight in my offerings of love.

Abba, my King, I desire all spiritual wisdom and understanding. I want strength in my inner man. For I want to know the length and depth and fullness of the knowledge of *Yeshua ha Mashiach,* Christ, my Lord. That I can go out this day forth and declare the love of *Yeshua,* to declare His truths and grace.

The only way I can do this, my King, is with the power and might that raised *Yeshua* from the grave. That Your *Ruach* comes with such strength and power that I am not in command of this vessel.

Take control of this ship, my King. Let it travel the seas to the destination of Your desire. Let me not be a Jonah, running away from the situations You put before me. But let me go in with an open heart. Knowing that Your *Ruach* is in control and will make all things happen for Your good and Your glory if I allow Him to be in command.

Be pleased with my offering, my King. My sacrifice is not money or wealth, for this I have not. But my offering is of myself, my time and my talents. For if it were not for You, I would have not.

My heart belongs to You alone. Mend it and hold it in Your right hand, then I will be safe and secure all eternity long. Amen and amen.

June 9

I Am Not Alone

Adonai—*He is the One who goes before you. He will be with you. He will not fail you or abandon you. Do not fear or be discouraged."*
Deuteronomy 31:8 TLV

Abba, I have been so discouraged. I have seen my enemies all around me. I have been going through deep, deep water and no one will come to help. They just stand waiting to see if I will drown.

This trial has been consuming me like a fire and I feel the flames scorching my clothing. Abba, please send a wave of cool water for my refreshing. Give strength to my bones. Let me see You before I cannot stand.

Abba, You promised that You will go before me. That You will never abandon me. I am trusting only in You, for You are my strength and my defender. You have always been faithful and I am standing on this promise as I press into You.

I am not alone on this journey. Because You will be with me, carrying me through this fire, mending all of my wounds and restoring my soul.

To You, my King, I give all honor and praise. Amen and amen.

June 10

Watch The Giants Fall

*This very day **Adonai** will deliver you into my hand, and I will strike you down and take your head off you, and I will give the carcasses of the Philistines' camp today to the birds of the sky and the wild beasts of the earth. Then all the earth will know that there is a God in Israel, and so all this assembly will know that **Adonai** delivers not with sword and spear—for the battle belongs to **Adonai**—and He will give you into our hands." Then when the Philistine rose and began to advance, drawing near to meet David, David ran quickly toward the battle line to meet the Philistine. David put his hand in his bag, took from it a stone and slung it, striking the Philistine on his forehead. The stone sank into his forehead, so that he fell on his face to the ground. So David prevailed over the Philistine with a sling and a stone, struck the Philistine down and killed him. Since there was no sword in David's hand...*   1 Samuel 17:46–50 TLV

    Adonai, there are giants all around. They are blocking my way stating they are going to take me down.

    But You are mightier and more powerful. You are capable of doing things unseen. Things normal humans cannot understand. But You make them no greater than a grain of sand.

    So I am going to stand like David, with child-like faith. And shout to that giant, my God is with me. He will take you down with one stone. Then I will feed you to the lions. For if God is with me, who can be against me. So move out of my way Satan, because Christ has pointed the way and You are not in it.

    I praise You, my King, and I will not be afraid. For You are with me always! Amen.

June 11

Light Shines In The Darkness

The light shines in the darkness, and the darkness hasn't overcome.
John 1:5 TLV

Abba, I praise You from the depths of my soul for loving me and showing me Your light that I might have life in You!

My Lord, It is so hard to look around and see true darkness in people and in places. To feel Your absence, that void, the evil that is around. Yet I felt You and Your peace within. How blessed I am, my Lord, that Your love is so strong that You cover me with Your wings and keep me safe from harm in places that evil lurks!

Abba, there have been times when I have spoken Your words, Your truth to others who are still walking in the shadows. Yet they hear me not. It hurts my heart so to see them struggle in pain because of the absence of You. I lift them up, my King, and lay them at Your feet. I cry out to You for their salvation and for all who do not believe. All I can do is speak Your truths and pray, my Lord, that these seeds I have planted will take root, for I walked in darkness for many years and it was the prayers of the saints that helped to set me free.

My Lord, take hold of me and direct me this day. Let Your light shine bright within my soul that I could never be mistaken for an unbeliever. No matter the circumstances, no matter the dangers, let Your words of truth be spoken and heard through me.

Thank You, my King, for hearing my prayer, that You cover me in the shadows of Your wings. Thank You that no matter how dark the moment or place may be, You will never leave me nor forsake me, because I am Yours through eternity.

To You, my King, I pray forever and ever. Amen.

June 12

I Will Follow You

He said to them, "Come after me, and I will make you fishers of men."
Matthew 4:19 WMB

Yeshua, I want to follow You, so I will go where You go. Where You stay I'll stay. What You pray, I'll pray. For I only want to be in Your presence, my King. I only want to please You.

This world is dark and confused. But where You are there is light and love. My body hungers for the bread of life, the sweet taste of fruit that only comes from the branches fed by the living water.

For You are *Adonai* and good and life and love reside in You alone.

Make Your precepts burned on my heart, so what You say I say, what You pray I pray, that I may be a fisher of men. Let all I do, I do for You alone.

To You, O God, I pray. Amen.

JUNE 13

I Am Yours

Not lagging in diligence; fervent in spirit; serving the Lord.
Romans 12:11 WMB

Abba, I stand on the mountaintop shouting out that I am Yours. I stand on the streets proclaiming that all I am, I give unto Your hands.

Here I am before You, my God, giving everything I have to You. My heart is on fire for Your *Ruach* to overtake me. Come from heaven, burn in my soul, O God. Let nothing stand between You and me.

I Lift up my hands to You, O Lord, standing with my arms wide open, to *El Olam,* the Everlasting God. Proclaiming, I am Yours!

Let me serve You with every breath I take. Let me use my hands to give all I have to help the orphan. May I help the widow find Your love, the homeless, warmth for their soul. May my feet not grow weary for all I do I do for the great I AM!

To You forever I proclaim my love. Amen and Amen.

June 14

Power In The Name Of Jesus

These signs will accompany those who believe: in My name they will drive out demons; they will speak new languages; they will handle snakes; and if they drink anything deadly, it will not harm them; they will lay hands on the sick, and they will get well."   Mark 16:17–18 TLV

Yeshua, You have called me by name and I believe. I have seen miracles performed through the power of Your name.

I stand here in awe of You. For Your *Ruach* fills the atmosphere and overcomes me, my Lord. It is through the power of the *Ruach ha Kodesh,* if I speak Your name, the demons have to flee. It is through this power when I have laid hands on the sick, I have watched them rise again free of pain.

For Your name breaks every chain Satan tries to bind us to. He hath lost all power, all threat of him disappears when You are near.

So I have no fear of snakes or anything deadly this world has to offer. Because You alone hold the key to heavens gates and of hell's fury. You alone are the great Judge of us all. It is only in You and Your power that I need to fear.

So let me become more aware of Your presence. Let me behold the glory of Your goodness. *Yeshua,* come fill my heart, let me speak in Your name that people may be saved. So we can stand together in the throne room of grace, singing songs of praise to You alongside the elders, forever more. Amen and amen.

Seal Upon My Heart

*Set me like a seal over your heart, like a seal on your arm. For love is as strong as death, jealousy as cruel as **Sheol**. Its flames are bolts of fire, the flame of **Adonai**. Many waters cannot quench love, nor rivers wash it away. If one gave all the wealth of his house for love, it would be utterly despised.*
Song of Songs 8: 6–7 TLV

Adonai, You are relentless in Your love and devotion to me. You will not stop until You have it all. So be a seal upon my heart, like a seal upon my arm. Let You and I become one.

Allow the *Ruach ha Kodesh* to consume me like a fire. That many rivers cannot quench or remove it from me.

I have nothing to give You in return for Your love. But I give You my heart, my soul and my mind. You may have it all!

Be relentless in my life. Take all of me. Take anything I have and use it to satisfy Your kingdom.

You are the only thing I hunger for: my Lord, my God.

In *Yeshua's* name I pray. Amen.

June 16

War On Death

"Death, eherre is your sting? Sheol, where is your victory?"
1 Corinthians 15:55 TLV

Abba, death has no sting, for the stone was rolled away and Your body was raised from the grave. You are our resurrected King. How beautiful is Thy Holy name.

Nothing Satan can put before me can separate me from You. For You have risen from the grave. And You, my Lord, are to be glorified throughout all eternity.

It is so hard to imagine, this amazing fact. But it is in faith alone that I stand. For on that day 2000 years ago, You bore the pain for me. You took on Satan at his best. You have showed him, he will not withstand the test.

He will be bound for 1000 years. Then You will take him to hell where he can never hurt anyone again.

Oh how I love You, my Father, my God. For You are the Holy One who will reign forever and ever. Amen.

June 17

Lilies Of The Fields

"And which of you by worrying can add a single hour to his life? So if you cannot do even something very little, why do you worry about other things? Consider the lilies, how they grow. They neither toil nor spin. Yet I tell you that not even Solomon in all his glory was clothed like one of these.
Luke 12:25–27 TLV

Abba, truth be known, I feel like I am taking on the weight of the world. This is not mine to take. For I cannot even add a moment to my day by anything I do or say. So how can I think I have the ability help others or take on their burdens?

But You can, my Lord! So I lay it all down at Your feet. For Your *Ruach* to breathe through me prayers of incense that bellow up before Your throne. Prayers that are according to Your will. Prayers that conform to Your word. Prayers that bring me and those around me closer to You. That we become steadfast in our life. That we allow our bodies to be used as a holy Temple for Your *Ruach* and through this may we be healed in our mind, body and spirit. Standing as the lilies in the field, a testimony, glorifying You.

I give You all that is happening before me, all that is happening in my mind, to cultivate, so the harvest will bear much fruit.

How I praise You for answering this prayer *Yeshua*. For You are King! Amen and amen.

June 18

Physical Training
⊰◈⊱

For bodily exercise has some value, but godliness has value in all things, having the promise of the life which is now, and of that which is to come.
1 Timothy 4:8 WMB

Abba, this world is so consumed with the flesh with; what designer clothes am I wearing? How big is my home? What kind of car do I drive? How muscular is my body and how young do I look?

It's not that any of these things in their own are bad, but none of these are helping in the furthering of Your kingdom. None of these will build up our treasures in heaven.

Abba, let me not to be consumed by the things of this world which are tempting to my mind. But let my heart and my soul be consumed by ALL that is godly. That I shall be blessed both in this life, but moreover in the life to come. For this life is temporary, but life with You is eternal and that is the reward I am working for.

If I need to be poor, or need a thorn in my side to keep my mind on godly things, then this is my desire. If I can have multiple blessings so I am able to pour out blessings on others in the furthering of Your kingdom, then pour them out on me! Bless me, my Lord, with what I can handle in the ways that are of You and only for You!

For I love You, my Lord, and I want so much to please You. For I understand that this life is two dimensional, with somethings that I cannot see. But the two dimensions is a reality I am working in. Let me pray about such things. Seek You in all things. And work on being as godly as I can be at this moment in time.

For it is through the power of the *Ruach ha Kodesh* and the love of Christ that I can pray to You this day. Thank You, my King! Amen and amen.

JUNE 19

Refuge Under Your Wings
➤❁⋖

You are my hiding place and my shield. I hope in your word.
Psalms 119:114 WMB

Abba, my hope for everything in this life and the next rest in You. All my desires for this life I put in Your hands.

For there are things you are having of me, I would have never expected to do. Then there are dreams I am praying for, hoping they are things You desire for me too.

But whatever may come my way, both the good and the bad. I take refuge under Your wings. For You created everything with the touch of Your hands.

You knit me together in my mother's womb with a purpose and a plan. You know every hair on my head. You've inscribed my name upon Your hand.

You have designed for me my earthly family with love that is true. There is nothing You would not do for me. For I could walk on the waters if I walked next to You.

I will put my shield in my right hand and the sword in my left. Will You hold up my arms as I am put through the test.

Whatever Your desires are for me, I know are better than anything I can imagine. All my hope is in You, my Lord, for Your love is more beautiful than I can fathom.

I love You and I give You this day. May I rest in Your arms until my dying day.

In *Yeshua's* name I pray. Amen.

June 20

A Gift Of Thanks

*"Give thanks to **ADONAI** for He is good, for His mercy endures forever."*
1 Chronicles 16:34 TLV

Abba, there are not enough words, there is not enough time to praise You. To say thank you for Your mercy and grace.

One could never repay You for Your love. There is nothing good enough I could buy, as a gift of thanks.

But what I will do is lift Your name up in song and praise. I will teach others of Your goodness and love.

I will offer my hand to a stranger in need. I will show my children how to live as a daughter of the King.

I will read Your word and abide by Your truths. When I fail, I will bow down before You and cry out to You for mercy and grace.

I will walk in peace with my fellow man. I will confront a liar and instead of being angry, I shall pray for them to find You and to seek Your truths in all things.

I know my best is as rags of dirt. Nothing I can do is good enough to repay You for all You have done for me. But You delight in my offerings, so I offer my life and all I have up to You!

In *Yeshua's* name I pray. Amen and amen.

JUNE 21

Free Of Burdens

Blessed be the Lord, who daily bears our burdens, even the God who is our salvation!   *Psalms 68:19 WMB*

God, I am asking that You hold my burdens today. That You, being the perfect Father, knows how to give good gifts to all His children.

So *Abba,* give me this one day to be free from my burdens, to enjoy my earthly family and for You to build me up in strength. Allowing me to face tomorrow renewed and refreshed in You!

I praise You for making the ultimate sacrifice for me. For my sins were many and You bore many slashes on my behalf.

My Lord, Your love truly exceeds all my understanding! Help me to understand this love and to bear my brothers' and sisters' burdens. Help me be Your hands and feet to those I know and to those who live on the streets.

Thank You for being all things to me. For what an amazing God, a wonderful Father, You are to me!

In *Yeshua's* name I pray. Amen.

JUNE 22

Life In You

Whoever pursues righteousness and mercy finds life, prosperity and honor.
Proverbs 21:21 TLV

Abba, this world is a wicked place, where selfishness and lust abound. And it seems the older I get the more and more I see this. The more and more I understand how Satan uses us and this earth to get to You.

But Lord, I can't seem to keep my mouth shut. I seem to want to let everyone know, that a life in You has so much more to offer. For You will give us love, honor, prosperity and truth.

Lord, You know it is hard for me to understand someone who does not want to turn from their evil ways. But in turn, I know I had thought I had gone too far for You to ever love or forgive someone like me.

So help me to memorize the verses in the Bible. Have Your *Ruach ha Kodesh* to speak through me that when I see someone who is like me, I can witness to them. So they too can find You and seek Your love.

For You love all of man-kind and it breaks Your heart for anyone who turns away from the truth. But You throw a celebration in heaven every time someone turns and seeks Your face.

For Your desire is that even the most evil change and come to know You. Because then they will see that in You is love and life, honor and truth. For then their lives will be changed in the twinkling of an eye. And instead of death, they will offer love and blessings to those around them.

You are such an incredible God. For You don't have to love us, who are evil in this way. But it is who You are, and You will never change!

I love You, Lord, and forever shall I praise Your Holy name. Amen.

June 23

Don't Be Anxious

In nothing be anxious, but in everything, by prayer and petition with thanksgiving, let your requests be made known to God.
Philippians 4:6 WMB

Abba, I am at a cross road. I do not know whether to go this way or that? I have my hopes, my dreams and my desires, but are they Your desires for me?

I need You to show me Your will without a question in my heart! For I was at such peace thinking I knew and then everything changed and it has left me in a quandary.

Abba, what is my next step? For I do not want to be out of Your will. Give me dreams, give me visions. Let Your *Ruach ha Kodesh* speak to me! Let me not have a doubt in my mind what journey I am to walk with You.

For You, my God, are my rock and my refuge. I do not trust myself to make the right decision. But I trust You in everything! Help me this day to see You in everything I do.

For it is in *Yeshua's* name alone I pray. Amen.

June 24

Faith Without Works Is Dead

Even so faith, if it has no works, is dead in itself.   Jacob 2:17 WMB

Adonai, to have "faith" is more than an intellectual exercise. It means to act on what we believe.

So if we have such a faith and we act on the teachings You gave us, why aren't more Christians stepping up and tending to others' needs?

For we live in a society where self-gratification comes first. But we are to be aliens of this world, where self-gratification comes last.

If all the Christians would pray 5 minutes out of the day, for their country, the homeless and the needy. If we would put a baggie of food in our cars to give the homeless on the streets, if we would spend 10 minutes a day, helping our neighbors in this land. What would America look like? I believe the non-Christians and the next generation would have a very different plan.

For me these are goals I set forth every day. I pray all Christians would stand and do more than ever before. Let us show the non-believers our God is not dead. He is just waiting for us to move forth, showing His hands.

I love You, my Lord, and I am grateful for all that I have learned. For my faith is not dead if I put Your desires first.

In *Yeshua's* name I pray. Amen.

June 25

I Will Extol The Lord

*I will bless **Adonai** at all times. His praise is continually in my mouth.*
Psalms 34:1 TLV

Abba, Satan tries every day to steal my joy. He sends some things that really hurt. Even little things if I'm not careful, I let get in the way. But the truth is, no matter how hard this life is, I get to spend eternity with You. So as long as I have breath in my mouth, I shall sing praises to Your Holy name.

This life is fleeting, here today and gone tomorrow, for no one knows when they shall take their last breath. But I have no fear, for You will never leave my side. You will come one day to take me home, where I will forever be Your bride.

My Lord, I know others are watching, for some have told me so. So help me to be careful, with every word and in all that I do as I walk along this road. May I show them Your constant grace, for it is what captivates the lost. Because You are the only God who loves without wavering, for it was all paid for upon the cross.

May those who don't know You become curious as I sing. May they watch as I praise You, through hurts and joy, in everything. May they hunger for this joy that they truly don't understand. May I be a vessel You use, so on that day, You take them by their hand. Help me be this vessel today, no matter what the cost. So when I enter through those gates I see those I met who once were the lost.

I will praise Your name forever, my Lord, because You sent others in my life, who showed me Your love in ways unexpected, unusual but completely true. I will praise You forever for loving me in all the ways You do.

Amen.

JUNE 26

Strengthen Us
➤|┆|⬅

*This is the day that **Adonai** has made! Let us rejoice and be glad in it!*
Psalms 118:24 TLV

My Lord, I praise You for this day, for this moment in time. That we can give in love, hope and devotion to others.

My Lord, Satan must have thought he had won by making changes that will affect our way of life. But You, O Lord, knew that this day would come. You knew that this evil lurks all around us. That is why You have given us the *Ruach ha Kodesh,* to strengthen us and to teach us Your truths so we can stand the test when they come.

So, my Lord, how do we respond to our children and their children when asked, why are people like this? How do we show them love and at the same time let them know this is not of You?

Abba, help me to respond by saying, God has given us another day on this earth, to love one another, to give to one another, to help one another as Christ gave to His church. And that no matter what, God loves all people and wants everyone to be His child. That is why He sent His son *Yeshua* to die on the cross for our sins.

Loving all and teaching Your commandments for sinners sometimes can seem contradictory, my Lord. Because they are not of You and just do not understand. So help me learn how to do this effectively, lovingly, but with such knowledge and strength from the *Ruach ha Kodesh,* that it causes those who hear to seek Your truths.

For some people will want to speak with a tongue that is pleasing to the ear. But, my Lord, keep my heart in check, that this is never me!

This is my prayer, my Lord. To stand on the living Word of God and Your truths forever, no matter the cost. Amen and amen.

JUNE 27

Born Again

*"Then **ADONAI Elohim** formed the man out of the dust from the ground and He breathed into his nostrils a breath of life—so the man became a living being.* Genesis 2:7 TLV

Abba, how I praise You! To think that Your *Ruach,* Your Spirit, Your breath was breathed into my nostrils the day I was conceived. And again on the day I let You take me in.

For You first gave me life, then allowed me to choose. But Your amazing *Ruach,* kept wooing me. How could I refuse?

For as You breathed into Abram and made him Abraham. You breathed into me so I could live again.

My first life I led was full of selfishness and ignorant pride. But now I live for You and I choose to put all of those aside.

For when Your *Ruach* moves inside of me, it humbles me and drops me to my knees.

Thank You for loving me in all the ways You do. How I praise You for giving me the gift of being Your daughter too.

In *Yeshua's* name I pray. Amen and amen.

June 28
To Act In Faith

"For this reason I remind you to fan into flame the gift of God, which is in you through the laying on of my hands. For God has not given us a spirit of timidity but of power and love and self-discipline."
Timothy 1:6–7 TLV

Adonai, I am a shy person at heart, and do not like to talk to strangers. But once I saw a lady crying in the bathroom at the airport. You impressed upon my heart to ask her if she needed prayer. To my surprise, when I asked her, she put her hands out to mine and cried out yes.

That act of faith was hard for me. But I stood bold in You, not timid as I usually am. For I know I will never see this woman again. Nor will I know if the seeds I planted will grow. But what You did in that moment for me was great! For that, I how I praise You so.

For You showed me how to love in that moment, someone I did not know. You showed me how Your grace passes through cultures and any barrier Satan tries to claim. That if I fan the flame, if I operate not on my own, but in the Spirit of the living God ... All things are possible.

My Lord, I ask that You give me opportunities to act in faith for You today. That it not only builds up the church. But that it builds up my strength too.

Thank You, my King. For every day is a gift from You!
In *Yeshua's* name I pray. Amen.

June 29

Heal Us, O' Lord

Adonai, in the morning You hear my voice. In the morning I order my prayer before You and watch expectantly. Psalms 5:4 TLV

Oh, my Lord, I beseech Thee this morning for guidance, understanding and joy. For I am trying to be joyful in all things, but I am only able to do this in You.

For there are so many I know in pain. It's hard to watch, not knowing what or if there is anything I can do. But Lord, You are our Creator. You made the heavens and the stars. There is nothing too hard for You.

Abba, as I enter Your throne room, I lay these petitions at Your feet. That You heal their earthly bodies. That You take away their sufferings. That the pain they have endured can be used to testify of Your love. That others may see and Your will be glorified. For You are the *Jehovah Rapha* and I know without a shadow of a doubt, You can heal them and make them whole.

Heal me, O Lord, of all my hurts, my pains, my illnesses, and my sorrows. Let me be strong so I can walk this earth and testify of Your love. It is to You alone I pray. Amen and Amen.

June 30

Hearing Your Voice

For it is God who works in you both to will and to work, for his good pleasure.   *Philippians 2:13 WMB*

My sweet precious Savior, why has it taken me so many years to understand how to hear from You? And why is it that there are times still I feel I am not sure what You are saying?

But Your *Ruach* is so sweet, so gentle and so kind, that He speaks into my soul Your longings for me. And it is I who allows the chatter of this world to be louder than Your soft voice.

Help me, my King, to turn down the volume of this world and turn up the word of God! Let this be the radio station of my soul. Let people see me worship and praise You with no music on and ask why am I so cheerful. Then I can say, my love is blessing my heart this very day.

Every time I listen to You, I am blessed. Whether the answer is to go forward or to step back, You tell me what stones are safe to walk on and which one will give way. This, my Lord, has kept me from drowning so many times. And when my volume has been down, You have even blessed me by blocking the way.

Thank You, thank You, Thank You, my King, that there is not a day You do not hold and cherish me. I praise You for the miracles You have performed before my eyes. I praise You for the hard times for they have stretched me and taught me of Your goodness. I praise You for the good times, for I have beheld Your sweetness.

For I love You from the depths of my soul, for it is there You reside. And it is there I will dance with You as You serenade me through this life. And I cannot wait until I can look into the eyes of love, forever and ever. Amen.

July 1

Rest In You

*For Benjamin he said, "the beloved of **Adonai** rest securely beside Him. He shields him all day long. Between His shoulders he rests."*
Deuteronomy 33:12 TLV

Oh, my Lord, what peace enters my soul as I read these words. To rest between Your shoulders. To be protected and loved all the day long!

For Your shoulders are as broad as the rivers and as strong as bronze. As I lean into them, I can hear my beloved's heartbeat, with such a love for me that grows stronger with every minute with every beat.

I praise You, my King, for I know there is nothing that can harm me while I rest in Your arms. For this is the place I run to at night. A place that I alone can tell You of my day, my delights, my hurts, my desires and my pain. It is there You tell me of Your love and all that You have planned for me.

Adoani, as I go out into the world this day. Send forth Your angels to surround me, to minister and protect me throughout this day.

Let all I do and say be as sweet as honey to Your lips and a pleasing aroma to Your nostrils. May it bring warmth upon Your heart and a smile upon Your face. For this is my desire, my King.

I praise You for each breath I take and the opportunities that lay before me this day. Let me make this day count for the furthering of Your kingdom.

In *Yeshua's* name I pray. Amen.

July 2

Never Leave My Side

"Finally, brothers and sisters, whatever is true, whatever is honorable, whatever is just, whatever is pure, whatever is lovely, whatever is commendable—if there is any virtue and if there is anything worthy of praise—dwell on these things." — Philippians 4:8 TLV

Abba, it is so true that we get caught up in the day to day life. That we forget to stop and ponder, to praise all the good that You have done for us each and every day.

But I want to praise You in the storm. Because never do You lose control or sight of me. I praise You in the trials of my life. With every step, You are teaching and stretching me to be more like You. I praise You for the times I feel unworthy and all alone. For You are there picking me up and taking me to a higher elevation in You. I praise You for all the earth, the skies, the people that surround me. For in them, I see the beauty of You.

No matter the day, how easy or hard it might seem. You are *Jehovah Shammah* and You never leave my side. You promised never to leave me nor forsake me. For this, I owe you my life.

I praise You in all things. For You can turn it into good, as long as I offer myself as a sacrifice, to love no other God, but to love only You.

You are my heartbeat, the expression of my life. Only to You do I give praise. All day and all night, it's hard to imagine, but I love You more every day. How much more will I love You, on my dying day and a thousand years after I leave this earth.

I'm looking forward to our wedding day, my Lord. And I can't wait to see the dress! But the best part will be, when we all stand before You, not one of us a guest.

I love You, my King. I praise You for today and every day here on this earth. Thank You for the way You love me and how it grows more and more in every way. Amen.

JULY 3

My Flesh Lingers For You

*How lovely are Your tabernacles, **Adonai-Tzva'ot**! My soul yearns, even faints, for the courts of **Adonai**. My heart and my flesh sing for joy to the living God.*   Psalms 84:2–3 TLV

Adonai, You are the almighty God! How blessed is the man who trusts in You!

My flesh lingers for Your touch. My mouth awaits Your kiss. My soul hungers to be in Your presence, to see You in eternal bliss.

How long must I wait to be held in Your arms, for I long for the lover of my soul.

For You created me to worship You and to be Yours alone.

How blessed am I, for I trust in You. You are preparing a wedding of splendor just for us to share.

Blessed am I among the multitudes, for I shall dwell with You in Your Holy kingdom forever and ever. Amen.

July 4
Choosing To Make A Difference

*Pray that the eyes of your heart may be enlightened, so that you may know what is the hope of His calling, what is the richness of His glorious inheritance in the **kedoshim**, and what is His exceedingly great power toward us who keep trusting Him—in keeping with the working of His mighty strength.*   Ephesians 1:18 TLV

My Lord, I am thankful to You, for I have awoken to another day, able to worship You, able to read my Bible. Currently, I am able to share my love for You with those who are around me. But our rights and freedoms are slowly being taken away and I fear it may be one day real soon.

My Lord, I turn on the TV and most the shows have plots or things in them that can destroy our minds. I can drive to the beach and see folly and lust all around. I hear of wars and the murder of Christians around the world. And here at home we are fighting each other over the color of our skins.

Adonai, Satan is having a great time. He is playing in the minds of unbelievers and working hard on oppressing those of us who believe.

But I am choosing not to watch the shows that have evil within them. I am choosing not to go where folly is at play. I do not desire to dress where others have thoughts of me that are not pure. I choose to pray for all who are being persecuted around the world. I am choosing this day to think and pray on what is good, honest and lovely. I choose to pray that hate leave the minds of others and that we choose to love all people as we love ourselves. Because You created all men equal. You really love us all the same! I am choosing to praise and worship You no matter what the circumstance.

I love You, my Lord, and I choose to follow Your precepts in all things. And what I choose this day, is to make a difference for someone for their eternity. You, my Lord, are Holy and just, and in You all things are made new every day. Amen and amen.

JULY 5

Wisdom In Leading

*Then King Huram of Tyre, replied in a letter that he sent to Solomon, "Because **Adonai** loves His people, He has made you king over them."*
2 Chronicles 2:10 TLV

Abba, I need Your wisdom in the leading of my people. I need an understanding of all that needs to be done. For everything I do must glorify You, my King, and everything must be done to bless and teach the multitudes.

But who am I, my King, to lead in such a manner? I am not a scholar or astute in the ways of man. But in You lies the greatest of wisdom. And it's only with You commanding me, I can move forward and take a stand.

Give me step by step instruction. Give me my helmet, my sword and my shield. Help me lead us into victory and build a wall of protection around us. So that the enemy knows where he stands. Which is outside these walls and he cannot enter in.

My work is Yours, my Lord. It is not mine to lead. I am going to walk through those doors grateful, every day! For until You remove me, these are the people I am supposed to feed.

In *Yeshua's* name I pray. Amen and amen.

JULY 6

From Your Word Comes Wisdom

"But he who does the truth comes to the light, that his works may be revealed, that they have been done in God." **Yochanan** *(John) 3:21 WMB*

Abba, all that I do I want to be done for Your glory alone. Help me not to be prideful, boastful or such. For then what was to be good, becomes detestable to You. And the last thing I want to do, is to displease You!

Abba, it is evident in my life. That I, by myself, am incapable of doing good works. For no matter how I try, I'm not smart enough, strong enough or financially able to do good unto others.

But as I read and meditate on Your word, wisdom comes. If I stop and pray before I act in a situation, You give me strength. If I do not spend on needless things, if I'm faithful in my tithing, then You bless me and allow me to share in this blessing with others.

So I pray, my King, that whatever time I have left on this earth. I spend it doing Your work, for Your glory alone. For it does not matter what man sees. Except that what they see is only You working through me.

For You are my life, my breath, the very heartbeat of my day. I don't want to exist without Your word pumping through my veins.

So give me wisdom this day that is beyond my abilities. Give me strength to do the impossible for others this day. Help me to be a lender and not one enslaved to debt. Let me be a blessing with every step that I take and with every breath.

I love You more and more with every passing day. And I give all of me to You, this and every day. Amen.

JULY 7

He Knows My Name

*But now, thus says **Adonai**—the One who created you, O Jacob, the One who formed you, O Israel: "Fear not, for I have redeemed you, I have called you by name, you are Mine.*   Isaiah 43:2 TLV

Abba, I have had trials and tribulations in my life, some small and others devastating. But there is nothing that has taken You by surprise, because You are omniscient and know all things. For You formed me, You called me by name. You knew all I would go through and created me anyway.

I praise You that it does not matter the mistakes of my past. For I have been forgiven. All that matters is where I am going and who I believe in; and, my King, I believe in You!

Though I may not be the most beautiful person in the room. I may not be the smartest on the streets. I may not have much money. I may not have many friends or a spouse to wake up to, but I have You, and this is all that matters. For I am the most loved person on earth. Because You love me and have called me Your own!

You have called me: chosen, treasured, adored, beloved, forgiven, accepted, adopted, cherished, prized, victorious, valued, sealed, daughter, righteous, wonderful, flawless, and Your bride. Adonai, I cannot wait to see the name on the stone I shall receive in heaven. When I see You face to face in all Your glory, standing next to all the saints who believe.

In *Yeshua's* name I pray. Amen.

July 8
Tell My Heart To Beat Again

Adonai is close to the brokenhearted, and saves those crushed in spirit.
Psalms 34:19 TLV

Adonai, there is so much that has transpired that I don't know how to forgive and forget, though I know this is what we are called to do.

I do not know that my heart can be repaired. No surgeon can fix what is wrong with it. But You, *Jehovah Rapha,* the Lord my Healer, You are the only One who can repair the damage and the pain. I need Your blood running through my veins. I need You to tell my heart to beat again!

Let me close the door to yesterday. Let me put it behind me. If I need a heart transplant, let it be. But, my Lord, do not let the recovery time take years. Let me open a new door to a new beginning, a new journey in You this day.

I am on my knees, my Lord, for I am crushed in my spirit. But there is nothing You can't do. For You collect my tears and record each one. You know every hair on my head. You know my every thought. So, my Lord, help my heart to beat again.

I am standing here with my arms stretched out wide, waiting on You. Trusting in You and in Your plan.

In *Yeshua's* name I pray. Amen.

JULY 9

Where You Go, I Will Go

Do not plead with me to abandon you, to turn back from following you. For where you go, I will go, and where you stay, I will stay. Your people will be my people, and your God my God.   Ruth 1:16 TLV

Adonai, Ruth understood what the true meaning of love was, for she would not abandon Naomi. She loved her like a mother, with the same kind of love You have for us. She trusted Naomi with her life. You delighted in Ruth and even though she was not a Jew, she became part of the lineage of *Yeshua* the King.

My King, may I follow You with the same love and trust. For where You go, I will go. Where you stay, I will stay. May I make all Your people, my people. For You are my God, the same God of Naomi and Ruth.

Let me follow You and Your *mitzvot* and be adopted into the lineage of Christ. To be Your child. For You will never abandon me, You will always show me the way. Then may others see me and want to follow You—to become Your people, too.

I am Yours. Help me to make the *mitzvot* something I enjoy following. Because I delight in You and Your love. That all my heart desires is to please You now and forever more.

In *Yeshua's* name I pray. Amen and amen.

JULY 10

Adonai

***Adonai** is my strength and song, and He has become my salvation. This is my God, and I will glorify Him, my father's God, and I will exalt Him. **Adonai** is a warrior—**Adonai** is His Name!*   Exodus 15:2–3 TLV

Adonai, You are my strength, my song. You are an all-consuming, everlasting fire. A faithful God, who is here to stay, forever and always the same!

Adonai, You are a warrior, the commander in chief. Nothing escapes Your hands. Justice prevails when You are near. Be near me and with me forever my God. Let my stand be on the side of the scales that stands for justice and grace.

Adonai, You are love, a love that human minds cannot fathom. For it is selfless, pure and holy. Envelope me in this love, let my heart know no other.

Adonai, You are always present. So show me Your glory. Show me Your power and majesty, my Lord. Show me how to walk before You in Your strength, my King.

I love You and will exalt the name of *Adonai* forever. Amen and amen.

July 11

You Are My Everything

Then I looked, and I heard the voice of many angels around the throne and the living creatures and the elders—their number was myriads of myriads and thousands of thousands. They were chanting with a loud voice, "Worthy is the Lamb who was slain, to receive power and riches and wisdom and might and honor and glory and blessing!" And I heard every creature in heaven and on the earth and under the earth and on the sea and everything in them, responding, "To the One seated on the throne and to the Lamb be blessing and honor and glory and power forever and ever!"   *The Revelation 5:11–13 TLV*

Yeshua, You are my everything. Oh how I adore You. For it is only by Your sacrifice on the cross that I will enter into Your throne room of grace and behold all that these verses foretold.

When I hear the Revelation song, it brings me to my knees. I feel like I have entered into Your presence with the angels. Singing Holy, Holy is the Lord God Almighty, worthy is the Lamb who was slain.

I try to imagine the power of Your presence. With lightning bolts flashing, the universe and the rocks crying out with all the angels singing praises to Your name.

I can only imagine falling prostrate before You, unable to move. Being awestruck by Your power and Holiness, by Your knowledge of all I have done wrong, yet seeing me through Christ's eyes. I would not know how to stand!

Yeshua, worthy are You, my God, worthy of all power and praise. You are my everything and I will forever adore You. Amen and amen.

July 12

Broken

For you don't delight in sacrifice, or else I would give it. You have no pleasure in burnt offering. The sacrifices of God are a broken spirit. O God, you will not despise a broken and contrite heart.   Psalms 51:16–17 WMB

Abba, I welcome You to come and fill this place. Be a consuming fire and heal this heart of mine. Burn a love in me that will spread the continents. A love that is deeper than the oceans, counted greater than all the grains of sand. A love that resembles You!

Abba, I do not have things to offer You. I do not have wealth or knowledge. But all of me, is Yours for the taking.

I want nothing of this world. For there is nothing this world has to offer but pain and sorrow. But in You, I have abundant life.

Hear me, O God, delight in me as I delight in You. Give me my daily manna. Give me an increase of Your presence this day.

For You were broken for my transgressions, broken that I might be saved. How I praise You that no matter my brokenness, You can make all things new in every way.

How I love You more, my Lord, for all You do for me, with each passing day.

In *Yeshua's* name I pray. Amen.

July 13

Seeking You

*Hear, **Adonai**, when I call with my voice, be gracious to me and answer me. To You my heart says: "Seek My face." Your face, **Adonai**, I seek.*
Psalms 27:7–8 TLV

Adonai, my Love, how I need You this day.

I seek Your face, my King. For I need to find You in all that is transpiring in my life. For You are *Jehovah Rapha,* my healer. You are *Jehovah Machseh,* my refuge. You are more than enough for me,, for there is nothing impossible for You.

So as I am seeking You in Your word, what amazes me, is the more I seek You, the more I find You. For You reveal Yourself to me in ways totally unexpected, totally just for me.

My heart is overwhelmed with love. For I can feel Your heartbeat and Your hand guiding me. For You are *Jehovah Shammah,* the one who is always there. And in this, I can stand.

Adonai, hear my plea and be gracious to me. Pour Your love over me like Niagara Falls and let me drown in Your living water this and every day. Amen and amen.

July 14

I Need You

We are pressed on every side, yet not crushed; perplexed, yet not to despair; pursued, yet not forsaken; struck down, yet not destroyed.
2 Corinthians 4:8 WMB

Abba, I come before you, battered, beaten and bruised. For in this world there have been people who have hurt me, situations that have been outside my reach. I ask now that you forgive them for what they have done and to start a forgiving heart in me.

My Lord, there are things in my life I am ashamed of. For I have sinned in your eyes, my King. Forgive me, O Lord, and restore me anew, that when others see me, what their eyes behold is not me, but only You.

My Lord, I no longer want there to be a chasm between us. For I only want to sit before You and worship at Your feet. I love You, my King, with all my heart, soul, and strength. And I can't wait to come before You, as Your bride, through all eternity.

I need You more than the air I breathe. More than anything this earth has to offer. I praise You, Abba, and I run to You for Your arms to envelope me now and forever more. Amen.

July 15

My Soul Longs For You

*For you did not receive the spirit of slavery to fall again into fear; rather, you received the Spirit of adoption, by whom we cry, **"Abba**! Father!" The **Ruach** Himself bears witness with our spirit that we are children of God.*
Romans 8:15–16 TLV

Abba, as I awake and call out Your name, my spirit longs to see You and my soul hungers for You.

Come to me, O God of Abraham. Let me see Your wonders. Let me hear the angels sing, "Holy, Holy is the Lord Almighty, who was and is and is to come." For this is what You have created me for. To sit before Your throne and praise You through all eternity.

My Lord, I love the blessings You have given me. I cherish my family and my friends. But I long to be before You, my Father. To be held in my daddy's arms. To look into Your eyes, the one who created everything, the one who created me with love.

I can't imagine anything greater, my Lord. I can't imagine the joy of this day. But until I am able to see You face to face, I will enjoy the blessings that You give. By letting my spirit experience Your presence, in the gentle ocean breeze, the fragrant flowers and in the birds of the air.

For it is in the precious name of *Yeshua* I pray. Amen.

July 16

Lord, Bless Me

*Blessed is the one who considers the wretched—**Adonai** will deliver him in the evil day.*   *Psalms 41:2 TLV*

Abba, my King, how merciful You are to me. For You protect me from thine enemies. You bless the work of my hands. You have set my feet upon a solid rock, and it is there I shall take my stand.

Abba, may You search my heart and change in me anything that is not of You. And put in my right hand Your sword to defeat my enemies and all the evil they try to do.

Bless me, my Lord, with many blessings from above. And may I be a good steward of all I have. For You are the reason I live and the reason that I love.

So keep my heart from growing angry, but may I rejoice in You instead. May I sing praises to You all day, and sleep peacefully when I go to bed.

For You, my King, can protect, give, and take away. May there be moments throughout this day that I am rejoicing, for You have taken my breath away.

Abba, I love You and I give You this day all the good and the bad. Help me give every moment up to You in rejoicing. Let me focus on Your grace and Your mercy. Let me be consumed with all that is Holy, right and just in my head.

You are my King, and I love You more than gold. May I treasure Your goodness and Your righteousness may I uphold.

In Christ Holy name. Amen.

July 17

Increase In Me Your Wisdom

*For **Adonai** gives wisdom. Out of His mouth comes knowledge and understanding.*   Proverbs 2:6 TLV

Adonai, there is so much that man seeks after in this world; money, fame and success, just to name a few. But Your wisdom rises above them all. For people perish for a lack of wisdom.

My Lord, I need wisdom from You to walk this life I have. I need it to get me through each day. For it will teach me how to use the money I have and how to bless the poor with it. It will teach me right from wrong and who to trust and who to follow. It will show me how to gain true success in walking in Your light each day. It is all I should ever need or want. It is what I pray for this very day.

Adonai, give me wisdom to understand the intents of others' hearts; are they full of Your love, or are they really speaking with a lying tongue? Give me wisdom with my finances, so that all I have is used to serve, bless and glorify You! Give me wisdom when I open my mouth. That what I speak is Your truth, never with malice or with hate. But may Your love and wisdom come forth from me, even when my heart is in pain.

Adonai give me Your wisdom to walk right behind You. May I be so close that Your footprints still be warm. Lord give me Your wisdom on leading others. For this is a weak point for me. So I am trusting in You alone to impart Your wisdom and to cover me. For You say where I am weak, You are strong. So live strong in me this way.

Increase my territory that I may serve You more. Increase my finances that I may bless others in many ways. But most of all increase in me Your wisdom, that all I do and say will not come back to haunt me on that great and righteous judgement day.

I love You, my Lord. Help me to look more and more like You in each and every way. Amen.

July 18

Take Away Any Anger

Don't judge, and you won't be judged. Don't condemn, and you won't be condemned. Set free, and you will be set free.   Luke 6:37 WMB

Abba, this verse has always hit me between the eyes and it is the one I needed to hear again today.

We are so quick to judge and condemn those we don't agree with or do not understand. But that is not our right, for we do not hold the scepter in our hands.

For this is all Your position, my God. And I am truly grateful that it is.

For some people harbor ill will in their hearts. Others are just going through things that we might not know of and we are the outlet of their frustration. For we can't see inside of them, but You, O Lord, can.

Abba, take away any anger or resentment I might be harboring in my soul towards others. Help me to truly forgive, to forget and to forget. That I am free of this burden and able to shake this dust from my boots and move on. May I walk shod with the shoes of peace daily.

For I, being human and full of so many faults and inabilities can ONLY do this with the help of Your son Jesus Christ. For He forgave those who persecuted Him, even those who put Him to death.

So help me, sweet *Yeshua,* to love the way only You know how to love, this day and forever more. Amen.

JULY 19

Help Our Fellow Man

*"We have come to know love by this—**Yeshua** laid down His life for us, and we also ought to lay down our lives for our brothers and sisters."*
1 John 3:16 TLV

Adonai, I want to pray for the police officers, fire fighters and military who put their lives on the line for us every day. I also want to lift up their families for knowing this and accepting it as a way of life.

But in the world that we live in today we all need to be prepared to be there to help our fellow man. But we first need to look at our hearts and ask ourselves, are we prepared for the day of judgement? Are we willing to help someone in that way?

Abba, help me live my life as if You were coming to take me home this day, so that my life is right with You every step of the way. For no one knows the day or hour of Your return or the day of our last breath. And it's not inconceivable that it could be today.

Let me be there to help my fellow man. May the Holy Spirit take command of me in this area of my life so that whatever it is You ask of me, I will be willing and obey.

For I may not know the person You are asking me to help. But to help them is to love You. Then this is the way I want to live out each moment of each day.

For You created me to love. Not in the usual ways, but in ways unseen. In ways that will stretch and grow me and those I meet. Let my life not be some ordinary story. But may it be extraordinary, because I live to love and worship You each day! Amen and amen!

JULY 20

Be Strong And Courageous

*Have I not commanded you? **Chazak!** Be strong! Do not be terrified or dismayed, for **Adonai** your God is with you wherever you go." Joshua 1:9 TLV*

Abba, be with me today and make me strong. Do not let those around me bring me down.

Let me keep my eyes encouraged and on You. Keep my heart full of love and Your grace on my lips too.

Abba, You have today. It's already written down. Let me walk with my sword in my hands, Your praises on my lips, wearing my righteous wedding gown.

For You are the Lord of Lord's and the mighty King of all. But You are my knight in shining armor and I am waiting for my call.

I love You, my King. With all my heart, I'll shout and pray. For I'll do anything for You, and I shall do this until You whisk me away.

In *Yeshua's* name I pray. Amen.

July 21

Praying For The Homeless

*Trust in **Adonai** with all your heart, lean not on your own understanding. In all your ways acknowledge Him, and He will make your paths straight. Do not be wise in your own eyes; fear **Adonai** and turn away from evil. It will be healing to your body and refreshment to your bones. Honor **Adonai** with your wealth and with the first of your entire harvest. Then your barns will be filled with plenty, your vats will overflow with new wine.*
Proverbs 3:5–10 TLV

Adonai, help me not to look to man for comfort, strength or wisdom. But to look into Your word, to come before You each day. To have the faith that all I lay before You, You hear and will act on what is truly best for me.

Give me the wisdom to know who and when to give to and who just to lay at Your feet. For some who stand on the streets are not in as much need as they make you think. But there are those who are starving and need food, medicine and a place to sleep.

Lord, since I am not wise and cannot see the hearts of man, I will lift each one up to You. Then, if You desire, quench my heart to give a helping hand.

I don't want to be as the rich man, who would not give Lazarus a plate of food, and I don't want to give to those who do not need it. So You will have to show me when and who.

Thank You for hearing this prayer my righteous King. For all the wisdom and riches come from You. I am Yours to do what You want. I praise You that I am not one begging for food. Amen.

July 22
Praying For My Enemies

"But I tell you who hear: love your enemies, do good to those who hate you, bless those who curse you, and pray for those who mistreat you."
Luke 6:27–28 WMB

OK, my Lord, this is the first verse You put before me this morning for a very good reason.

I need to pray for my enemies. I need to release my hurt to You and allow You to work in both of our lives. For until I give this disappointment, this frustration and anger over to You, I will never be healed

Lord, I allowed Satan a foothold, which I do not ever want to give him again. So, my Lord, here it is: I give it to You at the cross. I surrender it all! If I have done wrong in any of this, please show me. Help me to show mercy and forgiveness for what has been done towards me. There is nothing in this world worth holding over someone, because You paid for this and every sin and hurt on the cross. So it is forgiven in Your heart. I too must forgive.

Thank You for forgiving all my past, present, and future sins. Thank You that You do not hold anything over my head, that each day You extend grace, love and peace to me instead. Whatever the situation may be, may I do whatever I can to emulate this to others.

For it is only in You I can be this person You so desire me to be.

Thank You *Yeshua* for loving me so true. Amen.

July 23

A Lighthouse

Be careful that you don't do your charitable giving before men, to be seen by them, or else you have no reward from your Father who is in heaven.
Matthew 6:1 WMB

Good morning my Love, I thank You for this day, and every day You offer grace!

Abba, when I was young I was confused by this verse. For You say let Your light shine on a hill. But You say to do alms in secret, is to gain our rewards in heaven.

As I have matured in Christ it's so easy to see. That as a Christian, my whole life should be a witness, I should be like a lighthouse guiding the way. But if I want to do something special, to give to the poor or to help the beggar on the street; this should be done in secret, for it is a gift from the Holy Spirit not from me. And it will bless the one who receives it and any whom may see. But it's not something to brag about. It's something between You and me.

Then I can look forward to seeing what's in store, for You are the greatest at giving gifts. The Holy Spirit has poured gifts out on me now, but in heaven it will be times ten.

Fill me with You this day, let me be the light on the hill. If there is more You want from me, show me, Lord, so I can give to others as Your will.

In *Yeshua's* name I pray. Amen.

July 24

Do Not Worry

Therefore do not worry, saying, 'What will we eat?' or 'What will we drink?' or 'What will we wear?' For the pagans eagerly pursue all these things; yet your Father in heaven knows that you need all these. But seek first the kingdom of God and His righteousness, and all these things shall be added to you. Matthew 6:31–33 TLV

Abba, I must confess, I have been worrying a lot lately. For when people start losing jobs, it affects my business and my parents' health; the list goes on.

But what can I do by worrying? I have no power, no control to change a thing. So I lift up to You all my concerns, all of my doubts and worries, and I lay them at Your feet.

For You have a plan for me that is perfect. Some that may not be easy, so as to refine me in a fire. But in this refining process, my King, let the heat not be turned up so much that I am scorched. But only to where I am bendable and shapeable to Your likeness, my Lord.

You know my needs before I ask. You know the steps my feet must take. Carry me when the water gets deep. Do not let me drown in this world and its sorrows. But may my eyes see You in every moment, whether in a smile of a child or in a kiss from a friend.

Please continue to give me reminders throughout this and every day. That You are there. That I do not walk through my troubles alone. For You will give me all I need in this life and forevermore.

For You are not only my King, but my husband who counsels me. Who wants life and blessings to come my way. For this, I will stay on bended knee this day and every day, thanking You, *Yeshua*, for Your love and Your faithfulness is great! Amen.

July 25

Your Instruction

I will instruct you and teach you in the way which you shall go. I will counsel you with my eye on you.   Psalms 32:8 WMB

Abba, I praise you for Your instruction, for without it I would live astray. But with it I see Your glory, I see the beauty that only You are able to give.

Abba, I have a desire which lies within my soul. But I don't know if it is from You. So I will sit still here in Your word, and I will not move until I hear from You.

For Your word is alive and quick, sharper than any two-edged sword. For it speaks clear and precise to my soul. And this desire of my heart will not just affect me, but many, my King. So I only want what is right, what is true, and what is of You.

Thank You that Your eyes never leave me and that Your hands go before me. I praise You that Your *Ruach* never departs from me and that I am forever safe in Your arms. Your plans for me is to prosper in Your love, to look more like You every day. So show me in Your word how to do this, not just for my sake, but for all You cast my way.

I love You, my King, and I give You all that I am. For it is in my beloved's name that I pray. Amen.

JULY 26

I Can Only Imagine

But as it is written, "Things which an eye didn't see, and an ear didn't hear, which didn't enter into the heart of man, these God has prepared for those who love him."   1 *Corinthians 2:9 WMB*

Adonai, I have tried to imagine the streets of gold, the gates of pearl, the foundation of heaven made from different jewels. But I know there is nothing that I can imagine that could compare to what You have created.

For I imagine heaven to be more beautiful than a sunrise, more brilliant than the highest mountain. To be more breathtaking than Niagara Falls, more peaceful than lying in a field of lilies.

It has to be the most incredible place, not just because of the descriptions in the Bible. But it is a place where You reside, the King of all kings. It would have to be just to contain Your presence there.

I can only guess that when I walk through the gates, that I will be consumed with an overwhelming joy. That the ultimate peace that You speak of will fill my soul. For my eyes will behold the most beautiful place, one I can't even imagine. But, my Lord, to see Your face, in all its glory ... nothing in this world or the next could take the place of this.

How I can't wait for this day, my King. I can't wait to see all You have prepared for those whose hope lies in You alone.

For it is in *Yeshua's* name I pray. Amen.

JULY 27

On Bended Knee

*For the word of **Adonai** is upright and all His work is done in faithfulness. He loves righteousness and justice. The earth is full of the love of **Adonai**.*
Psalms 33:4–5 TLV

Search my heart, O God, help me make it true. Search my heart, O God, for I want to be like You.

You know me *Adonai,* better than I know myself. Help me to change anything that is not of You. Fill me with Your love and righteousness too.

For Your love is what I hunger for. It's all I'll ever need. I would hunt the whole world for You if I would have to. But all You ask is to be on bended knee.

So here I'll sit and here I'll stay, on bended knee every night and day. Crying out to You and telling You of my love. Come to me my darling, encircle me like a dove.

I give to You my heart and my life. I am devoted only to You. Change me in any way that I need, my King, so in the mirror I can look like You.

In *Yeshua's* name I pray. Amen.

JULY 28

To Wait On You

*"Have I not commanded you? **Chazak!** Be strong! Do not be terrified or dismayed, for **ADONAI** your God is with you wherever you go."*
Joshua 1:9 TLV

Adonai, did You not prove this verse to me again, just yesterday. For I have been trying for many years to get resolve. But I just needed to wait on You instead.

For to be able to *Chazak,* to wait on You with love takes faith, courage and strength. I want to ask You for forgiveness, for anytime I stood dismayed!

For on the day I asked You to be, my Lord, all my problems You put in Your hand. Help me to leave them there with You, for You can do more than I can!

I am so grateful that You take care of me so. I promise to tell and show others just how You never let us go.

For I know in my heart no matter the trial, no matter the circumstance, if I stay faithful and strong in You, my enemy does not stand a chance.

Praise be unto Thy name, forever and ever. Amen!

July 29

The Righteous Live By Faith

*In it the righteousness of God is revealed, from trust to trust. As it is written, "But the righteous shall live by **emunah**."*   Romans 1:17 TLV

Abba, I am very sad this morning about an attitude I see in most people. For when someone does what is wrong, instead of speaking up, they turn their head and look the other way.

For there have been women raped on beaches while others stood by and watched. Children abused and family members stay silent. It goes from small things to the large and people just say it's none of their business.

This world is so corrupt, my Lord. And as long as this is people's attitudes, it will continue to get worse.

Please *Abba,* help me to be bold and speak out where evil exists. Help me not to be accountable to You for this. For it may cost me family members. It may cost me friends. But when my life on this earth is done, who am I answering to? It's only You, Lord, not them.

May I speak with love, but speak truth and of Your goodness. May I show them a better way, a way of righteousness that blesses and offers hope.

For this is my prayer. In *Yeshua's* name I pray. Amen.

July 30

Acting In Righteousness

*Blessed are those whose way is blameless, who walk in the Torah of **Adonai**. Happy are those who keep His testimonies, who seek Him with a whole heart, who also do no injustice, but walk in His ways.* Psalms 119:1–3 TLV

Abba, help me to be more like this daily. That when life happens and people frustrate me, let me learn to handle them in a way that is righteous and true. That even if I have a reason to be angry, I do not sin in my anger. That if there is a consequence that I must give, that I am fair in giving this. And if it is not my responsibility to give the consequence, I gladly give it over to You.

Abba, if I have wronged my brother, please convict my heart that I can make everything right. If I see someone hurting, may I pray with them and offer them Your word. If I see affliction, may I stand with the sword and fight against the evil one. If I see someone hungry may I buy them some food.

Let me pay any and every one that I owe. Let me walk in the light and not the dark. Let me be as blameless as I can be, my Lord. For I already have enough in my past to answer for, I do not need to add to my lot.

For You were scourged for my sins. Put to death at my cost. I can't fathom what pain You went through for me and all who were lost.

I praise You, my Father, that each day is new. Let me work hard to walk blameless today, my King. But the only way I can is if I let You walk it through me this day too.

In *Yeshua's* name I pray. Amen.

July 31

The Lord Is Patient

The Lord is not slow concerning his promise, as some count slowness; but he is being patient with us, not wishing anyone should perish, but that all should come to repentance. 2 Peter 3:9 WMB

Abba, I praise You for Your patience with me. For being slow to anger and quick to offer grace. For I have done so much wrong in my life. But You used all these things to show me a better way.

As humans, we want You to be patient with us, to forgive and forget our stupid, arrogant ways. So why are we so hard on our fellow man? Why would we not want for them the same?

Help me know who to show grace to, who to teach and who to walk away from. Let me hear their hearts in the words that they say. But if I walk away, may I bend a knee and offer a prayer for their heart too. For I know it's through others prayers that I came to know You!

I love You so much, my King, for all that You do for me daily. Some that is seen and most that is not. And since Your *Ruach* lives within me, may I only go where You would want me to go and do the things You have shown me I ought.

For it is in the precious name of *Yeshua* I pray. Amen.

AUGUST 1

A Love That Never Fades

But we all, with unveiled face beholding as in a mirror the glory of the Lord, are being transformed into the same image from glory to glory—just as from the Lord, who is the Spirit.   2 Corinthians 3:18 TLV

Abba, how I praise You for every day. You unveil Your goodness to us in so many ways. I hear it in the songs we sing, and in the love we have that will never fade away.

For I hear it in the testimonies we give. Of how You take the hungry and the needy and pull them out of the depths of the seas. I see it in the majestic oaks, for they cover the ground just as You cover us from all our enemies. I feel it in my soul for it rumbles with fire and yet You have tenderized it too. Now I can't stop crying whenever I speak of You.

You are my King, in who all honor is given. But You are my Savior, who died for me so my soul can now be risen. You are my God who formed me in my mother's womb. You are my Husband, and through eternity, may I have that slow wedding feast dance, just with You!

Take me in Your arms and hold me until that day. Forever I will be with You. For in the death of this body my spirit becomes alive in You in a whole new way.

How I praise You, my King, and I give You each breath. Nothing will keep us apart, no nothing, not even death.

It is all for the love of Christ. I pray. Amen.

August 2

Your Grace

For I know the plans I have for you, declares the Lord, plans to prosper you and not to harm you, plans to give you a hope and a future.
Jeremiah 29:11 TLV

Adonai, Your grace is unending. Like Niagara Falls which continually flows and it never ceases. Your grace is eternal, having neither a beginning, nor an end. It was put into motion before the world was formed and it continues beyond the grave.

You fore-knew as You knit me in my mother's womb, what Your plans for me were and how You are going to see me through. You thought through every single detail of my life. My King, I am choosing to walk hand in hand with You as Your bride.

I cry out to You to put Your grace before me as You did with King David. For You anointed him as a young boy from a lowly family. Everything he did, he succeeded in. This was not because David was able in his own right, but Your grace was with him.

So since Your grace is unending and goes before me, I have faith that all I do in the name of *Yeshua.* That is done with the right heart and motives. I will succeed in all these things, for I want to only do things for You, my Lord, now and forever. Amen.

August 3

Teaching Others

*Thus says **Adonai**: "Egypt's toil, Ethiopia's merchandise, and the tall Sabeans will come over to you and be yours. They will walk behind you in chains. They will bow down to you, and pray, saying, 'Surely God is with you!' There is none else—no other God!"*   Isaiah 45:14 TLV

Abba, all knees will bow and every tongue confess that You are Lord of all! There will be no more judging of color, no more rich or poor. For everyone is equal in Your eyes and this is how it will be forever more!

But until the day You come for Your bride, let those who do evil see in us a value, a worth they desire to have. Let them come to us in all their splendor and say; nothing on this earth is as valuable as what you have. Teach me that I may walk in this way.

That day Lord will be a day to remember! That is a day I will pray for until You come and take me home. That I can plant seeds for the harvest. That I can nourish those who think they have everything and pray for them when they find out, that they have nothing at all.

For in You is life, hope and the fulfillment of all that is good! The world is just a foot stool for Your feet and everything underneath is Yours for the taking. Not just for now, but all eternity long.

Take me in Yours arms and hold me this day. I am Yours for the taking, now and forever more! Amen.

August 4

To Be Prepared For Battle

"When the strong man, fully armed, guards his own dwelling, his goods are safe. But when someone stronger attacks him and overcomes him, he takes from him his whole armor in which he trusted, and divides his plunder.
Luke 11:21–22 WMB

 Abba, You have called us not to be weak but strong! Not to just stand on the street corner handing out daisies saying bless you all day long, but to put on the full armor and to take a stand against evil. To prepare our hearts and minds for battle as if we were in the gym preparing our bodies for a physical battle.

 It is better to protect a stranger from walking in front of a moving vehicle than just to say "be careful" as they get hit by the car, but this is the stance I see most Christians take. They don't want to offend. They think it's better only to show the gentle side of *Yeshua* than the strong and righteous one. *Abba,* those who believe that way don't do You justice at all, for You are Holy and Righteous. One day You will return with an army of angels and cast Satan and all who follow, into the eternal pit of fire!

 Help me as I go out into this world, understand that I might step on others toes. But let me always walk in the shoes of peace, that I am not looking for fight, but I standing firm on all that is right. Let me wear the helmet of salvation knowing I am Yours now and forever more. Let me wear the breastplate of righteousness, protecting my heart against a crafty man's words. Let me put the shield of faith in my left hand, knowing that where I am, You will also be. Let me hold the sword of the Spirit in my right, fighting off my enemy. May I wear the belt of truth, so I do not give a reason for others not to believe. May I stand firm on You the rock, so the ground I am on does not waiver beneath my feet.

 You are my rock and my salvation in Whom I shall stand. Forever may I be with You, as my feet walk upon this land. Amen.

August 5

Lord Of All

He is the image of the invisible God, the firstborn of all creation. For by Him all things were created—in heaven and on earth, the seen and the unseen, whether thrones or angelic powers or rulers or authorities. All was created through Him and for Him. He exists before everything, and in Him all holds together. He is the head of the body, His community. He is the beginning, the firstborn from the dead—so that He might come to have first place in all things. For God was pleased to have all His fullness dwell in Him and through Him to reconcile all things to Himself, making peace through the blood of His cross—whether things on earth or things in heaven! Once you were alienated from God and hostile in your attitude by wicked deeds. But now He has reconciled you in Messiah's physical body through death, in order to present you holy, spotless and blameless in His eyes.
Colossians 1:15–23 TLV

My King, where would I be without You? Where would I go? What would I say?

I would be as a tumbleweed in the desert, going where the breeze would take me, having no purpose in life … I would be a grain of sand, lost in the multitudes, of no worth, to count for nothing…. I would be as a ship sailing in a storm, unable to keep the ship afloat, for the waters are taking me under.

But in You, I am everything. You have paid the price for my sin and called me Your bride. And You being Lord over all the universe, over all the inhabitants on the earth and the heavens, chose to pay the debt for my sin. I owe You everything, my Lord. I am grateful to be Your bond servant throughout all eternity.

You my Majesty, are Lord of all creation and Lord of my heart. Forever will You reign and Lord of all. Amen.

AUGUST 6

Peace

If then you were raised together with Messiah, seek the things that are above where Messiah is, seated on the right hand of God. Colossians 3:1 WMB

My Lord, on the days I focus on heaven and not on the things of this earth. Those are the days I have the most peace, the most contentment, the most joy, ever since my rebirth.

For here on earth there is strife, anger and stress. But in You, my Lord, there is unmeasurable love, peace, and rest!

Since I wear my armor and the helmet of salvation is the first piece I put on, I have the assurance of knowing that one day, I'll be in your arms.

Teach me today any precepts I need to learn. Give me a new heart. For only to You, my King, do I turn.

Today I live only for You and look forward to heaven alone. And I can't wait to see You sitting there, on Your magnificent Sapphire throne.

Thank you, my Lord, for hearing this prayer. For You are always there with me, no matter where.

In *Yeshua's* name I pray. Amen.

August 7

Rest In Your Arms Forever

Greater love has no one than this, that someone lay down his life for his friends. **Yochanan** *(John) 15:13 WMB*

My Lord, in this life I have seen selfishness. I have seen people ignore others in their time of need and pain. There are people who gang up on others, raping and unfortunately beating even sometimes to death. Where no one stops to lend a hand. No one cries out to help the one, in fear of what they may incur.

My Lord, I pray that if I ever am in a situation where someone's life is at stake. That I do no sit idly by in their need. I pray that *the Ruach ha Kodesh* will take over me and the situation and allow the enemy to run in fear. May I trust in You and do only what You would have for me to do on that very day.

I pray for all fire fighters and police officers as they work selflessly to serve and help those who are in need. May You keep their feet on solid ground and keep their heart in Your hands for all eternity. For no matter the cost, they lay it down for us every day.

Thank You, my Lord, for my life and all the blessings You bestow upon me each day. Thank You for saving my soul and that I never have to suffer the eternal pain I so deserve. May You be my strength and my song and all I need this day and forever more. Amen.

August 8

My Salvation

*Behold, God is my salvation! I will trust and will not be afraid. For the Lord **Adonai** is my strength and my song. He also has become my salvation."*   Isaiah 12:2 TLV

Adonai, how could I go through one day and not realize the depth of love You have for me.

For I arise to another day, because of Your grace. I'm able to use my hands in service, because of Your mercy. I'm able to spend time with those I cherish, because You love me. How beautiful, how marvelous are You, my King!

I walk the street, not in fear, for You are my protector. I speak Your truths to others, in reverent fear of You. I rejoice when I hear the cries of a baby. I pray when I see the tears of our youth.

How I pray this day for all the souls who walk this earth, especially those who are lost. For they know not the eternal suffering they shall behold, until it's too late and there is no way to recover what they lost.

You, O God, are my refuge and my strength. You care for me, no matter the cost. For You saw how lost this child of Yours was, so You sought me, and purchased my soul on the cross.

You, my Lord, are my strength and my song. Forever I shall praise You, all eternity long! Amen and amen.

August 9

Following You Alone

Ruth said, "Don't urge me to leave you, and return from following you, for where you go, I will go; and where you stay, I will stay. Your people will be my people, and your God my God.   *Ruth 1:16 WMB*

Adonai, where You go, I will go, and where you stay, I will stay. My Lord, I am lost without You. I have no meaning in this life. No one cares for me or searches my heart the way You do.

Take my very breath from me, if I cannot stay in Your presence. For this life is not worth living if I do not have Your love!

I bow before You, my Lord. For unlike Naomi, telling Ruth to go back home. Your desire for me is to follow in Your footsteps. Praying the prayers of the saints. Staying in the places You stayed, seeking You with my whole heart.

Yeshua, You are God alone! It is You alone who holds the key to my heart. My soul is in Your right hand and no one can remove it!

You are the lover of my soul and know every desire of my heart. You are the essence of each breath. You are the only reason I exist. So where You go, I will go. Where You stay, I will stay. What You pray, I will pray. To You alone, I give my soul for eternity. Amen and amen.

August 10

My Rock And My Fortress

For it was not by their own sword that they took possession of the land, nor did their own arm save them. But it was Your right hand, Your arm, and the light of Your face—for You favored them. You are my King, O God—command victories for Jacob! Through You we push back our foes. Through Your Name we trample those rising up against us. For I do not trust in my bow, nor can my sword save me. For You saved us from our oppressors and put to shame those who hated us. Psalms 44:4–8 TLV

Abba, You are my rock and my fortress. In You alone I trust. Give me the hands that will move into victory. Give me the land beneath my feet. Show me exactly who I can trust, my Lord, and who is my enemy.

For enemies come in sheep's clothing. They tend to blend in and act inconspicuously. But when they are ready to attack me, Lord, their teeth are like lions, tearing apart the meat.

But You, O God, are my protector and my Father, who can move the mountains to the seas. You would change the rotation of the universe, if that is what is needed to defeat the enemy.

Only You know the day and hour of Your return to take me home. Only You know if this will be with the multitudes or if I will go that day alone. I do not care what day and hour You chose for me. I just can't wait to see You and to dance with You on the golden streets. Then the problems that I faced on this earth will fade. For I will be with my King forever, engaged in His presence that never goes away.

Thank You for Your protection as I still walk upon this land. I will wait patiently for the day when You put Your ring upon my hand. Amen and amen!

AUGUST 11

His Eyes Watch Over Me

*For the eyes of **Adonai** are on the righteous and His ears open to their prayer, but the face of **Adonai** is against those who do evil."*   1 Peter 3:12 TLV

Abba, I am so far from perfect. But I try to live a life of piety and grace daily. I see why I need Jesus so desperately. No matter how hard one tries, it's impossible to walk perfectly straight!

You, O Lord, know my heart and how much I love Thee. You know that my desire is to be before Your throne throughout eternity. So turn Your eyes upon me, my Lord. Hear and answer my plea!

Adonai, I put all my work in Your hands. Do with it as You please. May it prosper and be a blessing to all who I serve and meet.

My Lord, help me have clarity of thought. Help me to do all that I need to do. To bless and increase the territory in which I serve. May I honor and worship You daily, so my walk is so close to You. That moment by moment I can hear Your heart beat.

I praise You that You heard these prayers of my heart. And that You, my Lord, will answer each one.

For it is in *Yeshua's* name I pray. Amen.

AUGUST 12

Salvation Unto Our Children's Children

*But the mercy of **Adonai** is from everlasting to everlasting on those who revere Him, His righteousness to children's children, to those who keep His covenant, who remember to observe His instructions.*
Psalms 103:17–18 TLV

Abba, I don't think there is a person who hears Your voice that would not hang on to this promise!

For if we truly love You, we will surrender all and obey Your commands. And if we truly love our children and their children, we will emulate You to them and teach them Your statutes.

Adonai, embed Your word within my soul. Burn Your love into my heart. Let me live a life that will bring all my family to walk in Your ways and to serve You only.

The only desire I have greater than this is for You to love me. For without Your love inscribed upon my heart, I could never show it or teach it to others.

This is my request, not just for today, but for eternity. That my children, their children and I shall stand before Your throne, bowing down to the one true King. Serving and praising You through all eternity.

For its only through the blood of Christ that I can ask these things.
In *Yeshua's* name I pray. Amen.

August 13

I Long For Thee

*My soul yearns, even faints, for the courts of **Adonai**. My heart and my flesh sing for joy to the living God.*   Psalms 84:3 TLV

Adonai, all the earth longs for You. For I hear the song of the birds in the morning singing praises to Thee. I hear the drops of the rain upon the ground and the flowers rise to behold Your glory. How much more my soul longs to behold You in all Your majesty, sitting upon Your sapphire throne of grace!

I can't imagine the courts before You; the color, the fragrance and the unending praises of all the angels and the saints. Singing forever their love song of praise.

To be standing before You, knowing there was nothing I did that allowed me there. I'm there only because of the love You have for me. How I have tried to imagine this day, but nothing in this earth can explain what this day will hold.

I can only imagine on the day when I behold Your face, that I will fall prostrate before You, unable to move. Your holiness will be too much for my soul to contain. So You will pick me up, hold me in Your arms, and tell me all the love You have for me.

For I love being in Your presence. I love You *Yeshua* my God, my redeemer and I will forever!

To You, my *Adonai* I pray. Amen and amen.

August 14

Instruct Me

*One prudent in a matter will find good Blessed is the one who trusts in **Adonai**. The wise in heart is called discerning, and sweetness of lips increases persuasiveness. Insight is a fountain of life to one who has it, but folly leads to the discipline of fools.*   *Proverbs 16:20–22 TLV*

Abba, may You instruct me in Your ways. May You be the light unto my feet. May I always come to You alone in and for everything I need. May I do and be what You created me to be this day.

How I praise You, *Abba,* for these women You have put in my path. May we lift each other up. Teach each other and hold each other accountable all the days of our lives. For we are sisters in Christ, one body in You. There should be nothing one should need that the other does not offer. No sin too great that we should not step in to intercede. We are Your daughters, Your bride, Your examples to live in this life. May we be worthy to proclaim the blood of *Yeshua ha Mashiach.*

Cover these women with Your perfect *Shalom* and allow Your glory to be revealed in and through all they do! And for those who do not have someone to be there for them. They struggle in life by themselves and are all alone. *Abba,* I ask that Your presence falls upon them life a waterfall. That they never are lonely again! Amen.

AUGUST 15

My Yahweh

God Answered Moses, "I AM WHO I AM." Then He said, You are to say **Bnei-Yisrael,** *I AM has sent me to you.*   Exodus 3:14 TLV

Yahweh, faithful God, I praise You, that You are here to stay. You are always the same, never changing, never ceasing to love in a manner that is beyond what man can conceive. For You forgive us even as we are failing. You are the great I AM. You are whatever I may need at that moment in time.

You are *Jehovah Jireh,* my provider.

You are *Jehovah Rapha,* my healer.

You are the Alpha and Omega, my beginning and my end.

You are my "*Hey*" the very breath that I breathe. You are more than I could ever want, more than I would even know how to ask.

Yahweh, You are all powerful, for You will condemn Satan to the grave, never to harm Your children again.

Yet You are the Lover of my soul, tending to my hurts and pain with the gentleness of a dove.

I love You, my God, with all that I am. If there is anything I can do to please You, to repay You for all You have done and will do for me, let it be, Lord. Let it be!

To You, my King, I give it all this day. For You are the Lover of my soul, now and forever more! Amen and amen.

AUGUST 16

Profitable For My Soul

"He will be like a planted tree over streams of water, producing its fruit during its season. Its leaf never droops—but in all he does, he succeeds. The wicked are not so. For they are like chaff that the wind blows away. Therefore the wicked will not stand during the judgment, nor sinners in the congregation of the righteous." Psalms 1:3-5 TLV

Oh, my King, how grateful I am for Your grace. For it cleanses me from all my sin!

I praise You for the doors You have opened before me and for the ones You have closed. For it has been through this pathway that I have grown in You! All Your hands have created is at my disposal. But You give me only what is profitable for my soul.

Adonai, I ask that You take me to a higher place in You! If that means closing many more doors, then I welcome this, my King! For I want to stand by the streams of Living water, producing fruit that is sweet and delightful just for You.

Put in me seeds of righteousness, that I can flourish and be strong and withstand any storm that comes my way! Let my branches not break from the weight of the fruit, because Your hand is holding it all the day through.

Adonai, I pray for the lost souls of this world. For they know not the gravity of their destiny. May I have an opportunity this day to plant a seed of righteousness before them. So Your Living water may bring life and make them grow.

In *Yeshua's* name I pray. Amen, and amen.

AUGUST 17

Who Am I?

We proclaim Him, warning and teaching everyone in all wisdom, so that we may present every person complete in Messiah. To this end I labor, striving with all His strength which is powerfully at work in me.
Colossians 1:28–29 TLV

Abba, who and what am I. Who and what am I to become?

The one truth I know, is that I am a child of the living God, an heir to the throne of Christ. That when I pray to You, I have access to the heavenly host. To help me in accomplishing what is good, right and holy.

Abba, help me this day in all wisdom. That I may speak Your words and save one soul who does not believe.

Be with me *Adonai,* captivate my soul. Help me in ways I would not know to ask and lead me into righteousness this day. May I labor in love for You, this day and forever more. Amen and amen!

August 18

Not Good Enough

*Enter His gates with thanksgiving and His courts with praise! Praise Him, bless His Name. For **Adonai** is good. His lovingkindness endures forever, and His faithfulness to all generations.* Psalms 100:4-5 TLV

Abba, I am so thankful that You love me and understand me.

For no matter how I try to do what I think is right, to be in Your will and to help others, I always seem to let someone down. I am never able to satisfy those I love.

I feel like such a failure, like my life does not count. For not matter what, someone is always upset with me.

Show me what You want from me. I need to be right by You. No matter what anyone else thinks. If You need to remove me from my surroundings or the situation at hand. Whatever the cost, I am here, my *Adonai,* just for You.

My life belongs to You alone, this day and forever more! Amen.

AUGUST 19

Be Still

*Be still before **Adonai** and wait patiently for Him. Do not fret over one prospering in his way, over one carrying out wicked schemes. Psalms 37:7 TLV*

Adonai, I sit before You and tell You of my worries, of all things concerning me. For I am seeking an answer from You. My Lord, I need You desperately!

You state that the word of God is living and effective, able to discern the reflections and thoughts of the heart. So I know that You know mine and theirs. Please Lord, keep us from being torn apart.

Show me the way, my King. What is right and just and true. Show me what You want me to do, my King. Not what I want or what others tell me to.

For You know what is best for me and for them. You know our hearts and how to make them soft and to search for You.

So let me know Your desire for me, and if it is hard, I will need Your strength. For I do not like to displease others, but sometimes in doing what is right, it is what I have to do.

I will be still and wait until I am confident of Your word for me. For if there is a way to diffuse this situation, this is what I want to do. But if I have to remove it, I can't do that without You, my King. I will need You to carry me through.

Thank You for always listening. For knowing what is best and for helping me guide my way. I lay this at Your feet, my Lord. Please let me hear from You this day.

In *Yeshua's* name I pray. Amen.

AUGUST 20

Unusual King

Behold, I am sending My messenger, and he will clear the way before Me. Suddenly He will come to His Temple—the Lord whom you seek—and the Messenger of the covenant—the One whom you desire—behold, He is coming," says **Adonai-Tzva'ot**. *Malachi 3:1 TLV*

Yeshua, how I praise You for sending John the Baptist, who declared Your name. For He foretold of Your coming, baptized You and never wavered from the truth.

Then You came down from glory to be put to death. So unusual for a king to do for his subjects, but You are no ordinary King! For You are *Adonai,* Lord and Master of us all. Your desire was for us to share in Your kingdom forever. Not just to worship You. But to enjoy and partake in all the marvelous things You have prepared for us in the heavens.

How I long for Your coming. To see You and the splendor of Your glory. To see Your face delight in the pleasure of all You have prepared for me. But the greatest treasure that awaits, is for me to lay my crown at Your feet.

I love You with all that I am, my *Adonai.* Hold me in Your arms this day. Amen and Amen!

August 21

Staying Pure

How can a young man keep his way pure? By living according to Your word.
Psalms 119:9 WMB

Adonai, our culture is one where if it feels good, do it. "It's your body; you have the right to use it how you wish."

It's a culture where shame and pain from this attitude is way too often. Because each time you give up of yourself in this way, you give up a piece of you with it.

How long will we say to our children, "It's OK, just don't get pregnant?" How long will we stand by and allow this self-destruction to continue?

Help this country stand for purity. Forgive our past sins and let us start anew. May each person be pure in their hearts, their souls and in their minds. Let us keep our bodies, Your temple, pure too.

Let us start today teaching this to our youth. That our future generation is known for its love and devotion to You!

I pray this in the Holy name of *Yeshua,* my Lord. Amen and amen.

AUGUST 22

Awaiting Your Return

So Messiah also, having been offered once to bear the sins of many, will appear a second time, without sin, to those eagerly awaiting Him for salvation.
 Hebrews 9:28 WMB

How often do people say they are looking forward to Your return. But do they really mean it, or are they just wanting things to be going easier in their lives?

Are we looking forward to our Groom to come and take us to the home, to the place He has prepared for us? Are we ready to leave this world and all its wonders to a place of the unknown?

If we truly believe the word and all that it says, if we love You with all our hearts, our souls and our minds, then we should be anxiously awaiting Your return. To spend eternity with You. To see all the wonders and majesty this world could not possess.

For the greatest part of Heaven is You. To see You on the throne of grace. To behold the elders and the angels praising Your name. To see the beauty this world could not contain. To receive a flawless body, with no more suffering no more pain. To look upon the face of *Yeshua,* who gave it all, so I could gain.

I am awaiting Your return *Yeshua ha Mashiach.* For in You, all my dreams will come true. Amen and amen.

AUGUST 23

Crowns The Humble With Victory
➤╬⬅

*For **Adonai** takes pleasure in His people. He crowns the humble with salvation*
Psalms 149:4 TLV

 Abba, during this time of trouble and turmoil, let me be victorious in You. Let me rise up with a sword in my hand. To speak what is right by You and not by man.

 I give all these trials in this process to You. For I believe deceit, jealousy, and anger have made a plan. But You are stronger, bolder and wiser than Satan. You can thwart these evils from every man's hands. Take them and cast them into the seas. Let this time be about You and Your promised land.

 I love You, *Adonai.* Don't let them take this from me. Keep me from allowing Satan a footstool. For it is all about You, not anyone else, or even me.

 Let me walk in victory of Your love and grace. Let me win over my enemies for You this day. But even if I don't see an answer to this prayer anytime soon, I will trust in You. For Your ways are higher than our ways. Your plans are perfect for me and for all who surround me.

 So I will trust in *You* alone!

 In *Yeshua's* name I pray. Amen.

August 24

To Die Once

Inasmuch as it is appointed for men to die once, and after this judgment.
Hebrews 9:27 WMB

Adonai, am I completely ready for this day. Have I done all I can in this world to the best of my ability? Have I forgiven others of their wrongs? Have I made amends for the wrongs I have done?

I am so looking forward to seeing Your face. But help me get to this point, my King. For I have done enough sin in my past to be judged for. Help me to make all wrongs right.

Your forgiveness is what I seek. Your grace and Your mercy I hunger for. For on the day of judgement the only thing I can say, is that *Yeshua* is the only reason I am able to stand before You, the King.

Let me give You my crown, my life and my soul to keep. I cling to You *Yeshua,* for You alone are my everything.

I love You and it's to You alone I pray. Amen.

August 25

Success

He has said to me, "My grace is sufficient for you, for my power is made perfect in weakness." Most gladly therefore I will rather glory in my weaknesses, that the power of Messiah may rest on me.   2 Corinthians 12:9 WMB

Adonai, I did not go to Harvard. Nor was I born a genius like others in my family. I struggled in school, thinking that I could never be anybody or do anything.

So I want to tell You, my Lord, how grateful I am for all the blessings You have bestowed upon me. To have owned a business for 20 years, where we spoke of and taught others about You. For the people and family You have put in my life who love me, teach me, and help show me Your way.

Adonai, I praise You for Your word. For each day I can find in it wisdom, strength, and love. In it I have found that I am somebody special. Because You created me in Your image. For where I am weak You are strong. So in the moments I have no answers, Your word provides the way.

I praise You because it does not matter if the world thinks I'm successful. If I have You in my life. If I am following Your commands. If I am searching for You as gold. If I have faith as small as a mustard see, then to You I'm successful and that is the only thing I need to know.

In *Yeshua's* name I pray. Amen.

August 26

Anger

Anger doesn't rejoice in unrighteousness but rejoices with the truth; bears all things, believes all things, hopes all things, and endures all things.
1 Corinthians 13:6–7 WMB

Abba, please help me to be more like these verses. For I find myself frustrated with certain people in my life. For when I see and hear of foolishness, of arrogance and pride, I just want to go and shake them until they understand the truth and all that is right.

I don't wish harm or trouble for anyone. For I am a peacemaker, and I want everyone to get along in the manner in which You have said. So when I get angry and frustrated with others, am I the arrogant one? Who should be on bended knee instead?

Help me as You walk me through this lesson. Help me to see and love others in the manner in which You do. May this be a lesson I learn quickly. For its one I will be faced with all my life through.

In *Yeshua's* name I pray. Amen.

AUGUST 27

Works Of Thy Hands

As you don't know what is the way of the wind, nor how the bones grown in the womb of her who is with child; even so you don't know the work of God who does all.   Ecclesiastes 11:5 WMB

Adonai, I see the works of Thy hands. But the knowledge of how You have accomplished all things is beyond all my understanding.

For I see the earth and all its grandeur. How the mountains rose to praise Your name. I have gone down into the ocean where there is no light. But when my flashlight was turned on, the beauty of the colors cry out of Your majesty.

I have experienced the growth of a child inside my womb, the love that I felt with every movement. No one is able to create this, but You. For only Your Spirit can speak and life exists.

I praise You for Your unseen hands guiding our way. That even in the midst of troubles, You are there. I praise You that in this life I will never comprehend the power and majesty of Your name. But soon, I will have all eternity to start learning all You have planned.

Thank You for Your *Ruach* entering into my bones and setting this captive free.

In *Yeshua's* name I pray. Amen.

August 28

Valued

*However, I don't consider my life of any value, except that I might finish my course and the office I received from the Lord **Yeshua**, to declare the Good News of the grace of God.*   Acts 20:24 TLV

My Lord, this was my prayer last night. Then to open up my Bible app and this be the verse of the day.... I should not be surprised!

For You know my inner thoughts, my every desire. You just wanted me to know You heard my cries! What a precious *Abba* You are!

Help me to finish the course You have put me on. Help me to stay positive and not look at the situations. But to keep my eyes focused on what matters. Which is for me, those I live with and those I meet to learn of, grow in and to preach the love of *Yeshua* our Lord.

To You, I give each moment of every day. In *Yeshua's* name I pray. Amen.

August 29

Giants

So then, those who suffer according to God's will—let them trust their souls to a faithful Creator while continuing to do good.   1 Peter 4:19 TLV

Adonai, my King, it is hard when we are doing what is right and yet we suffer for it. Give us the strength we need to stay the course. May we put on the armor and stand firm, waiting for Your command.

For no matter the giants in the battle. No matter how many scars we walk away with. With You in command and the strategies You give us to follow, we will rise victorious in the end.

For You parted the seas for Moses. You tore down the walls for Jacob. We stand anxiously awaiting what You have planned for us.

We give You this day. Show us how to approach our enemies, knowing they are not flesh and blood but the powers of darkness. Show us how to slay them and assure they will never return, moving us closer to our Jericho this day.

In *Yeshua's* name I pray. Amen and amen.

August 30

Your Bidding

*For if we keep on sinning willfully after we have received the knowledge of the truth, there no longer remain a sacrifice for sins, but only a terrifying expectation of judgement and a fury of fire about to devour the enemies of God. Anyone who rejected the Torah of Moses dies without compassion on the word of two or three witnesses. How much more severe do you thing the punishment will be for the one who has trampled **Ben-Elohim** underfoot, and has regarded as unholy the blood of the covenant by which he was made holy, and has insulted the Spirit of grace? Hebrews 10:26–29 TLV*

Abba, I need You more than words can say. I need You more than the air I breath. I need You more than the manna You give me each day. I need You more than all this life has to offer. I need You, my King. Please show Yourself to me this day.

Adonai, You are the very essence of my being. Without You my heart wont beat, for the blood will not flow through my veins. Allow my lungs to open up so I can breathe You in!

Keep my feet from sin, my King. Don't let me sway to the left or the right. Remove me from this earth if I shame You, my Lord. For I never wish to trample You underfoot! I only wish to uphold the beauty and majesty of Your name. I am weak at times so I need the *Ruach ha Kodesh* to be bold and strong in me. Taking control of the situation and giving me an escape route if I need one.

Help me to look at my tempter and say, "My King is Holy. My King is worthy of all my love, and I will not sway because He is the Lover of my soul. It is to Him alone I wish to please."

May I sing of Your goodness. May I sing of Your worth. May I kiss Your feet with my lips of praise. May I feed You grapes with the sweetness of my testimony and love. It is only You I desire to please! Amen and amen.

August 31

I Exalt Thee

*I will exalt You, my God, the King, and I will bless Your Name forever and ever. Every day I will bless You, and praise Your Name forever and ever! Great is **Adonai**, and greatly to be praised—His greatness is unsearchable.*
Psalms 145:1–3 TLV

Adonai, my Lord, my God, Thou art exalted far above all the earth. Thou art exalted far above all. I exalt Thee, O *Adonai,* my God!

I shall sing praises and tell of Your splendor and majesty. For You created all things far above the heavens and far below the earth. The universe cannot contain Your greatness.

You, my Lord, watch over all who love You and uphold those who fall, bringing them into Your bosom and putting Your loving arms around them.

You are great, O King. For Your scales of justice will prevail. No one will escape the great judgement in heaven. There is nowhere to hide, there is nothing that can be said. So I lay my sins before You and the only thing I can say: I accept *Yeshua ha Mashiach* as my Lord and Savior, for He is the only way of eternal life and my heart is His.

I exalt You, O Lord *Yeshua.* For it is in You alone I can praise. Amen and amen.

September 1

Complete Trust

He who seeks his life will lose it; and he who loses his life for my sake will find it.   Matthew 10:39 WMB

Abba, I have found such love in You. In following Your precepts, in holding onto Your truths. You have blessed me and given me life more abundant than I ever thought was possible.

Adonai, with my eyes of flesh I see so much turmoil and unrest all around me. But how I praise You, my Lord, because Your peace resonates from within my soul. For I have chosen joy, my Lord. And though I do not have spiritual eyes, I see You actively working all around me; to strengthen me, to encourage me, guiding me to a deeper walk with You. A place of complete trust, knowing that whatever I am facing, I am not facing it alone.

How worthy are You, my Lord, of all worship and all praise! Show me anything in me that is not pleasing to You and may I walk away from it. For I know the more I do to show You my love, the deeper my love grows for You. This love is a wonderful and amazing thing, and I am hungry and thirsty for more.

You are the wellspring of water, the joy of my life. The one I need to light the way. The one I want to hold me at night. Be with me, Lord *Yeshua,* and let me be You to others this day. Amen.

SEPTEMBER 2

Light Of The World

Yeshua spoke to them again, saying, "I am the light of the world. The one who follows Me will no longer walk in darkness, but will have the light of life."
John 8:12 TLV

Abba, I have felt a dark cloud hovering over me. It has been there too long and has brought me sadness, hurt, and pain.

I am asking, Lord, that You cause this cloud to break apart and fall down from the heavens, like the rain. May it open up and pour a waterfall of grace upon me and all who surround me this day.

Then, Lord, Your light will show its way, peering through the clouds, shining Your love and peace down upon me and this land. Giving us the strength we need to face our enemies again.

Help me to forgive my transgressors. Help me offer grace after grace after grace. Because this is what I need from You, nothing less. For even in my efforts to do what it right, I fail You each and every day.

Abba, I ask that You show them their ways that are wrong in Your eyes and bless those who turn to You. Give them the desires of their heart and lead them into the life everlasting, which is only found in *Yeshua.*

I ask nothing less for me, my King. That I may come to You, humbly wanting to be in alignment with You in all of my ways.

For this is my prayer and it is in *Yeshua's* name alone that I pray. Amen.

September 3

Exalt Adonai Forever

*Halleluyah! How good it is to sing praises to our God. How pleasant and fitting is praise. **Adonai** builds up Jerusalem. He gathers together the exiles of Israel. He heals the brokenhearted and binds up their wounds. He determines the number of the stars. He gives them all their names. Great is our Lord and mighty in power—His understanding is infinite! **Adonai** upholds the humble. He brings the wicked to the ground. Sing to **Adonai** with thanksgiving. Sing praises to our God on the harp.*
Psalms 147:1-7 TLV

Adonai, in the morning my heart cries out in song: How great is our God for You are clothed in majesty. Worthy are You, my King, of all praise.

One day all will see how mighty and powerful You are. One day, every knee shall bow and every tongue confess that You alone are God.

For the Holy mountain has Your name carved on the stones and they cry out to You, O Lord. For You are the Alpha and Omega, the creator of us all.

You have healed my heart. You have healed all my wounds. You have called my name and made me Yours.

You are with me when I rise and next to me when I sleep. How I praise You, almighty God, for each breath and for taking care of me and my needs.

All power is Yours alone and yet You live within my soul. Causing all evil to fall by my side as I use the flame of Your sword. You are coming for the righteous and my praise now and then shall be: How great are You, my God, and worthy of all praise! For You have taken away my sins and You have numbered my days. You have given all to me that Your hands have made, for I am an heir to the throne of grace. You are my *Yahweh,* my Lord that reigns forever. Worthy are You of all praise! Amen and amen.

SEPTEMBER 4

No One Can Separate Us

*And He said to him, "You shall love **Adonai** you God with all you heart, and with all you soul, and wit all you mind. This is the first and greatest commandment."*   *Matthew 22:37–38 TLV*

Abba, I have been asked by another, "How do I love You so?" I am not sure how I am to answer. She says she hears in me a love for You that is different from most.

My Lord, all I know is: I searched for You as a buried treasure and found You! My lips were dry and parched and You quenched my thirst.

Then, You created in me a love hat is beautiful and true. For I love You like a child who adores her father. I love You like a bride standing at the alter saying her vows to her groom. My love for You is purer than gold. It is more radiant than all the diamonds. It reaches into the heavens, and it is as deep as the seas.

You are the essence of my life, my morning and my night. Speak through me today, let Your voice be heard. Let me say the words You want them to hear. Let Your living water flow through from me into hers and others' hearts this day. And may they too find this love that is so divine.

For it is *Yeshua's* name that I pray. Amen.

SEPTEMBER 5

Suffering Produces Perseverance

*'But my righteous one shall live by **emuah**; and if he shrinks back, My soul takes no pleasure in him." But we are not among the timid ones on the path to destruction, but among the faithful ones on the path to the preservation of the soul.* Hebrews 10:38–39 TLV

My Lord, on that day You come to take me home, let my name be called righteous. Let my life reflect Your love. Let me not be timid in the way I walk alongside sinners. May I show them that there is a better way. A way that is unlike anything they have ever experienced. For through faith, they can endure all things. Through faith, they can have a new life. Not just in the here and now, but in the hereafter. For in You everything looks different, everything changes.

Abba, You open doors and make possible the impossible for those who walk by faith. You never lose sight of us. No matter the troubles of this earth, You are there guiding our way. Just like the Magi, You guided them to Yeshua, You will guide us if we believe.

Adonai, I believe, for my life is so different, my heart is not the same. I exalt You, my King, for being bold in me. Taking one who was timid and giving her the strength that only comes from You.

My I always be one who is faithful, bringing, dragging if needed others with me to Your doorstep. Knocking for You to let us in. Beholding You face with all who stood strong in You.

I long for this day! I long to be in Your presence. Fill me with Your *Ruach* this day. For it is only by Him I can live a life worthy of the calling.

In *Yeshua's* name I pray. Amen and amen.

SEPTEMBER 6

Doing God's Will In The Darkness That Surrounds

*And she said to the men: "I know that Adonai has given you the land—dread of you has fallen on us and all the inhabitants of the land are melting in fear before you. For we have heard how **Adonai** dried up the water of the Sea of Reeds before you when you came out of Egypt, and what you did to the two kings of the Amorites that were beyond the Jordan, to Sihon and Og, whom you utterly destroyed. When we heard about it, our hearts melted, and no spirit remained any more in anyone because of you. For **Adonai** your God, He is God, in heaven above and on earth beneath. So now, please swear to me by **Adonai**, since I have dealt kindly with you, that you also will deal kindly with my father's house. Give me a true sign that you will spare the lives of my father, my mother, my brothers, my sisters and all who belong to them, and save our lives from death."*
Joshua 2:9–13 TLV

*Adona*i, You blessed Rehab for her eyes being wide opened to Your majesty and power. She acted on what she knew, even in the face of death she was faithful.

I know that Your *Ruach* had to have come to her in this time of darkness to give her strength.

Then after the Israelites seized Jericho, You saved her and her house and called them Yours. But the biggest gift was she was put In the lineage of *Yeshua*.

How Your love exceeds all human understanding. For You take that which is low and make them great.

Abba, with all the sins I have committed in my life. I ask that You do unto me as Rehab. Save me and all that are in my home and call us Yours! Do things in our lives that will allow us to do great things for You and all whom You love. Amen and amen.

SEPTEMBER 7

Show Me Your Glory

Adonai answered Moses, "I will also do what you have said, for you have found favor in My sight, and I know you by name." Then he said, Please show me Your glory! So He said, "I will cause all My goodness to pass before you, and call out the Name of *Adonai* before you. I will be gracious toward whom I will be gracious, and I will show mercy on whom I will be merciful." But He also said, "You cannot see My face, for no man can see Me and live." Then *Adonai* said, "See a place near Me—you will stand on the rock. While My glory passes by, I will put you in a cleft on the rock and cover you with My hand, until I have passed by. Then I will take away My hand, and you will see My back, but My face will not be seen."
Exodus 33:17–23 TLV

Adonai, I want to see Your glory! I want to see Your face! I am blessed to be Your people. I am blessed to be here in this place.

For since *Yeshua* came and walked this earth Your glory has been revealed. Since Your Ruach came like a fire upon the apostles, Your Ruach has come to live in man.

Adonai, show me Your glory! I want to see Your face! I am crying out to You, my Lord, fill me with Your presence this day.

You, my God, are righteous and holy. No man can gaze upon Your eyes and live. I can't wait until the day I see You face to face. I can't wait until You reveal it all to me, for then Your presence will have no end.

Adonai, show me Your glory! I want to see your face! I am blessed to be Your people, I am blessed to be here in this place. Amen and amen.

September 8
Worth The Wait

*"Better is little with the fear of **ADONAI** than great wealth with turmoil."*
Proverbs 15:16 TLV

Adonai, I know You have blessed me with much more than I deserve. But I am even more blessed that I do not have so much. That my eyes look to You for everything I need. Because only what is good, what is right and what is Holy comes from You. Everything else may give joy, but it's fleeting. But the blessings from You are eternal and everlasting.

There is no person, no pleasure, nothing this world has to offer, that exceeds the joy of Your presence. There is nothing I want more than to bask in the presence of Your glory forever. In the warmth of Your light and in sweetness of Your love. The ultimate concert of the Heavenly host singing "Holy is the Lord almighty. Worthy is His name."

Yes, *Adonai,* this is worth the wait. And it is the treasure I can't wait to see. Amen, my Lord, and Amen!

SEPTEMBER 9

Your Love Never Fails

Let me understand the teaching of your precepts! Then I will meditate on your wondrous works.   *Psalms 119:27 WMB*

My Lord, I see Your glory, Your wonders. For You created the sun and the stars to light our way. You created the plants for our food and for shade.

You created the flowers for our pleasure. You created man to be Your child. How grateful I am, my Lord, among the multitudes, for You created me to love.

Help me this day to discern Your precepts. Let me come to know You inside and out. For the more I learn about Your precepts, the more I learn of Your righteousness and grace.

Let me come into Your sanctuary, let me come before Your throne. Let me see You in all Your wonders. Let me life be for You alone.

I only want to please You, my King. The desires of my heart are all for You. Give me the ability to do a great work. Not for my glory, but for You.

Let me speak loudly of Your love. Let me stand strong in the midst of adversity. Let me not waiver when the mockers are screaming. Let my silence be louder than their voices.

Let me resemble You in every way possible. But it is only through meditating on Your precepts that I shall know what You would do. Burn them on the walls of my heart, so they will never leave me. It's only then I can resemble Your truths. Amen and Amen.

September 10

Joy In My Trials

Blessed are those who keep his statues, who seek him with their whole heart.
Psalms 119:2 WMB

My King, my joy is found in You alone. For there is nothing on this earth that stays the same, that continually renews and restores. But You are faithful in all things, no matter the circumstance, You are there seeing me through.

There are so many situations around me that is hurting my heart. Some with the way people are living their lives, knowing the destruction they are causing. Others are just angry with the world or with their own circumstance and making so many bad judgment calls. It is hard when seeing them walk in this way.

Help my walk be one where people take notice. May I not grumble in the trials but glorify Your name instead. May I speak of all that You are doing that is good, instead of focusing on the bad. May my strength in You be like angels singing praises, because I am consumed by the *Ruach ha Kodesh,* whose beauty cannot be contained.

My Lord, no matter how things may look at that moment in time. Show me how to walk in Your footsteps. Allow me to focus on the end result rather than the momentary pleasure of the flesh. To be grateful for each day that I have breath, for I have another with family and friends, another day to share Your love, another day to see a soul be saved.

My joy is found in You alone. How I praise You today for each breath! Amen and amen.

SEPTEMBER 11

All Yours

Therefore I urge you brothers, by the mercies of God, to present your bodies a living sacrifice, holy, acceptable to God, which is your spiritual service.
Romans 12:1 WMB

My King, I am not sure why You have me planted where I am at. But I know I would not be there if not for You! I'm not sure what all I am to do in this place. But I know as time goes on, You will reveal it to me.

I'm not sure how I, someone without much skill, without great talents or abilities can accomplish anything special for You!

But I do know that You, *Adonai* are at my right hand. You created the winds and the seas. You created the place in which I stand and You have put me here with a specific plan.

So I give it all to You, my work, my life, it all. Put me where I will serve You best! Teaching me, even in the times that I fall.

For whether I'm poor or rich, sick or healthy, surrounded by others or all alone. I dedicate all of my life to You.

It does not matter whether or not I succeed in the ways of man. As long as I succeed in Your eyes, for this is the greatest plan!

Help me, my King, not to act like the world, but to earnestly pray over every decision, to know without question before I make a move.

Then I know Your hands will cover me. I know You will see me through.

Praise You, my Holy Father. For I am truly blessed to be Your child! Amen.

September 12
Working On The Sabbath

*Thus says **Adonai**, "Guard your souls! Carry no burden on the day of **Shabbat** or bring it in through the gates of Jerusalem. Nor should you carry a burden out of your houses on **Yom Shabbat** or do any work, but keep **Yom Shabbat** holy—as I commanded your fathers." Yet they did not listen or incline their ear, but stiffened their neck, not hearing or accepting correction. "However, if you listen attentively to Me," says **Adonai**, "to bring in no burden through the gates of this city on **Yom Shabbat**, but sanctify **Yom Shabbat** and do no work on it, Jeremiah." 17:22–24 TLV*

Forgive me *Adonai*. For I have failed You. I have sinned against You so many times in this area.

For when I was a child here in America, most stores were closed on the *Sabbath*. Now, most businesses require us to work so they can be open and make a profit. I know, my King, that this saddens Your heart, that we have stiffened our necks to this command.

Help us *Adonai*, give credence to this. So You can bless us and we can take back our land. For right now evil doers are running our country. Our children bring guns to their schools. We wonder why people run amok. But it's because we are not showing and giving this honor to You.

Help me, my Lord. Forgive me for not keeping this command as I should. I pray that all who have an ear will start working hard to keep this and all commands. Then You will bless this land as You said You would in Your word.

You are my God, my Father and my best Friend. Let me pour out my love upon You. Let me make the *Sabbat* holy in my home, my Lord, once again! Amen.

September 13

Hear My Cry

I will instruct you and teach you in the way you shall go. I will counsel you with My eye on you. *Psalms 32:8 WMB*

Morning by morning I call out to Thee! Please hear my cry *Jehovah Rapha*. Please, O Lord, may You hear my plea.

For many are suffering, from loss of family and friends, to loss of jobs. Hear my plea for Your loving arms to surround us. Hear my cry, my Lord, so we can see.

For nothing happens to us by chance. It is all in Your divine plan to teach us and build us in You. For Your angels are all around us, because protecting us is what You have them do.

You are the God of hope and I give it all to You today. Let me be an example of Your love. Let me show my family and others Your way.

In *Yeshua's* name I pray. Amen.

SEPTEMBER 14

The Lord Is My Shephard

A psalm of David. **Adonai** *is my shepherd, I shall not want. He makes me lie down in green pastures. He leads me beside still waters. He restores my soul. He guides me in paths of righteousness for His Name's sake.*
Psalms 23:1–3 TLV

Adonai, would You restore my soul this morning, will You strengthen me to see. For the journey You are taking me on will be long and winding. But in the end, there You shall be.

Help me to see You around each corner. Let me hear Your voice through the trees. For I will carry my lamp to get through the darkness but I will need You to be holding me.

Lord, I am not wise. I am a woman who in my past has done much sin. But You have found something of worth within me. Let others see Your reflection from within.

Father I am just an empty vessel. Please fill me up with You. I want to go where ever You are leading. So be my *Jehovah Rohi,* my Shepherd, my Lord, so I do not fail You!

I love You will all my heart, my soul and my mind. Please guide my steps this day.

In *Yeshua's* name I pray. Amen.

SEPTEMBER 15

Freedom In Christ

Stand firm therefore in the liberty by which Messiah has made us free, and don't be entangled again with a yoke of bondage.   Galatians 5:1 WMB

Abba, it is oh so clear to me this new life that You have given me. For You have taken me out of bondage and put my feet upon a rock. I praise You that I never have to go back to the days of old. That I am forever free in Your loving arms.

Abba, there are people I know who are suffering so, from drugs or alcohol and other addictions. I ask that You bind Satan and his demons from them. I beg that You cover them with Your wings of love and begin ministering to them a new. For they are in pain and agony and they need to find You this day and forever too.

Abba, will You search my heart today and take away anything that is not of You. Remove anything in my life that could put me in bondage or add pain. Help me to look more like You when I look in the mirror. Help others to see this reflection too.

I have many decisions that I need to be making. Many have come to me for a word from You. Lord let me be wise when I make these decisions and help me to find the words in the Bible when guiding others too. For all I want is to be in Your will. All I want is to steer others toward You!

For it is in Christ Holy name I pray. Amen.

September 16

Gifts

If I have the gift of prophecy and know all mysteries and all knowledge, and if I have all faith so as to remove mountains but have not love, I am nothing. 1 Corinthians 13:2 TLV

My King, I thank You for another day in which to honor and serve You!

I thank You for the gifts You have bestowed upon me. *Abba,* I ask that You increase the strength of, the knowledge in and how to use these gifts, that I might walk in the *Ruach,* edifying You and in the furthering Your kingdom!

I praise You for showing me Your existence. I pray that this Year my faith increases ten-fold. That I can move mountains in helping to lay a path that allows others a way to follow You!

But love, my Lord. This is the hardest to do. To love even those who persecute You. This is outside my ability…… So I open up my heart and cry out for this type of love to flow through my veins. That with each heartbeat, Your love flows through every part of my being. Then, my Lord, You can't help but be the essence of what others see in me.

I so want to walk closer to You! I do not want to let You down. But I know there is nothing I can do on my own that would ever be good enough. So I relinquish all authority of myself and ask that Your *Rauch* lives in and walks through me, this day and every day, my King!

For it is only through the blood of *Yeshua* do I have the right to come before Your throne and lay this petition at Your feet. I praise You and ask that the *Ruach ha Kodesh* will grant each request and build me up anew in You.

For it is in *Yeshua's* name pray. Amen and amen!

SEPTEMBER 17

Hearing From Your Lips

Enoch walked with God, and he was not found, for God took him.
Genesis 5:24 WMB

Abba, what a beautiful vision this is, of a love You have for mankind. For You created us. You walked with us and You sent *Yeshua ha Mashiach* to die for us, that we might have eternal life.

Very few people have ever lived who have walked with You. I can't imagine this experience. I can't imagine hearing from Your lips, the truth!

For You are omnipotent, the Holy righteous one. Whatever would come forth from You, would change all who hear forever.

So why is it so hard for people to believe the word of God? For You are the author, who spoke it to man.

If we choose to read it and apply it, we are changed and could never be the same again. For Your word changes us from the inside out. It is burnt on the walls of our hearts.

Let me hear from You in my spirit where You want me to walk this day and every day I am here on this earth. Change me from the inside out to where all who know me, know I am a child of the living God's.

In *Yeshua's* name I pray. Amen.

SEPTEMBER 18

Integrity

Righteousness guards the way of integrity, but wickedness overthrows the sinner.
              Proverbs 13:6 WMB

 Good morning my Love. How I need Your strength, how I need Your wisdom this morning. For You know the hurts of my heart and how much I don't understand the ways of others. How they love to repay evil with evil.

 For my love for You is more valuable than gold! It is stronger than the waves of the ocean crashing into the rocks. Where the current takes me to a deeper walk with You.

 So, my King, I lay these children of Yours at Your feet. Because I know the love You have for them is great. I ask that You heal all the hurts and all the pains deep within them. Let them not go a day without searching for Your truths and to walk in the righteousness of *Yeshua ha Mashiach,* Your Son! For we are all just sinners who need grace, and I know I definitely need Your grace, my King.

 So help me to go through this life blessing and loving; giving and caring for others. Help me to be a better sister, daughter, mother, friend, and witness of Yours, my King!

 Let me walk in righteousness, breaking the laws of evil with the laws of love and truth. Let Your light shine through all my brokenness. Let me be a vessel, a woven tapestry, a masterpiece just for You!

 For I can only do this through the power of the *Ruach ha Kodesh* living through me.

 It is in the precious name of *Yeshua* I pray. Amen.

SEPTEMBER 19

Came To Fulfill The Law

Do not think that I came to abolish the Torah or the Prophets! I did not come to abolish, but to fulfill. Amen, I tell you, until heaven and earth pass away, not the smallest letter or serif shall ever pass away from the Torah until all things come to pass. Therefore, whoever breaks one of the least of these commandments, and teaches others the same, shall be called least in the kingdom of heaven. But whoever keeps and teaches them, this one shall be called great in the kingdom of heaven. Matthew 5:17–19 TLV

Abba, I pray for our pastors, for all those who teach and preach Your word. I also pray for the leaders of this country and the leaders in our homes. That when they teach or talk about Your word, they are careful in what they say. That they don't speak unwisely about such things.

Because You did not say there are laws we can now ignore. So we should not pretend or say that times have changed, and if You are a loving God, You will understand.

For it is true that You are a loving God. But if we truly love You, which is the greatest command, then our hearts would want only to follow all of Your truths! To please You instead of our fellowman.

So, my King, I can't help myself. For I am compelled to tell others of Your love and grace. Help my lips be used by Your *Ruach ha Kodesh*. That they are worthy, and righteous in all I say. Let me never tell anyone something that would cause them to sin, or to turn from You. But let my words and actions compel others to want to find out for themselves Your truths!

Thank You for all the things You show me daily about Your love for me and how Your amazing grace has set me free.

For its in *Yeshua's* name I pray. Amen.

SEPTEMBER 20

When The Shofar Blows

Do not think that I came to abolish the Torah or the Prophets! I did not come to abolish, but to fulfill.   Matthew 5:17 TLV

Yeshua, so many have come and called themselves the Christ or the anointed one. But You are the only one who fulfilled every prophecy spoken by the prophets of old. You are the only one worthy to sit at the right hand of God Almighty. You are the only righteous Judge and may we all be ready for Your return.

Yeshua, just as the Hebrews were brought by Moses to mount Sinai to meet our God when they heard the blowing of the shofar; so it shall be at Your return. All who believe in You as Lord, Master and Savior will meet You in the air when the shofar blows. How we must be ready, how we need to be watchful, for this day will come like a thief in the night and only those who are prepared will rejoice.

Abba, keep my heart pure, keep my eyes focused on You. May I be an offering of love for You to others. May I be prepared, for the day draws near when my eyes shall see the glory of my God. For all I want is to hear You say: well done my child, for Your love of Me was shown to all you knew. May you enter My gates and rejoice, for the marriage supper of the Lamb is at hand.

And may we all sing Hallelujah and say Amen!

September 21

The Heart Of A Man

The good man out of the good treasure of his heart brings out that which is good, and the evil man out of the evil treasure of his heart bring out that which is evil, for out of the abundance of the of the heart, his mouth speaks.
Luke 6:45 WMB

Abba, this verse says exactly what I have always believed. That if you listen to someone long enough, they give themselves away.

There are many good people out there, my Lord, who do not know You. Who do good deeds, but their hearts are dead and are unable to speak Your truths.

Then there are those who know You, but whose walk is that of an unbeliever. For they have not been able to walk away from certain sins that are great!

I know that I have sins in my life I have to work on every day, my King. And I praise You that You, being the gentleman that You are. Do not show me everything at one time. For in fear and depression, I might turn and run the other way.

But I pray that those who have not seen or heard from me in 6 months to a year, or more can hear and see a change in me. A walk that is so close to You, that there is no denying I have a heart after Yours.

May my actions follow Your words to a point of amazement. That my convictions are so strong, I can stand in hard times, with joy, because I trust in You alone.

Remove from my life anyone or anything that gets in the way of You and me. Let me be an imitator of *Yeshua,* because HE is what lives in me.

May all I do and say edify You and bring honor to Your kingdom. For it is *Yeshua's* name I pray. Amen.

SEPTEMBER 22

Broken Vessel

***Adonai**, You are our Father. We are the clay and You are our potter. We are all the work of Your hand.*   Isaiah 64:7 TLV

Abba, I am mere clay from the ground, without beauty, without form.

I have tried on my own to be molded into a beautiful vessel. But others broke pieces off and crushed them back down into the ground.

Abba, will You take some fresh clay and start anew? Create a new work of art in me, just for You!

One that can sit alone on a shelf that You get great enjoyment from. Or one You put around many others. That adds a sparkle and completes the assortment.

Whatever You choose, my King, I am ready for the process. Because I know between the pressing and the firing it won't all be easy.

But I am ready for You to put me in Your hands this day and for everything to start fresh with You!

In *Yeshua's* name I pray. Amen.

SEPTEMBER 23

Love Does No Harm

Love doesn't harm a neighbor. Love therefore is the fulfillment of the law.
Romans 13:10 WMB

Love, true agape love, is the hardest commandment of them all. Because we, being selfish people, love ourselves more than others. So I know that this love is not about our feelings and it's not about our wants and desires. It is about *truly* doing unto others as you would have them do unto you: sacrificially, without anger or malice. To be there for them, not in words, like most people do on social media, but to be there in person and to give without wanting in return.

But the hardest of them all, is to pray blessings over those who have hurt you or despise you. That You God would do wonders and miracles in their lives and give them their hearts desire. This is tough, my King! To do these things to those I don't know and to those who have hurt me.

But I have made a promise to You, my King, that I would walk this life with intention. That I would do acts of kindness to those I don't know. That I would pray earnestly for those I love. And that I would ask the *Ruach ha Kodesh* to pray through me blessings over those who have hurt me, that I may be clothed in the righteousness of God.

So be with me this day, for Satan wants so much for me to walk in the hurts of my past. But Lord, You have that agape love for me. You are truly amazing! Speak through me this moment. Let my heart be turned towards You. Show me exactly what it is You would have me do for others this day and every day.

For as long as I have breath, my life belongs to You. I am Your bond servant, marked by the blood of Christ. Knowing that I must be intentional in all I do to represent You, my Lord, my King!

Thank You for Your love and living in me. Which allows me the ability, the freedom to walk in You. Amen and amen.

SEPTEMBER 24

Climb Into My Abba's Lap

"You will seek Me and find Me when you search for Me with all your heart."
Jeremiah 29:13 TLV

Abba, let me go to my secret place where I can find You. For this is a place that I have for us to meet. A place we can commune. A place I can give You my whole heart.

And there are times I am at work when things are going wrong. That I can't wait to go home to climb in Your lap and have my *Abba's* arms wrap around me.

I am surrounded by people every day, my King, but I am still alone. I tell others things of my heart, things that are the desires of my heart, and no one hears.

But I can come home to my secret place. And You are there, anxious to hear about my day, wanting to share in all my needs. Giving me Your love, filling my deepest desires.

My biggest and deepest desire, my King, is the indwelling of the *Ruach ha Kodesh.*

For it is only in Him I can find rest and peace. It is the only place where I have security and love.

It's in the precious name of *Yeshua's* I pray. Amen.

September 25

The Heart Is Deceitful

*The heart is deceitful above all things, and incurable—who can know it? I **Adonai** search the heart, I try the mind, to give every man according to his ways, according to the fruit of his deeds.   Jeremiah 17:9–10 TLV*

Abba, You are the God above all creation. You created all things for Your good. You created me in my mother's womb. So please, circumcise my heart, Lord. Make it pure! Let there be no crevice empty, where I can come in. But fill every part of it with You.

I have so many desires in my heart, but my heart can deceive even me. So show me what is good and pleasing for my soul, for You are the One who created me.

You hear my thoughts. You live in my heart. You know more about me than I know myself. Show me where the Living water is. So my body can be refreshed.

Take me to the *mikveh* pools, immerse me in Your *Ruach.* Take me to the desert, my King, and let me only eat Your manna. Search my heart, my *Adonai;* let it beat a song of praise. Speak to me whatever Your desires are. For my life is Yours this day.

How I praise You, almighty God, with my hands lifted up high. I give You all that I have, and all that I am, forever and ever amen.

September 26

Armor Of God

*But the wisdom that is from above is first pure, then peaceable, gentle, open to reason, full of mercy and good fruits, impartial, not hypocritical. And the fruit of righteousness is sown in **shalom** by those who make **shalom**.*
Jacob (James) 3:17–18 TLV

Abba, may the peace that passes all understanding flow in us and through us this day. May this peace confuse our enemy to a point of interest. May we stand strong and courageous and fight by the sword, which is the loving *Rhema* of God, not with the sword that slays mankind. Let us wear the belt of truth, so no lies can be found on our lips. May we use the shield of faith, because with faith, all things are possible. May we put on the breastplate of righteousness and protect our hearts, because it can easily be deceived. May we wear the helmet of salvation; and may others see that our God is the God above all. That You, Lord, can tear down the walls they think are protecting them, just as You did with Joshua at Jericho.

You are a mighty and Holy God. There is no place one can hide from You. I am praying Lord for the time is quickly coming for Your return, where peace and love will reign forever. But until then it will grow harder for us each passing year. Build in us Your strength, Your knowledge and Your love. May we tell everyone we know about You. May we understand who to fight and how, so as to win their heart and not turn them cold. May we have no fear of death, but may our testimony of Your love make death just a moment in time before we behold Your shining face in glory.

I will praise You, my Lord, forever; I want to lay at Your feet. Amen.

SEPTEMBER 27

Showing Mercy

And have mercy on those who are wavering— save them by snatching them out of the fire; but on others have mercy with fear—hating even the garment defied by the flesh.   *Judah (Jude) 1:22–23 TLV*

Abba, showing mercy mixed with fear is difficult at its best for me.

But for You, my King, this is Your character. A manner that is easy for you. But for us, it is a line that can so easily be crossed.

For Isis is so cruel, so much evil in their hearts. I do hate the way they think. The actions they take, the horror that they cause.

Showing them strength and fear is something, maybe the only thing they would understand. But how would You show these people mercy? Or would You just wipe them off the face of the land?

Our leaders need guidance. They need a revelation on how to handle this evil in Your way. I have no suggestions, but to lay this at Your feet, my Lord, and pray.

Abba, I know evil exists, and in it we can see just how good You really are! Help me in teaching this to others, both near and afar.

I pray for salvation, for restoration, for love to grow in the hearts of man. For I have tasted Your love and know that even the evillest of hearts can be changed to a godly man.

This is my prayer, my Lord, and I offer it to You today. Show me what I can do, to witness to others in Your perfect way.

In *Yeshua's* name I pray. Amen.

September 28

Love And Grace

"Now beyond question, great is the mystery of godliness: He was revealed in the flesh. Vindicated in the Spirit, Seen by angels, Proclaimed among the nations, Trusted throughout the world, Taken up in glory."
1 Timothy 3:16 TLV

May I only live to proclaim of Your glory, to seek truth and justice, to offer love and kindness.

Let me not repay evil with evil. Instead, may I repay deceit with truth and hatefulness with kindness. Help me, my Lord, to keep Satan beneath my feet and keep love and grace around my heart.

Let me be gentle in my flesh and bold in my spirit. Let this be because You are in control of all that I do and say. Let the words of my mouth be pure and may You equip me for the task ahead. Let all who come by me, hear Your voice, Your truths, see Your love, and feel Your peace.

For this is my one desire. That we walk together in the furthering of Your kingdom, so wounds can be healed and mountains can be climbed.

Thank you for always being there for me. And for seeing me through in all that I do.

In *Yeshua's* name I pray. Amen.

SEPTEMBER 29

I Give You My Soul

"I urge you therefore, brothers and sisters by the mercies of God, to present your bodies as a living sacrifice—holy, acceptable to God—which is your spiritual service. Do not be conformed to this world but be transformed by the renewing of your mind, so that you may discern what is the will of God—what is good and acceptable and perfect." Romans 12:1–2 TLV

Adonai, I have always thought of worship as singing as the exhortation of You. But it is also in the way we live, how we give and whom we love.

I knew these things showed of our love for You. Showed others what and who we thought our God to be. But it's even deeper. It goes right back to the core of why You created us.

We were created in Your image to worship and praise. Not as the elders do by singing Holy, Holy all through the day. But differently, by giving You every ounce within our souls. To give unto You so much of ourselves that there is nothing left for us to hold onto.

This is the praise that bellows up through the heavens. The ones that are sacrificial in our lives and in our souls.

Help me today, my King, sing and worship You with every bit of my being. Help me conform to be exactly who You created me to be. Let me cast away all the selfishness and pride so You can do a mighty work in me.

I thank You, my King, for allowing me another day to offer such a praise to You.

For it is in *Yeshua's* name I pray. Amen.

September 30

Mercy Seat

"For we must all appear before the judgment seat of Messiah, so that each one may receive what is due us for the things he did while in the body, whether good or bad."   2 Corinthians 5:10 TLV

My King, I am nothing more than the dirt on the ground. Filthy rags are cleaner than me. But You called my name and made me a new creature. So when others see me, they do not see the shame and filth I am. But I pray they see a magnificent God instead. I thank You my mighty King! For Your mercies are new every day.

Adonai, I praise Thee that I will not receive the judgement that I should. For salvation comes to me through You alone. But I pray, my King, for those I know, those I love, and those whom I meet. Let there be something in me, something I do, that mirrors You so beautifully that they want to know more. May I find a way to bring them to pray the prayer of salvation. That none may perish but all may have everlasting life.

I am so sorry, my Lord, for all the times I have failed You, for all the times I should have spoken a word or given out a hand in love.

But help me be an alien to things of this world and stand in the righteousness and holiness of *Yeshua ha Mashiach,* Jesus Christ our Lord!

Thank You for hearing this plea, my King. For my love for You grows deeper and stronger with every passing day. Amen and amen.

October 1

Mountaintop

*How beautiful on the mountains are the feet of him who brings good news, who announces **shalom**, who brings good news of happiness, who announces salvation, who says to Zion, "Your God reigns!"*
Isaiah 52:7 TLV

How beautiful is the name of *Yeshua*. For it is in the whisper of His name the angels come to encamp around me and protect me. It is in the crying out of His Holy name that the healing comes. In His majestic name, salvation comes to all who love and honor Him.

How blessed am I, Lord, that You have taken me to the mountain top to reside there with You. How blessed am I that You would bring healing and restoration to me and my family. How blessed am I, Lord, to be called a daughter of the King!

You, my Lord, are the very essence of every breath. Let me stay in this moment of Your presence, with Your arms wrapped around me, knowing I am secure and loved like no other. May everything I do and everything I say be done to edify You.

You are the Lord of Lords and the King of Kings. May You find favor in all who read these words. May they find restoration and love, healing and peace. May they follow You so closely that the dust from Your feet stays upon their face. May all they do be done for You.

To You, my King, I give today. To You, my *Adonai,* I give all praise. Amen.

OCTOBER 2

Blessing Others

*In all things I have shown you an object lesson—that by hard work one must help the weak, remembering the words of the Lord **Yeshua**, that He Himself said, 'It is more blessed to give than to receive.*   Acts 20:35 TLV

Adonai, my King, You have given so graciously to me. May I give according to that which You have given me, and may others reap blessings from the seeds which I have sown.

How great Your love for me is, my Lord. You take that which is good and bless me. And all that which would not help me in my walk with You, You hold back so I can grow closer to You each day.

I thank You for blessing me with Your presence, my King. For each night I lie down in Your arms of love and every morning I awake to Your words of life. Your understanding of my every need far exceeds the things of this world.

Hold me, Lord, and do not let me go. Make me like the dove; both beautiful and graceful. Make me like the lion; strong and courageous. Make me like Martha, where I am a gracious host. Make me like Saul where I can defeat the enemy. Make me like Solomon, wise with the ability to bless. Make me like Peter, with a clear understanding of Your word and with the desire to share it with others. Mold this jar of clay *Adonai*, to be the very essence of Your desires.

For it is in Your mighty name I pray. Amen.

October 3

Beautiful As Tizrah

You are beautiful, my darling, like Tizrah, lovely as Jerusalem, awesome as an army with banners.   Song of Songs 6:4 TLV

King *Yeshua*, I bow down before You, with love and thanksgiving in my heart. No matter what is going on all around me, You are there. No matter what I see happening in this world, Your *Ruach* is guiding me for a closer walk with You!

Adonai, You are more beautiful than the sunrise, stronger than the seas. Your grace pours over me like a waterfall and Your love covers me with peace.

Be my banner, be my victory, defeat my enemy and hide my shame. Let me shine, my Lord, because I have climbed the mountain and have proclaimed Your love.

Abba, Your eyes of love overwhelm me. Your beauty far exceeds that of Tizrah. May I be a sweet aroma to You. May I be as Your bride, beloved and beautiful. Let no one and nothing stand in the way of the day when we commune at the wedding supper of the lamb.

For You are my King, my Savior, my *Jehovah Nissi,* my banner, my hope and the lover of all who seek Your face. I love You, my Lord, and I give You all that I am. To You my Love I praise. Amen.

October 4

May Your Glory Fall On Me

Now may the God of hope fill you with all joy and shalom in trusting, so you may overflow with hope in the power of the **Ruach ha-Kodesh**.
Romans 15:13 TLV

Abba, put us in the crevice of the hills to protect our eyes from seeing Your face as You pass by. And at that moment, may Your glory fall on us so strong that we are forever changed as Moses was on mount Sinai. May the indwelling of the *Ruach ha Kodesh* be so strong in us that every day our gifts are strengthened in service for You.

Abba, You have given us this day to make a difference: to feed the hungry, to help those who are hurting, to lay hands on and pray for the ill and to confess of our salvation to others. May we not let a moment go by when we don't show others the majesty of Your love.

How I long for the day when You will descend from the heavens and call Your bride home. But until this day arrives, may You increase in us wisdom and discernment through the *Ruach ha Kodesh,* knowledge and visions of things to come. May Your army of angels encircle us and protect us. May each member of our households be saved!

May Satan flee because we are someone to be reckoned with. Someone of strength because we are alive in You. May the angels sing with rejoicing because each day our works are on bringing another person into the kingdom of God.

And on the day when our eyes may see You, may we hear those words from Your lips: "Well done, My fine and faithful servant, for it is you that I love."

To You we give all of our love, honor, and praise forevermore. Amen.

October 5

Need Refreshing

You, in Your loving kindness, have led the people that you have redeemed. You have guided them in your strength to your holy habitation.
Exodus 15:13 WMB

My beloved, I am lovesick for You and I am in need of refreshing. Bless me with raisin cakes. Let the *Ruach ha Kodesh* come upon me and may I have a deeper more intimate relationship with You. Take me to the promised-land. For it is there I will see Your face. It is there that I shall have rest.

My Beloved, this journey that I am on is long and winding. I have had mountains to climb and rivers to cross. But with each struggle, with each barrier I come to, where I feel there is no way out, You open the seas and carry me to the other side, to the land of milk and honey, a place of hope and promise.

I praise You, my *Adonai,* that even though I do not know what today may hold, I know You will be there with me. And if I can hold onto all the truths You have taught me, I will make a difference for You today. For all things work together for good to those whose trust is in Christ *Yeshua.*

You created me and You know me better than I know myself. Help me to become the most beautiful bride for You, adorned with jewels and white linen. May You be pleased with me, my Lord. May You long for Your bride.

To You, my King, I ask these things. It is in Your holy name I pray. Amen.

October 6

Newness Of Your Love

*Through **Yeshua** then, let us continually offer up to God a sacrifice of praise—the fruit of lips giving thanks to His name. Hebrews 13:15 TLV*

My dear Lord, as the beings that surround Your throne are crying "Holy, Holy, Holy, is The Lord almighty" all day and all night. May the words from my lips praise You forever. For every day I am fascinated by the newness of Your love. Every day, Your grace covers me in new and wondrous ways.

Continue to strengthen me my love. Continue to woo me from afar. For as I get closer to You, I am able to see all that needs to change in me, in order that our fellowship will never be broken.

Help me be strong in faith where I can cast the mountains into the seas. Help me find a place in ministry where I can make a difference for others and for Thee. You have sustained me in the winter, my Lord, now take me to the harvest! I am Yours forever, *Yeshua*. Help me find Your way.

My Lord, beckon me to Your throne room. May I be Your servant forever. Let me smell the fragrance of Your praises, let me taste the goodness of Your love. I am nothing more than ashes that should be buried in the ground. But it is in Your throne room where I am made new. So create in me something beautiful, something that looks like You!

For You are my King, my Lord, and You alone are the one I will praise forever more. Amen and amen.

OCTOBER 7

The Sabbath

*Observe **Yom Shabbat** to keep it holy, as **Adonai** your God commanded you. Six days you are to labor and do all your work, but the seventh day is a **Shabbat** to **Adonai** your God. In it you are not to do any work— not you your son or your daughter, or your slave or your maid, or your ox, your donkey or any of your livestock or the outsider within your gates, so that your slave and your maid may rest as you do. You must remember that you were a slave in the land of Egypt, and **Adonai** your God brought you out from there with a mighty hand and an outstretched arm. Therefore **Adonai** your God commanded you to keep **Yom Shabbat**.*
Deuteronomy 5:12–15 TLV

Adonai, this is a command that should be easy to follow. We should actually enjoy taking this day off to spend in Your presence alongside our family.

But there is a great debate. There are those who believe the Sabbath is Sunday and others Saturday. Then I have heard it said, that as long as you keep one day to the Lord, that this is fine, because it is the principal of the Sabbath, not the actual day.

This is extremely hard, my Lord. For we have to have doctors and police officers who work on Saturdays and Sundays. Then we have companies that will fire their staff if they don't work on those days too.

So *Abba,* I lay this command at Your feet. Because I want to obey, I want to honor You in all things. Show me Your truths in this teaching. Show me Your desires for me and others in obeying every command.

For I am Yours not just one day a week. I am Yours every day. Let me worship and praise, let me serve You all the days of my life. Let me give You my mornings, my nights and my hands during the day. Let everything I do, be unto You, my Lord.

It is to You alone *Jehovah Jireh* that I pray. Amen and amen.

October 8

The Fruit Of Your Love

May the Lord direct your hearts into God's love, and into the perserverance of Messiah.   2 Thessalonians 3:5 WMB

Abba, may I love You so much that my life is not just about being in Your presence and receiving Your love; but may my love be so strong that I may wash Your feet. May I pour out my finest perfume upon them. May I dry Your feet with the locks of my hair. May I kiss them with my lips to show You my deepest love.

May I spend the rest of my life giving of my time, talents and money where others can smell and taste the fruit of Your love in me. May I not grow tired and weary on this walk, but may this flavor be new and refreshing every day.

If I see someone hungry, may I give them food. If I see someone cold, may I give them a blanket. If I see someone hurting, may I share Your love. May I be moved by the *Ruach ha Kodesh* to know those You wish for me to help. So I am not seeing through my eyes, but only through Your eyes, my King. May I serve Your angels that are here among us with Your refreshing water. May I know in my heart that I have given to those whom You desired.

May I grow in Your knowledge, the awareness of Your presence and in discernment this day. I ask that You bind Satan from me, my family and friends and loosen Your angels around us and protect us. I ask all these things in Your Holy name! Amen.

October 9

Blessings And Cursing
❧❦❧

Out of the same mouth comes blessing and cursing. My brothers, these things ought not to be so.   Jacob 3:10 WMB

Adonai, my God, how I stand here in awesome wonder, considering all the universe Thy hands have made.

You have said that You have given us life, to live in abundant blessings. That whatever we have, You, my Lord, have given it unto us.

What makes us think we can grumble if things don't go according to our plans? Your ways are higher than our ways. Your thoughts are higher than our thoughts.

So I should sit and wonder and praise at all that You have given me; whether great or small, rich or poor. I am richer than the richest man on earth, if he doesn't have You. Great men have done great things in the eyes of man, but what matters is that am I doing things to further Your kingdom.

I cannot be furthering Your kingdom if I am blessing and cursing at the same time. So let me, Lord, be full of praise, full of truth, full of worship. Let all that I do and say and do be edifying and uplifting. If I have a disagreement with my brethren, may I go to them in secret and make it right. If there is still trouble, may the elders come and help us to make amends.

Help me put away a life of sin and work towards being a disciple that is worthy of Your calling. I cannot do any of this without You, my Lord. Fill me this day with Your Spirit. Give unto me strength that I can extend grace to those around me. Let Your eyes be how I see those who surround me, each and every day.

For it is in *Yeshua's* name I pray. Amen.

October 10

My Provider

*I have set **Adonai** always before me. Since He is at my right hand, I will not be shaken.*   Psalms 16:8 TLV

Jehovah Jireh, You are my provider. You give me all that I need and much more than I deserve.

I am holding on to You, my Lord, for strength! I am clinging to Your right hand! Go before me, my Lord, and make my paths straight. For with You, I cannot be shaken. Then the ground I stand on will not give way beneath my feet.

I praise You my Majesty that You have anointed my head with oil. That You have chosen to forgive me and have called me of all people, a saint. That I can serve You in Your kingdom forever! For You, my King, are a God of grace!

Let Your warriors arise! Let us shoot flaming arrows at the enemy. May he run and flee and not come near us or our families. May Your words of truth scare him, because he knows the great judgement is coming and his judgement will be that of the lake of fire.

May we stand arm to arm guarding those who are weak and afraid. Let them see Your army of saints along with the heavenly host praising Your holy name. For where You are the enemy cannot stand, for the ground beneath him is just sinking sand.

You are the Mighty One, the Holy One, the Rock of all ages, the Everlasting to everlasting and the King of all kings. You, my Lord, hold the key to my heart, the keys to heaven and hell. I am waiting, my King, for the day when You open heaven's gates so all the saints may enter in.

May today be a day of reckoning. Let this day be a day of truth. Let Your saints all stand up and sing "This is a day that The Lord hath made. May we all rejoice and be glad in it!"

For it is in *Yeshua's* name I pray. Amen.

October 11

Love For Others

For where jealousy and selfish ambition are, there is confusion and every evil deed.   *Jacob 3:16 WMB*

Abba, I am asking that You take my heart and put it in the palm of Your hands. That You would knead it as you would dough. Make it soft and pliable, my King, and work carefully around the edges, to keep them from getting hard and crusty.

Just like sugar which activates the yeast, may Your love activate in me a new love for others like I have never had before. A passion, an understanding, of what I can do for them and more.

Keep every selfish ambition from my heart, along with all jealousy, anger and hate.

But let my heart be tender, loving and giving. To a point that seeing You in me is absolutely no mistake. For You hold the key to my heart, my soul, to it all. So let me do everything I can to offer myself to others. But not for my own recognition, but for Yours alone.

I have seen this example in a few, my King. But I pray to see it more and more in others and in me. Help me to start a new wave of paying it forward. One that is everlasting and true.

My King, I thank You for each breath that You give me. For it is another opportunity to have this prayer come true.

In *Yeshua's* name I pray. Amen.

October 12

Heavens Proclaim Your Glory

The heavens declare the glory of God, and the sky shows His handiwork. day to day they speak, night to night they reveal knowledge.
Psalms 19:2–3 TLV

Adonai, as I look into the heavens, my mind cannot conceive Your wisdom and Your power.

For man can make beautiful objects such as sculptures, colosseums, oriental gardens, skyscrapers, and incredible jewelry.

But You made Niagara Falls, Mount Everest, and all the jewels we use in our jewelry. Man can only use that which You have made. For we do not possess the power or the knowledge of You.

But You created us with hands that are able to work the land. With a mind that is able to continue growing in knowledge every day. You gave us a working body, both for our pleasure and to serve. But I thank You most for putting a hole in our hearts that can only be filled by You.

For there are not enough words to express my love for You. And it is so hard for me to understand how a God so big can love someone like me. But day after day, You show me Your love, by the skies and through nature. But what brings me to my knees is when I feel Your presence embracing me.

Thank You for this love that surpasses all understanding. For always being there and guiding my way.

This world proclaims Your glory and I praise You for allowing me to live in it. But my heart's desire is to serve You in Your throne room of grace. Where I can gaze upon Your strength, Your wisdom and Your eyes of love forever.

For this is my prayer. In *Yeshua's* name I pray. Amen.

October 13
A Light On The Hill

But the wisdom that is from above is first pure, then peaceful, gentle, reasonable, full of mercy and good fruits, without partiality, and without hypocrisy.   *Jacob 3:17 WMB*

Lord You call us to be apart, to be the light on the hill; without hypocrisy, without hate and malice. To try hard to be Your example, but yet we are sinners who fall short every day.

Abba, so many times people judge Christians as if we are supposed to be perfect, as if we are like *Yeshua.* And because we fall short, they turn away from the church, rejecting You because our likeness is not who they want to be, or even should be.

Help us, the church, to take on the fruits of the *Ruach.* To share Your love with those we do not know. That we are not just Your example at church and around fellow believers. But that we are truly Your hands and feet everywhere we go.

Help those who stay away from the faith because of hurts and things they have seen in others, see for the first time who You really are. Let me be that vessel today and every day. Let me show them that no matter how hard I try I will fall short. And it is for this reason You had to come and give Your life. For it is the only way for my salvation.

I praise You, Lord, that You made a way for me. For I am lowly and should have no place in Your kingdom. But You, my Lord, loved me from the beginning of time. You have found a worth in me. Let me show others their worth in You this day and every day I walk upon this earth.

For it is only by the blood on the cross I can come before Your throne. And I lay this request at Your feet and I will wait in expectation for You.

For it is in *Yeshua's* Holy name I pray. Amen.

October 14

My Portion

My flesh and my heart fails, but God is the strength of my heart and my portion forever.   Psalms 73:26 WMB

Adonai, try as I may, my flesh fails You every day. But You are my portion, You are my strength. And when I fall down, You so graciously pick me up again.

You allow me to fail and fall so that I gain understanding and learn more about Your truths. You allow me to fall so the only place I can look, is up to You.

I praise You for all the trials, those I suffer in and those I rise up in victorious. Because in both, I grow closer and deeper in love with You. In both, I learn to hold on to Your truths.

I'm so grateful, my Lord, that You love this frail, faulty person that I am. Please continue to mold me to look more like You in each and every way that I can.

Thank you, Adonai, for You are boundless in grace and in love. Let me see You this day, guiding me from above.

In *Yeshua's* Holy name I pray. Amen.

October 15

Your Direction

*Trust in **Adonai** with all your heart, lean not on your own understanding.*
Proverbs 3:5 TLV

Abba, day after day I sit, trying to sort out what I am to do and how I am to get there. I sit in deep thought, what is it you would have of me? I would think this would be easy, my Lord. But there are times when I choose incorrectly and this makes it hard to ever trust myself again. So help me, my Lord. Make my thoughts be Your thoughts; my ways, Your ways. Because I surely do not understand the things of this life.

I am grateful that You know all things, You see all things. That Your ways are higher than my ways. I am asking for You will guide my life and work all things for Your Glory, honor, and praise. Then I know my life will be the richest it could possibly be, both in this life and the next.

So, Abba, I will put my trust in You alone. I will study Your word and pray. Believing in my heart I will hear an answer. And even if it takes along time, or when things get tough, I know that You will give me the strength to keep pressing forward. For You promised to never leave me nor forsake me and to work out all things out to good for those who trust in You.

Adonai, give me Your peace today. Let Your wisdom fill my mind. Let Your love flow through my thoughts. Let Your grace be spoken through my lips. That others may hear and learn to trust in You.

For it is in *Yeshua's* name I pray. Amen.

October 16

In Awe Of You

"But in all these things we are more than conquerors through Him who loved us."   Romans 8:37 TLV

Abba, I sit in awe of You this morning. For I know that what plans You have put in motion will succeed.

Therefore I have no worries, no dread of what will happen. Because You are the Commander of a mighty army who is sent before me. All things will come to pass that are for Your glory. All things that honor You and bring life and love to others.

I praise You, *Adonai,* that I am Yours! I praise You that You have called my name. No matter the circumstance, You will come to rescue me.

For You are the One true King, my Lord, my Savior, the Everlasting one who loves and will reign forever more.

The best part of living is; You love us so much, so deeply, that we will get to watch it all and live it all, praising You.

In *Yeshua's* Holy name I pray. Amen.

October 17

Orchestrating My Life

On God, my salvation and my glory is the rock of my strength. My refuge is in God.   *Psalms 62:8 TLV*

O Lord, my God, how I need You this day. I cry out to You for Your grace and love to be poured out on me. For Your wings to cover me and Your light to guide me. Please do not let anything that I may do wrong hurt those around me or those whom I love. Keep my mind clear that what I do is in alignment with You.

I praise You, *Adonai,* that You hold my head with Your left hand. That there have been many unseen circumstances that could have harmed me or taken my eyes off of You, and You protected me. Thank You for orchestrating my life and bringing me into a deeper love with You. To understand that, yes You are my Savior, but even more incredible You love me as Your bride. How blessed am I to know You this way. How great is Your love for all!

Give me today what I need and not more. For when there is less of me, there is more of You. Give me the ability to be a blessing and show others the hope we have in You. For those that need healing Lord, may Your hand be upon them and remove all iniquities. For those in financial stress, may a wave of blessings come their way. For those who need a job or a promotion, may You open the door for them.

I Love You, my King, and I lay these requests at Your feet, and it is to You I give all praise. Amen.

OCTOBER 18

Direct My Path

*The heart of a man plans his course, but **Adonai** directs his steps.*
Proverbs 16:9 TLV

My Lord, Holy and righteous are You. For You have taken me in a new direction. Down a path I did not think possible and You have called me by name.

For You have a purpose and a plan for me that is perfect and profitable for my soul. I had made a plan, my King, but I see Yours is better, stronger, and more profound! So help me to design this plan and make it exactly what You desire.

For You are the author of my life. And praise You *Abba,* this book has not been finished yet. I praise You, my Lord, for directing my steps, for opening doors and closing other ones. I praise You that no matter what, You are here guiding me, loving me through another day.

I praise You for my life and my breath.

In *Yeshua's* name I pray, Amen.

October 19

Kiss Me

Let him kiss me with the kisses of his mouth; for your love is better than wine.   Song of Solomon 1:2 WMB

My King, You are the adoration of my soul! You are the essence of my life. You have kissed me with Your love, and I will never be the same!

Take me into Your arms. Let me feel the beating of Your heart. Let me know the height and depth of Your love for me.

For I am waiting, my Lord, for You to put Your covenant ring upon my finger. That all shall know I am Yours forever. That no one and nothing will ever separate me from the love that *Yeshua* has for His bride!

For Your love is smoother than wine, sweeter than honey and more beautiful than a rose, and all I want is to bask in this love forever!

I will wait and prepare for this day of feasting, my King. For the day when You come for me, there will be no question where I am. The oil in my lamp will be full and my light will be bright. Shining that You shall find me, no matter how dark the world is all around me.

For I am Yours and You are mine. And no matter how long I must wait. I will stay right here waiting for You until the end of time.

Forever Yours. Amen.

OCTOBER 20

The Work Of My Hands

To this end I labor, striving with all His strength which is powerfully at work in me.   *Colossians 1:29 TLV*

Adonai, I awake to the aging of this world. My body has aches and pains. I'm tired, my Lord, but I must still work with my hands throughout this day.

Help me to work throughout this day with praise on my lips. May I toil for You and not in vain. Let me pay my debtors all that I owe them. Let me use the rest all in Your name.

Help me be grateful, for I am blessed beyond measure. Help me to focus on the good and not the bad. Let me show those around me the love You have for us. For it is a sacrifice of ourselves to make others glad.

Help those who are too ill to get out of bed this day, to spend this time in worship of You. May their spirits rejoice in great measure. Let their love increase and their witness too.

My Lord, please give me the strength to make it through this day. May this strength be in my spirit too. Help me, *Adonai,* to do all that You would have of me. For I can't make it in this world, not even for a moment, if I don't have You!

For it is in *Yeshua's* name I pray. Amen.

October 21

Whether I Have Little Or A Lot

*Then he said: "Naked I came from my mother's womb, and naked I will return there. **Adonai** gave and Adonai has taken away; blessed be the Name of **Adonai.**"*   Job 1:21 TLV

Abba, Job was a strong man of faith. He endured far more than I can possibly imagine or even want to.

I have very little, yet to me it is a lot and I would be devastated if I lost it all!

I know that I have everyone in my life and the clothes that are on my back because You have given them to me. Help me to treasure each one. Help me learn to show You and others my appreciation for these gifts. I need to be a better steward. I need to be a better friend!

Open my eyes to the needs of those around me and speak to my heart what I am to do. Help me to use my gifts, my talents in serving others and also in serving You.

Let me not be worried about what I might have for I can take nothing with me when I go. But let me use it all for Your glory. For this I want You to know: I love You for each breath, for the health of my loved ones. I love You for the clothes I have and that I have food every day to eat. I love You that I have a home and a soft, warm bed I can sleep in at night. I love You for having transportation where I can go visit family and serve You in many ways. I love You because I can go to work each day and speak of Your love to others. But Lord, I love You most because You have loved me and provided this great, divine hope in a life everlasting. To spend my eternity at Your feet: there is no gift greater than this!

Adonai, I will praise You for all of my life. Amen and amen.

OCTOBER 22

Hidden Treasures

He who trusts in the Son has eternal life. He who does not obey the Son will not see life, but the wrath of God remains on him.   John 3:36 TLV

Abba, as time passes, I meet more and more people who don't know You. From adults to children, they never go to church, much less open Your word.

How can it be that they don't see You? How can they deny Your name? For You show Your glory in every sunrise! You show Your power in the lightning and rain!

Help me to shout of Your existence from the moment I rise until I close my eyes each night. Let my life be a story that others want to read. Help me to show others that the hidden treasures of their desires are found when reading the treasure map of Your word!

Let me be bold like Moses, have the faith of Job, have the love of Hosea and strength of Jacob. Let me plant those seeds, my Lord, that possibly one more soul will not have Your wrath upon them. But may eternity await them in Your loving arms forever.

For it is only by *Yeshua's* name I am able to pray. Amen.

October 23

Renew My Spirit

What then shall we say about these things? If God is for us, who can be against us? Romans 8:31 WMB

Good morning my Father. How amazing is Your love. You covered me as I slept and gave me dreams of Your glory. May I meet You in this place, may I meet You in Your garden as Your bride; enveloped by Your love forever! Amen.

Abba, You have called me to be Your servant, my Lord, just as You served. You have called me to love; because You are love. You have called me to offer grace and forgive those who have wronged me; because You have forgiven my multitudes of sins. How I want to be this image of You, my Lord. Take me to the top of this mountain that I may grow in love and maturity in You.

Help me to walk not by sight, nor emotions or feelings, but by faith in You alone.

Abba, with every step that I take up this mountain, renew my spirit and reveal to me all that I need to change. May I not worry about what others say or do, but may my eyes stay focused on You. May I stand on the top of this mountain. May I wave the banner of victory. May my enemies fall and Your glory shine because I followed You all the way. For You, my God, are with me, so who can be against me?

Abba, You are more beautiful than the sunrise, more precious to me than gold. Make Your way for me this day and may I walk with You forevermore. Amen.

October 24

My Shepherd

***Adonai** is my shepherd, I shall not want He makes me lie down in green pastures. He leads me beside still waters. He restores my soul. He guides me in paths of righteousness for His Name's sake.   Psalms 23:1–3 TLV*

Adonai, no matter how hard things seem, You are there. You have walked me through some of the darkest times. You have shown me a way into the light. You have never left me, nor forsake me, no matter how far I have fallen. How I praise You, for You have been there, gently restoring my soul!

Abba, thank You for not abandoning me. Thank You for showing me step by step, things I need to change in my life. For not showing me the whole, but showing me how just one small change can make a big impact. Then the next change seems to come a lot easier.

I was so lost, yet You found me and carried me through the rough waters. You have carved my name on a rock, placed it upon the ground, where I will see it for eternity.

Lord, take this empty vessel and fill it to overflowing with Your grace. Let me pour out grace upon grace on others this day. Let me be used to bless those who curse me. Let me be a word from You to those who are lost. Let me show those who are hurting Your mercy and tenderness. Let me show those who are mourning, Your love that has no end.

May You live through me this and every day, my King. May I live giving back for all You have done. For You have restored my soul and given me life eternal. Let my life reflect this to all I know.

In *Yeshua's* name I pray. Amen.

OCTOBER 25

Robe Of Righteousness

My lover extended his hand through the opening—my heart yearned for him. I rose to open for my lover. My hands dripped with myrrh, yes, my fingers with flowing myrrh, on the handles of the lock.
Song of Songs 5:4–5 TLV

Oh, my Lord, thrust Your hand through the opening of my heart that I may be overflowing in grace. May Your love be dripping from my hands. As I remove my filthy rags, my garment of disgrace, may You cover me with a robe of righteousness that Your beauty is all others see.

Help me grow in maturity, to a deeper understanding of Your love for me. May I grow in wisdom of finances; in knowledge of Your word, with clarity of mind that I can recall scripture as I need it; to discern the spirits so I see the truth clearly; that I may be strong and faithful to withstand any test that may come my way.

Abba, put Your angels as guard over me and my household. Protect us from the evil one. Let no harm come our way. Build my household in You that all may be saved.

To You, my *Adonai,* I give it all. To You, my Lord, I sing songs of praise! And I ask all these things in Your Holy name. Amen.

October 26

Enjoy Where I Am

The grass withers, the flower fades; but the word of our God stands forever.
Isaiah 40:8 WMB

As the grass dies on my side of the pasture and I look to another's, I always wonder why theirs is green and mine is not. Help me, *Adonai,* to understand and appreciate the trials in my life. That instead of wanting things to be different, may I just enjoy where I am and cry out for a deeper walk with You. For You created the grass and the lilies of the fields. When the time is right for me, the lilies will bloom and cover my fields with both beauty and grace.

I thank you for the new discoveries of You. For taking me to a deeper understanding of being Your bride. For new revelations of this intimate love You have for me.

You are the Alpha and the Omega, the beginning and the end. And You know exactly what I need this day. Give me this day my daily bread. May I be immersed in Your love, filled with the *Ruach,* and strong in the faith.

I am devoted only to You my love. And I lay all my needs at Your feet. May You hear my prayers, my Lord, and may the angels sing: "Hallelujah to the Lamb, for You are worthy of all praise." Amen.

October 27

A Taste Of Your Wonders

As we look not at what can be seen but at what cannot be seen. For what can be seen is temporary, but what cannot be seen is eternal.
2 Corinthians 4:18 TLV

Abba, I have so much to lay at Your feet. May those who do not believe, find a glimpse of You so they can believe in what is unseen. May those who are ill or holding on to life with every breath, have Your mighty hand rest upon them. And even though this is unseen, may they feel this touch so strong that they know without question You are God and You are there.

Abba, You created the sunsets on the oceans and mountains covered in snow; the stars that dance at night and the songs of the birds in the air. Since this is just a taste of the wonders that Your hands have made, I know without question that You can do a miracle today and give to those who need spiritual eyes this gift so that they might believe. Please don't let this moment fade from their memory. May it be a life changing event.

Lord, give wisdom to those who seek. To those who are blind, give spiritual eyes. To those whose hearts have been closed to You: may this door be opened and they let You in. To those who are weak: may Your strength fill their bodies. To those who mourn: may the *Ruach ha Kodesh* give them comfort.

You are a God of hope and all my trust is in You. May I be who You want me to be this day. May I be a blessing to all I know. To You, my Lord, I pray and give thanks for all You do. Amen.

OCTOBER 28

What Matters

Bearing with one another and forgiving each other, if anyone has a grievance against another. Just as the Lord pardoned you, so also you must pardon others.   *Colossians 3:13 TLV*

My Lord, You have commanded that we love one another, for us to live in harmony and seek peace whenever possible.

You have asked us to forgive others their sins, because You have forgiven us. For how can we ask a Holy God for something that we ourselves are not willing to do?

Abba, I ask that You take away my sins and cast them into the deepest oceans where they are remembered no more. Help to forgive others in this same manner, my Lord. For in the end, most of our grievances really did not matter. For the only thing that mattered is if we showed *Yeshua* and won another soul. Whether it was the one who wronged us, or another watching, we need to always be reflecting You.

Help me to be like this more and more each day. May Yours be the reflection I and others see, whenever I look in the mirror.

I ask these things in Your Holy name. Amen.

OCTOBER 29

My Beloved

*And He said to him, "You shall love **Adonai** your God with all your heart, and with all your soul, and with all your mind." This is the first and greatest commandment.*   *Matthew 22:37–38 TLV*

    Abba, I am overwhelmed that You are blessed by our love. That not only do we long to be loved by You, but You long for us. In Solomon 7:10, it states: For I am my beloved's and His desire is for me. What an amazing revelation this is for me, what a truth that has set me free.

    Help me increase my knowledge in You. Make Your face shine upon me and pour out Your blessings and Your love on me. Don't let anything separate me from Your presence.

    Allow me to love others with Your love. Help me have compassion even for those who are un-loveable. For this is Your desire for me, but I cannot do it without You. May I be dedicated to You every day and in every way.

    To You, my Lord, I pray. Amen.

October 30

My Gift

*Now there are various kinds of gifts, but the same **Ruach**. There are various kinds of service, but the same Lord. There are various kinds of working, but the same God who works all things in all people. But to each person is given the manifestation of the **Ruach** for the benefit of all. For to one is given through the **Ruach** a word of wisdom, to another a word of knowledge according to the same **Ruach**, to another faith by the same **Ruach**, to another gifts of healings by the one **Ruach**, to another workings of miracles, to another prophecy, to another discerning of spirits, to another different kinds of tongues, to another the interpretation of tongues. But one and the same **Ruach** activates all these things, distributing to each person individually as He wills.*   1 Corinthians 12:4–11 TLV

My Lord, people say they see talents and gifts in me, but I do not see these. Lord, You created us to do a good work, but how am I, if I do not know the gifts Your *Ruach* has bestowed upon me?

For I don't have money, I definitely cannot sing. I am not a great cook. I am not an artist. I am not knowledgeable in medicine or teaching. I am not a preacher, an orator, or such. I have not any great gift that makes me shine above the rest, so what am I to do?

But I have two hands that can work. A heart that is open to Your will. May You put opportunities to serve You in my life daily. I may not be put on earth to do some grandiose thing, but if I feed one child, if I paint an old person's home, if I give someone help in paying their child care, it might be a grandiose thing to them.

Help me to remember this, my Lord: that it is the daily things that You created me to do. It is being there with arms opened wide. It is knowing that *Yeshua* was intentional to do these daily acts of kindness and love. Being His reflection is all I want to do. Help my eyes be open to those opportunities to serve You this day and every day. Amen and amen.

October 31

My Love For You

For God so loved the world, that he gave his one and only Son, that whoever believes in him shall not perish, but have eternal life.
Yochanan (John) 3:16 WMB

Abba, this verse is the one everyone holds onto. For it is the promise of all! The promise of eternity with You.

How could one so small as I, be something You would want to spend eternity with? I have nothing I can give that You do not possess. I am not brilliant in my thoughts, nor do I have great abilities with my hands. I am nothing but a speck of dust, blowing in the wind. Yet You looked near and far until You found me, and then You put me in the palm of Your hand.

I am in awe of Your goodness. I am astonished by Your love. For no one on this earth would have suffered the cross for me, knowing all the times I had done them wrong.

I praise You, my King, for this life and the next. Help me this day to show this verse to someone who is lost so their eternity is secure in You.

In *Yeshua's* name I pray. Amen and amen.

NOVEMBER 1

Commit To The Lord

*Commit whatever you do to **Adonai**, and your plans will succeed.*
Proverbs 16:3 TLV

Abba, this year is full of changes. Some are big and others are small. I cannot do any of them by myself. I can't even imagine trying!

Abba, these changes in my life do not compare to some of others, but they are significant to me. Help me in each decision-making process. Help me do what it right, fair and just. Let everything I do be bathed in prayer and with supplication. Let it all be given unto Thy name.

I praise You, my King, for I see Your mighty hand at work in my life. For by myself I am nothing, just a seed blowing in the wind. But with You, I shall burst forth from the ground and produce the most beautiful flowers, and the sweetest of fruits. Because my lips and my actions desire only to praise You, my Lord and King!

May everything within me and all that I have, be dedicated to a life of passion and service to You, my King!

In *Yeshua's* name I pray. Amen.

NOVEMBER 2

Just Ordinary People

Now as for these four youths, God gave them knowledge and skill in all learning, and Daniel had understanding in all of visions and dreams.
Daniel 1:17 WMB

Abba, You are no ordinary King! For You use ordinary men to do extraordinary things. You took four men and gave them gifts and knowledge beyond most. Then the faith they showed Nebuchadnezzar and all who witnessed were amazed and believed.

For as the three were thrown into the fire, neither fire nor smoke touched them, because You, *Yeshua,* stood in the fire with them.

Then Daniel speaking the King's dreams to him, no man has the ability to do this. It took You speaking to him and showing him this vision.

But because You used these ordinary people to do these extraordinary things, it changed the lives of many.

Abba, I am definitely a very ordinary person. I hold no special talents or gifts. So I am asking that You supply extraordinary abilities in and around me. That people take notice because of this and say it must be the God of Abraham, for only He can do these mighty things.

I am here not for me, not for my pleasure, but for You alone. Help me to show others that the miracles and power of Your mighty hand are still at work in this day and age. That You are not dead, but active in all our lives, if we just stop to look and see.

I love You and pray that I may be this vessel for You this day. Amen and amen.

NOVEMBER 3

May I Be

*So consecrate yourselves and be holy, for I am **Adonai** your God. You are to keep My statues, and do them. I am **Adonai** who sanctifies you.*
Leviticus 20:7–8 TLV

Abba, how refreshing is the coolness of this day. A sweet reminder of the promises You have made. How pleasing is this change in the season, so we may pick the harvest and enjoy the fruits of our labor. How faithful are You, my Lord, for giving us so much more than we need.

Lord, thank You for Your sacrifice. You knew I am incapable of living under the law. That it was Your blood that would have to atone for my sins. But help me to obey Your laws, all of them, that I may be pleasing to You.

My Lord, my King, may I worship You this day. May I seek to wash Your feet. May I pour out my love on You. May each tear I cry fall upon Your feet and be perfume to Your soul. For every tear that flows in is need of Your grace or in praise of Your love. For I am unable to do anything without You.

Abba, I praise You for my family and the love we share! I thank You for my friends and all the blessings they pour out on me each day. I thank You for my home and a safe place to lay my head. I thank You for my work and the opportunity to serve others. I praise You for being *Jehovah M'Kaddesh,* the Lord who sanctifies me. For without You, I am nothing.

Help me, my *Adonai,* to be Your hands and feet today. Give me strength to obey Your laws. Let be like *Yeshua* to anyone I meet.

I ask all these things in Your Holy name. Amen.

November 4

Your Bride

*I will rejoice greatly in **Adonai**. My soul will be joyful in my God. For He has clothed me with garments of salvation, He has wrapped me in a robe of righteousness—like a bridegroom wearing a priestly turban, like a bride adorning herself with her jewels.* Isaiah 61:10 TLV

My Lord, my Savior, how I delight myself in Thee, for I am just a girl in a faraway land, without anything of value to give.

But You were not looking for a bride with beauty and gold. You were looking for a heart open to Your every word.

So I will call out Your name, O Beautiful One. For my heart is longing for Thee. I want to see You in Your armor, because I know You will guard and protect me.

I want to hear Your words of love, for they will embrace my heart, my soul. I want to look into Your eyes of splendor, for in them I will see all I need to know.

For Thou art mine and I am His forever. Take this bride and adorn her in Your likeness, in Your jewels and beauty, forevermore. Amen.

NOVEMBER 5

Living Sacrifice

I urge you therefore, brothers and sisters, by the mercies of God, to present you bodies as living sacrifice—holy, acceptable to God—which is your spiritual service. Do not be conformed to this world but be transformed by the renewing of you mind, so that you may discern what is the will of God— what is good and acceptable and perfect. Romans 12:1 TLV

Abba, for years I contemplated how exactly do I do this? What exactly are You requiring of me? But the closer I draw to You. The easier it is to see. For I want to please You, my Lord, in every way.

I want to stay in constant communication with You. I want to hold Your hand and walk on the beach. I want to stand by You when visiting someone who is ill. I want to give myself to You in every way, my Lord. But You require even more than this.

You require that I serve You first and others second. It's the serving others before me that can sometimes really be hard! I am to bless those who curse me. This is not just a little hard—oh my, how I struggle here! You ask that when I see a stranger on the street, I should pray for them, then if the *Ruach ha-Kodesh* prompts me to act in any way, I need to obey. Well I don't like talking to strangers, so this is extremely hard for me to do!

But my Love for You exceeds my own selfish desires. It exceeds my hurt feelings. It exceeds my fears. So I know I can do all things through *Yeshua* if I just stay close to You!

So, Abba, hold my hand as I walk through this day. Whisper in my ears the sweet blessings I can share. Let me know that I am putting a smile on Your face and giving warmth to someone else's heart.

For I ask these things in *Yeshua's* name. Amen.

NOVEMBER 6

Heeding Correction

*One whose ear heeds a life-giving reproof dwells among the wise. Whoever avoids correction despises himself, but whoever heeds reproof acquires understanding. The fear of **Adonai** is the discipline of wisdom, and humility comes before honor.*   Proverbs 15:31–33 TLV

Abba, help me today to be wise, stay close to You, heed Your correction, love others beyond what is expected, and do things beyond what is the norm.

May all who see me know that what I do is only because I have the power and the love of a God so true living within me. For doing what comes natural to me is of the flesh. So I can only be wise with the *Ruach ha-Kodesh* living in and through me.

I am holding onto Your cloak, my Lord, and I am not letting it go. For then I shall only be where You take me, hearing Your every word, following Your commands.

Heal my body and soul dear Lord and give me strength to make it through this day. Doing what does not come naturally for me, but what is natural in You.

In *Yeshua's* name I pray. Amen.

November 7

Standing Firm

Be therefore imitators of God, as beloved children. Walk in love, even as Messiah also loved us and gave himself up for us, an offering and a sacrifice to God for a sweet-smelling fragrance.   Ephesians 5:1–2 WMB

Adonai, how can I be a fragrant offering to You today? What can I offer You that would give You great joy?

I have nothing but my life and to offer it as a sacrifice of praise in all that I do. To be an imitator of Christ. To press in so close to You that no one can see me in the things that I do.

I want to hear Your heart beat when I go to sleep at night. I want to feel Your breath upon my neck as I walk the streets in the day. I want the dust from Your feet to land upon my face. I want to hold the hem of Your garment in my hands while I pray.

Everything of You is what I want to be consumed with. Everything of You is what I want my heart to reveal.

Let anything in my life that might lead me astray be removed from me this day. Let my life be a sweet offering of praise to You my mighty King.

In *Yeshua's* name I pray. Amen and amen.

November 8

Look Upon Your Face

*Yes, in the way of Your judgments, **Adonai**, we have waited for You. Your Name and Your remembrance is the desire of our soul. My soul longs for You at night, yes, my spirit within me seeks You. For when Your judgments are in the earth, the inhabitants of the world learn righteousness.*
Isaiah 26:8–9 TLV

Abba, I long for the day that I can look upon Your face. To see Your glory and Your splendor in all its majesty. How, my Lord, will I respond? Will I cry? Will I laugh with joy? Will I sing Hallelujah? Will I fall prostrate before You? I imagine I might do all these things, my Lord. I imagine my soul will be filled with so many emotions, I will have a hard time containing these.

But until that day, my King, as my soul yearns for You each day. Search me my God and cleanse me. Show me if there is anything I need to change. For I want nothing standing between us.

Send Your judgements upon the earth. That all the people might be better for it. Let those who do evil be judged and tried. Let those who are humble and pure in their hearts be blessed. May the humble search for ways to teach the lofty and mighty before this great day of judgement comes.

I praise You that You have called my name. From the darkest seas, You searched for me. You hold my hand and have assured me, that on that day, You will rescue me! Hallelujah, my Lord is great! Hallelujah the Lord is One! Hallelujah for my God is the great I Am! Hallelujah, for He holds my hand!

In *Yeshua's* name I pray. Amen.

November 9

One Mediator

*For there is one God and one mediator between God and men—a human, Messiah **Yeshua**, who gave Himself as a ransom for all—the testimony at the proper time.*   1 Timothy 2:5–6 TLV

Abba, I thank You for hearing my prayers and even more for answering them. Some have been huge miracles and some have been small answers. And I thank You for even answering those prayers I have not spoken, and for giving me life this day.

Help me not to get angry, my Lord, but to look for how to make good out of every situation. Help me to speak Your word to those who curse You. Help me to pray for those who have hurt me and for those whom I have hurt.

I praise You, Lord Yeshua, for hearing this and every prayer of mine. For no matter how small or large, I can pray in my closet or in the street. As long as I am praying to You and not for man, You hear my prayers and will answer them.

You, my Lord, hold the key to heaven and earth. You alone are worthy of all praise.

I give You my life to do with as You please, my Lord. Just help me to be obedient to You in this every day.

For it is in *Yeshua's* name I pray. Amen.

November 10

The Word

Rejoice in the Lord always—again I will say rejoice! Let your gentles be known to all people. The Lord is near. Do not be anxious about anything—but in everything, by prayer and petition with thanksgiving, let your requests be made known to God.   Philippians 4:4–6 TLV

Adonai, I was asked yesterday, "Everyone comes to you to tell their troubles to. Who do you go to?" I replied I go to prayer to seek my Lord, for He is my Father, my redeemer, my friend.

I have not answers for anyone, but only that of which I know from His word. And I pray that anytime I guide someone, it is from His word alone. But I also say "you must search through the word for yourself to make sure what I say is in alignment with Him."

For I, like others, have many anxious thoughts. I pray Lord that I seek wise counsel. But let me never stop at that. Let me search through Your word. May I fast and pray, so You can affirm that which was spoken to me.

In Yeshua's name I pray. Amen.

November 11

Fighting The Enemy

*So David's men said to him, Look, it's the day **Adonai** spoke to you about, "Behold, I will deliver your enemy into your hand, so you may do to him as seems good in your eyes." Then David crept and cut off the corner of Saul's robe stealthily.*   1 Samuel 24:4 TLV

Abba, David was truly a man after Your own heart. For King Saul wanted David dead, and when David had the chance, he did not take Saul's life. He just showed Saul that he could have.

Let me show this kind of wisdom, love, and faith in my times of trouble. Let me be just, but cause no harm. Let me be wise and yet gentle, not giving a foothold to my enemy but giving them over to You. For You will always do what is best for our learning, best for our growth, best for our souls.

For there is no greater judge than You. No greater teacher! For You love all things, created all things, and give us each and every breath.

For as David knew Saul was anointed by You and only You should choose his destiny, I lay all my enemies at Your feet now and throughout this lifetime. You shall be their judge, for You will only do what is right for them.

How great are You, O God. I can trust You in all things, through all things, and for all things.

For I adore You, and I lay my life at Your feet. In *Yeshua's* name I pray. Amen.

November 12

Trust In The Lord

*Trust in **Adonai** with all your heart, lean not on your own understanding. In all your ways acknowledge Him, and He will make your paths straight.*
Proverbs 3:5–6 TLV

My Lord, I lay my enemies at Your feet. I trust in You alone to make all things right. If I have done any wrong, please show me. For You will say what is right.

You detest evil, my Lord, and all of their plans. Break any hold on me, with the strength of Your hands.

Show me Your plan for me in this, my King. For I stand ready for this fight. For I will call out Your name and my enemy has no choice but to take flight.

I would rather not fight, but for all this to go away. But if I must, my King, by my side may You stay.

Abba, I am not asking that You take sides. I would rather You take over. Let us all walk in peace and in Your love, forever and ever.

In *Yeshua's* name I pray. Amen.

November 13

Tempted

Let no one say when he is tempted, "I am being tempted by God," for God can't be tempted by evil, and he himself tempts no one. But each one is tempted when he is drawn away by his own lust and enticed.
Jacob 1:13–14 WMB

Adonai, every morning I rise I will face temptations. Some will be those that are familiar to me. Some will be out of anger or lust. And others will be so enticing because I know it would be fun.

But Lord, I also have a choice to make each day. Do I choose to follow my one true love? Or do I choose to please my own selfish desires?

For it was just yesterday when faced with one that I sat and said, "Yes, this would please me, but my God would not be pleased. And my God has rescued me from the pit, so why would I do this if it would displease Him?"

The only place I want to be is in Your arms. I want You to acknowledge me with love and a smile. When I see You face to face, I want You, the Lover of my soul, to say, "Job well done."

For Your ways are higher than our ways. Your thoughts are higher than our thoughts. For where You are, I could not be happier. Where You are, my soul can rest.

I give You all of me this day. Help me to stop at each temptation and think of Your love, of the gifts You have poured out on me, and of the way You would choose for me to handle the situation. For it is always for my good and the good of those around me. Then, my Lord, may I always choose You!

For it is in *Yeshua's* name I pray. Amen.

November 14

Crown Of Life

Blessed is a person who endures testing, for when he has been approved, he will receive the crown of life, which the Lord promised to those who love him.   *Jacob 1:12 WMB*

Abba, death is a funny thing. For some there is such peace! For it does not matter the pain they may be in. Your glory and the expectation of being in Your presence is so great. All they desire is to pass from this life and enter through the gates into heaven.

Then there are some who may not have lived as close to You as they should have. Who are scared of the unknown. Who do not want us to leave their side in fear of what is to come. For they know they will see Your face and enter into the kingdom, but the fear of Your disappointment is great! For they have not done the things in this life You have asked of them.

Then there are those who do not know You, my Lord. Some have lived an arrogant life style while others have walked in peace. I pray that before they close their eyes, they have one last breath to ask You to enter in. To ask for salvation, for forgiveness of their sins.

My Lord, I pray for all, for death escapes us not. That when our time comes, we are at peace. That we have the assurance of Your hand reaching down from heaven and taking us home. That we know we are sinners, but we know that the blood of Christ covers us, so there is nothing to fear. For we have lived a life professing Your love and giving up of ourselves, so that You may live in us. That Your glory may shine through us for all to see.

For this is my desire for my life and for all. For it is in *Yeshua's* name alone I shall stand before Your throne. Amen and amen.

NOVEMBER 15

How Great Are You, O Lord

Yours, ***Adonai,*** *is the greatness, the power and the splendor, and the victory and the majesty, indeed everything in heaven and earth. Yours is the kingdom,* ***Adonai,*** *and You are exalted above all.* 1 Chronicles 29:11 TLV

Abba, I rise and sleep to the splendor of Your name. Great are You, O Lord of the universe. For Your glory will reign forever. You created the heavens and the stars to shine and tell of your wonders. You created the mountains and the oceans to show of Your majesty. You created the birds and the flocks of the fields to show off Your goodness. Then You created man to exclaim of Your love and Your grace for all to see.

How great are You, O Lord. For You pour out Your love on this earth and on me daily. For not only do I rise each day, but I get to spend it with You! For You are showing me, through people, through signs and wonders that You have a plan for me. I am ready to go on this journey, my Lord. I shall go where ever You may take me. Fill my heart with love, my spirit with strength, and my mind with Your living word. Let me put on the full armor of a God so I am ready for the battle that will lie ahead.

Open the doors in front of me and lock the doors behind so I do not get confused about the direction I am going. Let each day my manna come from You alone. So I do not walk in my own knowledge, but the knowledge that everything I am and everything I have is a gift from above. Let me stand guard outside my home that nothing may enter that is not of You. Let me sleep peacefully in Your arms, knowing this is where I will stay forever.

For You are my Lord, my God, my provider, my friend. You are my Alpha and Omega, the Lover of my soul. For it is with You and You alone that I wish to spend eternity. Serving You, praising You, staring at Your beauty, now and through the end of all time. To You, my Lord, I give all praise. Amen and amen.

November 16

Your Glory And Majesty

God chose to make known to them this glorious mystery regarding the Gentiles—which is Messiah in you, the hope of glory! Colossians 1:27 TLV

Adonai, even though I know You have saved me. Even though I have seen Your hand at work in my life and others, I look in the mirror and see a person of much sin who is so unworthy to do any calling that is great.

But You, O God, maker of the heavens, keep showing me in ways that are so significant to me. That You have this, You are holding my hand.

Speak through me, O Lord, the words You choose for me to say. Give me visions and dreams of how You wish for me to show Your glory, Your riches, Your incredible love that is overflowing to all who will accept the sacrifice of *Yeshua*.

Give me the knowledge and wisdom to do this task ahead of me. That nothing of me is seen, but everything of You is revealed.

I praise You, my King, for showing me through a friend that I am Your child. Through a place unknown to her, but significant to me, she would pray for me. May You cover this journey You are leading me through. May I be covered and immersed in the power of the *Ruach ha-Kodesh*. May Michael be on the right and Gabriel on the left to the entrance of this place. May nothing and no one enter that is not of You.

Thank You, my King, for hearing and answering this prayer.

In *Yeshua's* name I pray. Amen.

NOVEMBER 17

One Christ

Your ears will hear a word behind you saying: "This is the way, walk in it. When you turn to the right, or when you turn to the left." Isaiah 30:21 TLV

Father, there are so many voices saying go this way or that. You must do this and you can't do that! Or "This is the *Mashiach* or it does not matter in whom you believe, all will enter heaven."

But there is only one way, one Christ and all must believe in Him and His sacrificial love in order to enter through His gates.

Abba, we must read Your word. We must pray to hear Your voice. Then the *Ruach ha Kodesh* will guide our feet and show us the way.

I hurt for those who do not read Your word and follow other teachings. For they will be led astray, not even realizing the destiny of their fate until it is too late.

Abba, You have given us this one life. And You have made it so easy to find You. Help me to show others Your way.

I pray for my family, my friends and all who surround me that they come to know You as I have. That they hear Your voice of love, wisdom, and discernment. That they search through Your word, for it is a treasure to their soul. That no one or nothing can take them, because they lay in the grasp of Your hand.

Then, my Lord, no matter what comes our way, we shall stand with You in victory until Your return.

I love You, my Lord, and I thank You for the opportunities You have given me in this day.

For it is in *Yeshua's* name alone I pray. Amen.

NOVEMBER 18

Author Of My Soul

I have hidden your word in my heart, that I might not sin against You.
Psalms 119:11 WMB

Abba, You are the author of my soul. And it is Your words that are written upon my heart.

So when Satan tries to sneak in his story, it's as if his pen has run out of ink. For the pages are full of Your writings and where there are any empty spaces, his ink does not seem to hold. For it just runs off my heart like water because Your grace comes rushing in to cleanse my soul.

How blessed am I among Your children. Adorned with love and righteousness in You.

Continue to fill any open spots with Your story. And may it be a romance novel, that others want to read and desire to have this same love with You.

In *Yeshua's* Holy name I pray. Amen.

NOVEMBER 19

Our Mortality

For the needy will not forever be forgotten, nor the hope of the poor perish forever. Arise, **Adonai,** *do not let man triumph. Let the nations be judged before You. Strike them with terror,* **Adonai.** *Let the nations know they are only human.*   Psalms 9:19–21 TLV

My Lord, this is something so many of us have a hard time with ... our own mortality. For in the present is easy. We see it, we feel it and we taste it. But what happens the moment we die, well ... That is in our hearts and our minds.

For those of us who have fallen in love with You and have become a bond servant of Christ, know in our hearts where we will go in the hereafter. But our minds can only imagine the setting of beauty, peace, and love that is in store.

There are so many people, my Lord, who can't think about the future. Only the here and now is what counts. I fear for their souls, my King. For their lives You could take even now.

Then there are those who are pure evil, my King. Who want to destroy everyone who doesn't agree with them. People who are demonically possessed. Lord, I pray for their salvation. For if they won't turn to You, their immortal bodies shall never find rest.

I can tell as every year passes, my body is slowly going away. As long as I am getting closer and closer to You, everything in this and the next life for me is OK.

My Lord, I ask today that You strike down those who do evil. Take back this world for You. For soon You are coming to judge us all.... I am ready, and I pray that many others are, too.

I love You, my Lord, and I love being a bond servant of Christ. Amen.

November 20

Captives

For this is God's will, that you silence the ignorance of foolish men by doing food. Live as free people, but not using your freedom as a cover-up for evil. Rather, live as God's slaves.   1 Peter 2:15–16 TLV

Abba, thank You for giving me the privilege of being born at this day and time in a country that is free. Especially when I hear of others who live in bondage. Of the oppressors who rule their land. I think of how easy I have had it all this time and yet I still complain. How foolish I can be!

My Lord, I have seen how freedom can take some people and turn them into the most selfish people on earth. Seeking desires of the flesh and not serving those around them but only their evil hearts. For they are truly prisoners, sitting in a cell with a door opened wide. And one day, my Lord, that door will shut and unfortunately, there will be no chance of them escaping.

My Lord, I do not want to live a life of freedom! I want to be a bond servant of Yours! I want to work from early morning until I close my eyes doing Your will. Let me not give anyone the ability to say that I am out serving other masters. If they speak evil of me, let it be because I serve You only. Then, my Lord, my riches of Your love will be given unto me. For even if I sit in a jail cell with the door locked tight, You hold the key, and You will come rescue me!

For there is only one true freedom, my Lord. And that freedom resides in the love of Christ! In the one who holds the key to heaven and hell. In the one who created everything! Let my freedom be in You alone this day and forever more.

In *Yeshua's* name I pray. Amen.

NOVEMBER 21
A Time To Share

Rejoice always, pray constantly, in everything give thanks; for this is God's will for you in Messiah **Yeshua**. *1 Thessalonians 5:16–18 TLV*

I turn to You, O Lord, in a time of need. For this season is a time for family gatherings, to enjoy the harvest, for lifting each other up and remembering the good times.

But Lord, many people are suffering. Many have lost loved ones, many are ill. Many are in financial trouble. Many have families who do not wish to be together.

But Lord may we remember that today is a gift from You. You have appointed us a time to live and to share. A time to give to others when we can love and pray for those who hate us. We are to visit the ill and to cherish in our hearts those whom we have lost.

I am thankful, my Lord, that in this season of trials and troubles, You have never left my side. As long as I call upon Your name, You are there. And even though I do not have much, I am richer than King Solomon. For You have blessed me beyond measure with Your love.

I praise You that You have given me another day to make right any wrongs I have done. To look at others to see where I might can help them. To love, not as the people do, but to love like You. With that special kind of love that never fails, that keeps no records of wrongs, that always perseveres and is always kind and true.

I thank You, my Lord, because I cannot be this person on my own. But that I have the *Ruach ha Kodesh* living in me and that I am able to let Him love others through me this day.

For it is in *Yeshua's* name I pray. Amen.

NOVEMBER 22

Your Protection

Because your loving kindness is better than life, my lips will praise you. So I will bless you while I live. I will lift up my hands in your name.
Psalms 63:3–4 WMB

Adonai, how sweet is the taste of Your love. For it is sweeter than honey and its smoother than wine. When I drink from Your cup I do not thirst. For You quench my soul with love so divine!

Your wings of protection, cover me both in the night and in the day. And I do not worry of harm that Satan may send my way.

For all I have to do is to cry out *YESHUA* and You will be there. With the sword in Your right hand. Slaying the enemy and all that are there.

I love You, my Lord, with every breath that I breathe. For I'm never alone. You give me all that I need.

I lift my hands to You. I'll proclaim of Your love. Encircle me forever, for You are my King here on earth and in heaven above.

How I love You, my *Adonai.* It is to You alone I pray. Amen and amen.

Thanksgiving

Enter into his gates with thanksgiving, and into his courts with praise. Give thanks to him, and bless his name.   Psalms 100:4 WMB

Abba, I am so thankful to You for Your grace! That You love me just the way I am. Even with all my flaws and the mistakes I make daily, You love me unconditionally, unwavering, and offer unto me total grace!

It doesn't mean You don't want more from and for me. That is why Your word is my guideline, the truth to get me through this life.

So let every word that comes forth from my mouth praise the *Yeshua ha-Mashiach.* Who was, and is, and is to come. For putting Your ring upon my finger and calling me Your own. For taking this sinner and making her set apart for Your honor and glory forever.

I give to You my all, my Lord. And I praise You with all that I am.

In *Yeshua's* name I pray. Amen.

NOVEMBER 24

Walking Hand In Hand

The Lord, you are my God. I will exalt you! I will praise your name, for you have done wonderful things, things planned long ago, in complete faithfulness and truth.   Isaiah 25:1 WMB

Abba, life was put into motion long ago. Your perfect plan that will not be changed. Why You chose me I am not quite sure. But, my Lord, I am so glad that You did.

For I love my family and would not want any other. I have everything I need and more. You have given me life, and given it abundantly. But You have even more in store.

For You want a more intimate walk with me. One where I see two footsteps walking in the sand. One is mine, my Lord, while the other is Yours. And as we walk together holding hands, You bring new things to my mind and heart. You bring people in my life who need a little help. But at times You want me go outside of my comfort zone, to give even more of me, so I can become a more perfected image of You.

I am willing, my Lord, to be a vessel. To go and do things of Your desire. So put opportunities in front of me and quench my heart. That I know without doubt, that this is planned by You. For even though I'm weak and full of fault. I'm just a mere mortal man. But with You, all things are possible. Help me be willing, to be the vessel of Your desire and go the direction of Your perfect plan.

Thank You. For even though I cannot see the future and I do not understand the things of today, all I have to do is to have faith. To walk hand and hand with You. For it is You and You alone, who will complete in and through me, Your perfect plan.

Thank You *Yeshua,* it's to You alone I pray. Amen.

NOVEMBER 25

Blessings

He who didn't spare his own Son, but delivered him up for us all, how would he not also with him freely give us all things? Romans 8:32 WMB

Abba, I praise You to the heavens this morning. For everything I have comes from You. For You have provided my home, my health and my family. For my work, my freedom, and even my gifts and talents are all given to me as gifts of love from You each day. Even the air I breathe is Yours to offer or take away.

I am truly amazed, my King, how intricate the design of my life is, that You have created. For You have woven a beautiful quilt of love that covers and protects me. How marvelous, how wonderful, how beautiful You are. To forgive me and bless me in this way!

May I, my Lord, treasure each breath, knowing it could be my last. Offering each one up as a prayer of incense before Your throne.

May each person I meet, every opportunity I have to speak, I use to share the name of *Yeshua ha-Mashiach.* That even in my weakest moments I am still finding a way to show others the majesty of You, my King.

For I can never repay You for anything I have, but I can offer my alabaster jar at Your feet. Thank You for this life and all the blessings You have and continue to give me daily.

For it is in *Yeshua's* Holy name I pray. Amen.

November 26

Take Captive My Thoughts

Whenever you stand praying, if you have anything against anyone, forgive him, so that your Father in heaven may also forgive you your transgressions.
Mark 11:25 TLV

Abba, I stand today asking help for the frustrations that I bear in my heart, and for You to work a forgiving heart in me. For how can I with a right heart, ask of You anything, if I have not forgiven my brother?

This can be so hard when they have done or continue to do the same thing over and over again.

But You, my Lord, are greater. Help me take captive my thoughts and pray for them each time it comes to memory. Let my thoughts be Your thoughts, Your word and not my own.

Then, my Lord, I will be able to come before You with a gracious heart, a heart that that is refined, glistening Your reflection.

Help me this day and every day, with every thought, think how Your grace can cover each person, including myself, all the time.

For its only because of *Yeshua* that I can come before Your throne of grace and pray. Amen and amen!

November 27

The Shepherd

He will feed his flock like a shepherd. He will gather the lambs in his arm, and carry them in his bosom. He will gently lead those who have their young. Isaiah 40:11 WMB

Ruach ha Kodesh, may You move Your *Ruach* upon this land. For where You are not, there is unrest and death. Where You are not, people cannot see. For they are blinded by the lies of Satan and all will suffer in his hands.

Abba, this land has turned from a God-fearing nation to one that does not recognize You. You speak of how in the end, people and families will turn on one another. This has not been as prevalent in my lifetime as it is now.

Abba, You have blessed me and filled me with the *Ruach ha Kodesh.* And I am calling out to You, O Lord, for a revelation. How can I reach the lost? How can I reach others who I have nothing in common with? How can I touch the lives of those I fear?

For these children were created by You. They are Your lost sheep that have gone astray. Help me to serve You in the gathering of Your sheep. Embrace us all in Your arms of love. Sustain us with Your mighty right hand. Let this country be reunited by You, my Lord. Let grace and peace cover this land!

Adonai, I lay prostrate before You. That we are changed from within. To have a hunger and thirst that only can be quenched by following the Shepherd to the watering hole. For You are all we need, nothing more, nothing less, through all eternity. Amen and amen.

November 28

The Lost Sheep

What do you think? If a certain man has a hundred sheep and one of them goes astray, won't he leave the ninety-nine on the mountains and go looking for the one that is straying? — Matthew 18:12 TLV

Abba, how easy it is in this day and age to stray. To get caught up in what most people say are silly, not harmful things.

But anything that is not holy can be a very dangerous situation to allow in our lives. We should run away and not dabble in the ways of darkness, or unfortunately, we have given Satan a victory, a foothold in our lives.

Let us be as blameless as we can be! For God hates the smallest of sin. For any sin is an abomination before our Lord. That is why He will leave the ninety-nine and run after the one, breaking his legs and carrying him back to the flock. So that this little one will not stray again.

How I praise You my heavenly *Abba,* my *Jehovah Rohi.* For You are my Shepherd, the One who tends to my every need. The One who leads me to the water when I thirst and protects me from the wolves at bay.

You are my Rock and the only One in who I trust. How I will praise You, my King, throughout eternity. Amen and amen.

November 29

My Failures

*A final word, when all has been heard: Fear God and keep His **mitzvot**! For this applies to all mankind. God will bring every deed into judgment, including everything that is hidden, whether it is good or evil.*
Ecclesiastes 12:13–14 TLV

Abba, I love You so much and I can't wait to sit upon Your lap and gaze into Your eyes of love. But I know how many times I have failed You. That I have disappointed You and brought tears to Your eyes.

I know that like my father on this earth, I have a reverent fear of You. For You hold the scales of eternity and You are mighty and Your hands are just.

How I praise You for Your sacrifice, otherwise my eternity would be in hell forever. For I have broken Your *mitzvots* so many times. Yet I stand here, white as snow.

Abba, my love for You is what makes me want to follow Your decrees. My fear of You is in where I should be going from the deeds of my past.

But You have inscribed my name on the palm of Your hand. So my destiny is forever to be with You!

How I love You, my King, my Love. Forever will I be before Your throne, looking into the eyes of pure love. Amen and amen.

NOVEMBER 30

How Blessed Am I

*Then as **Yeshua** was saying these things, a certain woman in the crowd, raising her voice, said to Him, "Blessed is the womb that carried You and the breasts that nursed You!" But He said, "Rather, blessed are those who hear the word of God and obey it."*   Luke 11:27–28 TLV

Yeshua, You told this woman that we are more blessed if we hear and follow Your *mitzvots,* than Your mother who carried You in her womb.

I can't imagine, carrying You, nursing You, taking care of You all the days You lived under my roof. And yet You said, "Rather, blessed are those who hear and obey."

Wow, how amazing this teaching is. How amazing Your love is! That no person is greater than another. For the only ones who are blessed are those who hear and obey. You say this so many times in scripture. Why don't people understand this truth?

Blessed are those who love You. For if we truly love You, we will obey Your commands even when it hurts.

I want Your blessings! The blessings of Your presence. The blessings of eternal life. Fill me with the *Ruach ha Kodesh* so He can help me on my journey to grow in You. Help me not be afraid in the storm, to trust, to understand that I do not have to know all things. I just need to hear Your words and obey, and then You will make a way for me that is perfect for my life and Your plan.

Thank You for Your unfailing love, my Lord. Amen and amen.

December 1

True To You

How can a young man keep his way pure? By living according to your word.
Psalms 119:9 WMB

Abba, this applies to both young and old. For the only way to stay true to You and pure is by the renewing of Your word: reading it, studying it, praying it throughout each and every day.

For You give us free will, which is good, but hard! And it is a choice we have every morning we wake, whether we are going to live by it or not.

For You said that it was better for You to go, so we could have the *Ruach ha Kodesh* living in us. For He convicts us, reminds us of Your words and always shows us another way.

If it was not for *Ruach ha Kodesh,* I could not imagine where I would be. To think about where this world that we live in would be.

For we live in a time when the moral depravity of this world looks like Sodom.

Oh, how I praise You. That I live at this day in time and that Your *Ruach* dwells within me. That I have the freedom to read Your word and speak it to others. That today, I can hopefully have an opportunity to show someone the power and the love of Yeshua.

How blessed am I that You knew my needs and have provided all I would need to live a life of purity and strength in a time such as this.

For it is by Your grace that I pray. Amen.

December 2

My Blessings

For God is not unjust so as to forget your work and the love that you showed for His name, in have served and continuing to serve the **kedoshim**.
Hebrews 6:10 TLV

Abba, just as You would never forget anything my hands have done. Do not let me forget the blessings You have given me in the past and through each day.

Let me remember that each breath comes from You alone. That when I eat, it is only by Your grace. The fact I have a roof over my head is by Your sweet provisions. But all those special moments that cannot be explained by man, the visions, Your forgiveness, those, my Lord, are given to me only by Your love!

Abba, please continue to give me those special moments, the visions, and Your grace today. For these are what gives me strength to get through the hard times.

And Lord, during this season of remembrance. Help me to pour out Your love on others. To build up new and wonderful memories for them. That they may be strengthened. Because what they have desired from You has been received. Let me hear from You and be obedient today, my King. For each day is all about You!

I thank You for the privilege of coming before Your throne. I praise You for hearing my prayer, and my lips will praise You forever more. Amen.

December 3

Walk With The Wise

One who walks with wise men grows wise, but a companion of fools suffers harm.
Proverbs 13:20 WMB

Abba, I am so thankful to You for the Christian fellowship You have put in my path. To have others to share my walk with, to be held accountable to, to be able to seek wise counsel from.

This has been one of the greatest gifts I have received from You, my King. For even though I know the only person I need is You! What joy, strength, and protection I find when I stand with the multitudes.

For where two or more gather together, there You are! When we pool our gifts, more lives can be changed. Even though one is all that is needed to make a difference. You made Eve for Adam.

This was Your design. To bless each other and teach each other about You!

Thank You for loving me enough and for putting so many in my path who love, honor, and obey Your commands!

For it is in Your precious name I pray. Amen.

December 4

Straight And Narrow

*Delight yourself in **Adonai**, and He will give you the requests of your heart.*
Psalms 37:4 TLV

My heart is Yours, my *Adonai*. Take me and use me as You wish. For You know me better than I know myself. So give unto me what would please You, for in this, I will be pleased.

Keep me on the straight and narrow. Don't let me sway to the left or to the right. Build in me strength and courage like Joshua. So that any walls they are separating me from You, are torn down.

Put Michael on my right side and Gabriel on my left. Let me wear my full armor today. Let this be how I walk every day: bold, confident, and ready to slay the enemy so I can fight for my family for this life and the next, being the servant You wish me to be.

My body and soul are awaiting Your *mitzvots*. Because all I want is to do what pleases Thee! Amen and amen.

DECEMBER 5

Walking In The Spirit

But I say, walk by the **Ruach**, *and you will not carry out the desires of the flesh. For the flesh sets its desire against the* **Ruach**, *but the* **Ruach** *sets its desire against the flesh—for these are in opposition to one another, so that you cannot do what you want. But if you are led by the* **Ruach**, *you are not under law.*   Galatians 5:16–18 TLV

Abba, teach us today how to exercise our spiritual muscles. May we work out our spirit as much or more than we work out our bodies. One day, our bodies will die, rot, and decay. But our spirit will live on for eternity.

May we live this life knowing we are not limited to just the natural realm, to what we see around us. But that Your *Ruach* living in us, that makes all things possible, things unseen, to those who believe.

For we are not walking just in the flesh. But we are choosing spiritual realities that affect our lives and others too each day.

I pray, my Lord, that for each person I speak to today or meet today, for each financial decision or decision of the heart, that I not only look at what is the effect of my words and actions towards them in the flesh, but what and how will I affect their spirits as well.

May we live each day with this in mind. May we look at each other as a spirit and soul and not as flesh and blood. Maybe then, my Lord, the actions of our flesh will mirror the actions of Your *Ruach*.

For it is in Your Holy name I pray. Amen.

DECEMBER 6

Let Me Work Unto Thy Name

And whatever you do, work heartily, as for the Lord and not for men.
Colossians 3:23 WMB

Abba, how many days do we get up and do the same old ritual routines? Whether it is a job that we do to earn money for our family or even, sad to say, work we do for You.

How often do we look at our finances, at our own abilities, our own desires and say we can't do this so we will let someone else who is more capable do it instead. Even though we know it would be pleasing to You.

How often we turn our heads and look the other way when we see someone in need because we ourselves may be struggling.

Help us Lord, the mighty King of Israel. Help us to change from the inside out. Let us look at work, at situations and how to do them, not by that which we are able. But let us look at each situation as *what can God do!* Then You can work in us and through us to serve others.

Because after all, You give us breath each day. So our work, our toil, our labor should reflect this knowledge. We should understand that if You did not want us here, You could remove the breath from our mouths.

Let me live today as God can do it through me. Let me live today in appreciation of each breath I have. Let me live today to give You my heart, my soul and my mind in everything I do.

For it is in *Yeshua's* name I pray. Amen.

December 7

How Deep Is The Love Of Christ

*For this reason I bow my knees before the Father—from Him every family in heaven and on earth receives its name. I pray that from His glorious riches He would grant you to be strengthened in your inner being with power through His **Ruach**, so that Messiah may dwell in your hearts through faith. I pray that you, being rooted and grounded in love, may have strength to grasp with all **kedoshim** what is the width and length and height and depts., and to know the love of Messiah which surpasses knowledge, so you may be filled up with all the fullness of God.*
Ephesians 3:14–19 TLV

Abba, I pray for all the saints to be strengthened by Your *Ruach.* That through all that might be going on in each of their lives, they can see how deeply You love them. That no matter what the schemes may be that Satan lays before them, they are more than conquerors in *Yeshua.* For it is through faith and the reading of Your word that we receive the knowledge with which to fight.

I also pray for the health of the saints. Let them be strong and victorious, so they can share the gospel with unbelievers and those who are weak in faith.

I pray for a financial blessing upon them, my Lord. So they are able to pay their debtors and also able to share food and warmth with those in need.

I pray for safety as many travel as many go shopping among the thieves.

I praise You my *Abba,* my Comforter, my Friend. I praise You for giving us this day to spend at the feet of *Yeshua.*

For it is only by Your grace I am able to pray. Amen.

DECEMBER 8

The Great I Am

Then God said, Let Us make man in Our image, after Our likeness! Let them rule over the fish of the sea, over the flying creatures of the sky, over the livestock, over the whole earth, and over every crawling creature that crawls on the land.   Genesis 1:26 TLV

I praise You this morning, my Lord, for Your love surpasses all the glorious riches on earth. For You have shown me all that I could ever need, I have found in You!

For You are *Elohim,* my creator: You created me in my mother's womb and You know every hair on my head. You created me for a purpose, which is to serve, honor, and love You this day and forever more.

You are *Jehovah* God, the Unchangeable intimate one, who knows every thought, every desire of my heart. My desire this day, my King, is to know You more and more.

You are *Jehovah Jireh,* my provider. Without You, I would have nothing. But I praise You, my Lord. For with You, I have food and shelter, and I am clothed like the lilies of the fields.

You are *Jehovah Yatsar,* the Lord who molds me. You have been molding me for many years, my Lord, but I am in need of more refining. Cut away any darkness from me, Lord, so all my facets will shine brilliantly for You!

You are *Jehovah Shammah,* the God who is here. Father I feel Your arms embracing me. I feel the kisses of Your word. I know all I have to do is to cry out Your name and there You will be, dressed in armor battling the enemy for me.

Abba, You are the great I Am. Whatever I may need, whenever I may need it, there You stand! I praise You that Your love for me is stronger than the forces of the seas. That it is wider than the universe, far greater than I could ever see. And You are the Lover of my soul and all I will ever need. How I love you, my *Adonai.* Amen.

DECEMBER 9

Your Vessel

__Adonai__, You are my God, I will exalt You, I will praise Your Name, for You have done wonderful things, plans of old with steadfast faithfulness.
Isaiah 25:1 TLV

Lord, You planned long ago the meaning to my life. I am grateful though that even though You know each day, all that will transpire and how I will respond. I love the fact that they unfold new and fresh to me each day.

This way I can take what was wrong, where I messed up at yesterday and work on making it good today. I can truly see my own heart in the responses I make to others when I am stressed, and how it should have been.

I praise You, *Jehovah Yatsar,* for gently molding me into the vessel of Your desire. But because of Your gentleness, You are not overwhelming me with all the changes I need to make at one time.

Abba, I have been frustrated lately about things not going according to my plan. But I know that my plans are not always Your plans. That sometimes because of my selfishness, or stubbornness to change, those plans need to be put on hold until I am in a better place. Or to find out that You had a much better plan for me.

Thank You that as You are molding this hard clay into a beautiful vessel for You. That Your living water is what is used to soften and mold it so its perfect design is unique and not like any other. Thank You for taking Your time in molding me. I just pray, my Lord, that this vessel will eventually become the design of Your desire. That I can be used in Your kingdom, forever more. Amen.

December 10

Warrior For Christ

When Moses held up his hand, Israel prevailed. But when he let down his hand, the Amalekites prevailed. Moses' hands grew heavy, so they took a stone, put it under him, and he sat down. Aaron and Hur held up his hands, one on each side. So his hands were steady until the sun went down. So Joshua overpowered the Amalekites and his army with the edge of the sword. **Adonai** *said to Moses, "Write this a memorial book, and rehearse it in the hearing of Joshua, for I will utterly blot out the memory of the Amalekites from under heaven." Then Moses built an altar, and called the name of it* **Adonai-Nissi.** *Exodus 17:11–15 TLV*

Abba, You are a Holy God, righteous and true! Your name is above every name. For You parted the seas for Moses, You gave them manna to eat and water from a rock to drink. Then when the Amaleks came to destroy them You made the Israelites victorious over this dreaded army. But with each miracle You gave, You asked Moses for a sign to show his people he was trusting in You.

Abba, I trust in You! Help me this day and forever more stand strong in my battles. Help me hold up my sword so victory can be mine. And Lord, I know in the battles, some will be long and hard. Some will seem like I might not win the fight. Bring to me at this time my family and friends to help me hold up my sword to You, that You see our faith and we are victorious in You. For You are *Adonai (Jehovah) Nissi,* God my Banner! I shall stand victorious in all I do, when I am standing by You!

Let me always remember to kill all my enemies, sin, in the fight, to blot them out completely. For when You say remove it all from your life, we must obey and not leave any remembrance of this sin. So this sin cannot turn back on me as it did Saul and destroy me. Let me start every battle on bended knee. Let me wear my armor this day. May I stand victorious in Your army, my Lord. Let me be a warrior for You, *Yeshua!* Amen and Amen.

December 11

Build Me Up

He was not the light, but was sent that he might testify about the light.
Yochanan (John) *1:8 WMB*

What a perfect witness of the faith, was John the Baptist. For he was strong, pure and righteous. He foretold the coming of our Lord and clung to all that was true. He was a great and holy man. For even *Yeshua* said there is none greater than John!

My Lord, I am amazed by so many in their strength and walk with You. For they have done wonderful things in the moment of tragedy and stress. They have stood strong in the midst of temptation and even death.

Adonai, I love You so, but I am weak. So I need You to be strong for me. This world is a very dark place, because fewer and fewer Christians are living by faith. Help me even in my weakest moments to be a testimony of Your love.

Let me be a light, because Your light shines from within me. A person with knowledge, not mine, but Yours. A person who understands and uses the gifts You have bestowed upon me in the furthering of Your kingdom. To become the person You created me to be.

This is far greater than I can do on my own. So I surrender it all to You. Walk through me. Speak through me, love through me. For this is my desire, my hope, my deepest need.

For it is through the power of the *Ruach ha Kodesh* I ask these things. Amen and amen.

December 12

Miracle Of The Menorah

*Then came **Hanukkah**, it was winter in Jerusalem. Yeshua was walking in the Temple around Solomon's Colonnade. Then the Judean leaders surrounded Him, saying "How long will You hold us in suspense? If you are the Messiah, tell us outright!" **Yeshua** answered them, "I told you, but you don't believe! The works I do in My Father's name testify concerning Me. But you don't believe, because you are not My sheep. My sheep hear My voice. I know them, and they follow Me. I give them eternal Life! They will never perish, and no one will snatch them out of My hand."*
John 10:22–28 TLV

Abba, my King, during this time of Hanukkah, I want to re-dedicate my life and all I have to You. For You have me in Your right hand and Satan cannot have any hold on me!

What a great and mighty God I serve who tends to His sheep with such tenderness, with such love and strength. That any wolf in sheep's clothing will be exposed and tossed down as long as I stay close to You.

That You would hear my cry and want to answer! Let's me know that all I am only belongs to You!

Thank You for the miracle of burning the Menorah for eight days! I am looking and expecting for a miracle from You in my life during this time of re-dedication!

In the Holy name *of Yeshua* I pray. Amen.

December 13

Things Hoped For

Now faith is the substance of things hoped for, the evidence of realities not seen. For by it the elders received commendation. By faith we understand that the universe was created by the word of God, so that what is seen did not come from anything visible.   Hebrews 11:1–3 TLV

Adonai, You give me the assurance daily in my walk with You.

First You give me life, then You give me certain tasks. Then You affirm with signs and wonders that these tasks are of You. To serve You, to honor You in ways I could not do in my own strength or knowledge.

You affirm to me daily Your love for me. By the people You have put in my life and all the answered prayers. You affirm my salvation over and over again, my Lord, because I know where I have been and where I am now and where I want to go. I know the desires of old and I know the change within.

There is no way these things could have taken place in my life without You! There is not even a reason for them to. But You saw in me something of value, something of worth and You have given me life and given it abundantly.

I praise You, *Adonai* for Your love. Help me to honor Your name this day by the proclamation of faith I have in You!

For it is in *Yeshua's* name I pray. Amen.

December 14

Ultimate Trust

*But the angel of **Adonai** called to him from heaven and said, "Abraham! Abraham! He said "**Hineni**." The He said, "Do not reach out your hand against the young man—do nothing to him at all. For now I know that you are one who fears God—you did not withhold your son, your only son, form Me." Then Abraham lifted up his eyes and behold, there was a ram, just caught in the thick bushes by its horns. So Abraham named that place, **Adonai Yireh**—as it is said today, "On the mountain, **Adonai** will provide." The angel of **Adonai** called to Abraham a second time from heaven and said. "By myself I swear—it is a declaration to **Adonai**—because you have done this thing, and you did not withhold your son, your only son, I will richly bless you and bountifully multiply your seed like the stars of heaven, and lie the san that is on the seashore, and your seed will possess the gate of his enemies. In your seed all the nations of the earth will be blessed—because you obeyed My voice." Genesis 22:11–18 TLV*

Abba, help me today to be more like Abraham. To be willing to give up anything and everything to You because of the deep love and reverence I have for You. Let me not begrudge the things You ask of me, but may I give it with joy and gladness. And even if it takes something of joy from my heart, may You fill me with the knowledge it is the right thing, so that the affirmation of You being pleased with me replaces the object that was lost.

Be my *Jehovah Jireh* today, the Lord who provides. Provide for me all that is necessary for me to be sustained and then all I need to serve You. Provide for me a clear understanding of the task You have laid before me. Show me the talents and gifts that I can use. Show me who and what to use around me. May it all be to the glory of You! Amen and amen.

DECEMBER 15

New Each Day

*Because of the mercies of **Adonai** we will not be consumed, for His compassions never fail. They are new every morning! Great is Your faithfulness. **Adonai** is my portion, says my soul, therefore I will hope in Him. **Adonai** is good to those who wait for Him, to the soul that seeks Him. It is good to wait quietly for the salvation of **Adonai**.* Lamentations 3:22–26 TLV

Abba, how I love You, my Lord. For You make everything new each day. For my love for You this morning is deeper and stronger than yesterday. And yet I know there is more in which we can grow.

For even though I am covered in darkness with the sin in my life, You see the beauty within me. Man may see me like the tents of Kedar, dark and unattractive. But You, O God, see me as beautiful, like the curtains of Solomon.

Cleanse me, O Lord, remove any desire to sin out of my life. Renew me in Your love every day. Let me be drawn after You, with a heart like David's. A woman whose husband is blessed because she tends to His every need.

Let my life be cultivated by the things of You. Take away all doubts that I might have in my abilities to serve You. But let me see that You will place in me what and where You wish me to be. If I trust in You, You shall give me the words and ability to do exactly what You desire.

Change me, O Lord, from this earthen vessel, to one who is the beautiful bride, adorned with love of her groom.

In *Yeshua's* name I pray. Amen.

DECEMBER 16

Faith

Without faith it is impossible to be well pleasing to him, for he who comes to God must believe that he exists, and that he is a rewarder of those who seek him. Hebrews 11:6 WMB

Abba, there are so many prayers that have been laid at Your feet. Some prayers of illness, some of sorrow, some of finances and some of loneliness. Father, may You hear our cries! May You answer our plea! Give us a new love for You that is deeper than the seas.

Let our relationship grow deeper with You in ways we would not even know how to ask. Let there be such a renewal in our hearts, in our minds that we conquer the demons of our past.

Let our strength in You be so powerful that the evil one runs in fear! Let no one and nothing come between us, my Lord. Let us know that You hear.

Let our hearts be full of such joy that the saints stand on the streets and cry "Holy, Holy is Lord God almighty. Worthy is the Lamb who was slain." Our God is the One and true God of Israel. Who will answer your plea, if you call out to Him in faith.

In *Yeshua's* Holy name I pray. Amen.

DECEMBER 17

I Have Found You

All Judah rejoiced at the oath, for they had sworn with all their heart, and sought him with their whole desire; and he was found by them.
2 Chronicles 15:15 WMB

Abba, I have sought You and found You. I have searched for You as gold. I went into the wilderness, and You came and brought me home.

How wonderful, how marvelous You are. How beautiful to me. May I stay forever before Your throne! For You are the one true King!

Let me always stay in Your presence! Let me always stay at Your feet. Let me fight for what is right in the eyes of my Lord. Let me stay on bended knee.

For You are a mighty King. The Warrior for our souls. I will trust my soul only to You. For You treasure it as gold.

I don't understand why You love me the way that You do. But I never want to leave Your presence. May I go forever before You, now and all eternity through.

In *Yeshua's* name I pray. Amen.

DECEMBER 18

Doing Right

*To do righteousness and justice is more acceptable to **Adonai** than sacrifice.*
Proverbs 21:3 TLV

Abba, Father, I feel so under attack right now. I feel the dark forces against me. There were times last night when I wanted to cry and walk away, but then, my Lord, I stopped to think of You.

If I am striving to do what is right and what is Holy and acceptable to You, then Satan is going to shoot flaming arrows at me to try to get me doing everything outside of Your will.

So may I put on the full armor today. May my shield block the arrows from hurting me. May I seek justice, but offer mercy. May my name, which means grace, be exemplified through me.

Let me choose joy in the midst of troubles. Let me seek the good in every situation before me. May you put Michael on my right side and Gabriel on my left. May nothing come to me that is not of You!

My Lord, during this time of trials and frustration, help me look outside of myself. Help me look to the lessons I can learn in them. For then I can be a better example for others to follow. But most importantly, may I be acceptable to You in everything I do!

For it is in the precious name of *Yeshua* I pray. Amen.

December 19

Teach Me

*Though **Adonai** gives you the bread of adversity and the water of oppression, your teachers will no longer be hidden but your eyes will see your teachers. Your ears will hear a word behind you saying: "This is the way, walk in it. When you turn to the right or when you turn to the left."*
Isaiah 30:20–21 TLV

Adonai, teach me in the midst of adversity. Show me in my affliction the ways of You, O Lord. Help me to seek answers that only come from Your word. For then I can bear fruit. Then I can take joy in my affliction.

Lend me Your ear, my King, that I may always hear Your voice. Lend me Your hand that I may offer it to others. Light my path that I can see in the darkness. Hold me in Your arms so I know I have a safe place to run home to.

Let me seek You in the morning so my day starts off with You. Let me praise You during the day for Your love will get me through. Let me read Your word in the evening so my eyes can see Your truths. Let me pray to You each night, for forgiveness of myself and blessings for others, too.

For You are my Lord, my God, who teaches me each day. May I rejoice in my affliction, because then You, my King, will come rescue me and embrace me until my dying day.

I love You, *Adonai*. I give to You my heartaches, my afflictions, my moments of joy and of sorrow. For when I am in Your arms, none of this matters anymore.

In *Yeshua's* name alone I pray. Amen.

December 20

Peace On Earth

*"Glory to God in the highest, and on earth **shalom** to men of good will."*
Luke 2:14 TLV

Adonai, Your angels came and proclaimed "peace on earth, good will toward men."

But I cry out in despair. For I see destruction. I hear the hate. The children are without fathers. The countries are without leaders. Men run around seeking self-pleasure and trample on anyone in their way.

And yet, in heaven the bells are ringing.... I hear the Angels singing, "Peace on earth, good will toward men."

For Your plan is in motion. *Yeshua ha Mashiach* was born. He was a baby, yet the Mighty Counselor.

For He died, marred and laid in a tomb. But He rose again glorious for all to see, and He holds the key to heaven for you and me.

He will come again with a mighty trumpet blast. So then all the nations will hear the angels as they sing: "Peace on earth, good will toward men."

For then, my King, it will be not for a moment, but for eternity!

Praise be the Holy name of *Yeshua ha Mashiach* the King! Amen.

December 21

Lord Bless You And Keep You

***Adonai** bless you and keep you! **Adonai** make His face to shine on you and be gracious to you! **Adonai** turn His face toward you and grant you **shalom**!* Numbers 6:24–26 TLV

My Lord, I need You this much! For Your face to shine on me, bless me, and give me peace—I can't think of anything sweeter, or of anything more that would get me through each day than to have You look at me and say, "I love You and I always will, every day."

For that is what this verse speaks of to me. It's of truth, love, and protection. All of what a father does for his child.

Abba, I am Your daughter, humble and meek. And I am yearning to sit on the lap of the one who created me.

You, my Lord, are so much wrapped up into one incredible gift. May I share this gift with others, during this Christmas time.

In *Yeshua's* Holy name. Amen.

DECEMBER 22

Eternity Mindset

Let's therefore draw near with boldness to the throne of grace, that we may receive mercy and may find grace for help in time of need.
Hebrews 4:16 WMB

Abba, teach me how to ascend unto Your throne room of praise. Teach me how to come before Your throne of grace. Let me kneel before You my Heavenly Father. Let me show You that You are worthy of all praise!

Abba, Paul prayed that we, his brothers and sisters in Christ, would never stop growing in the love and knowledge of Your will. That Your word would abide in us and prepare us for battle.

That we, being of small mind, would allow Your Ruach to live through us a life of sacrifice and praise. That we would learn to live a life of eternity mindset rather than an earthly one.

That we would move forward each day knowing that Satan is around the corner ready to devour. But we, who are in Christ, would be willing to unsheathe our swords and battle for what is truly ours: a life in abundance through Christ.

Grant us this day a life fully devoted to You. For You descended from heaven that we may have life eternal with You. So may our lives be an offering of praise and worship that ascends before Your throne. May our lives be the example that causes others' hearts to hunger to know You, my King!

For it is only through the grace of Christ that I can lay this prayer at Your feet. Amen.

December 23

I Am Not Ashamed

For I am not ashamed of the Good News of Messiah, because it is the power of God for salvation for everyone who believes, for the Jew first and also for the Greek.   Romans 1:16 WMB

Adonai, I am not ashamed of the gospel of Christ, but so overwhelmed with joy for its offering!

For man hath no power over me and my destiny, but You cause each breath to come forth from my mouth. For You alone hold the key to heaven gates. And its only You who can decide who can enter through.

Yeshua, it is Your blood, Your ultimate sacrifice alone that covers my sins and allows me to have eternal life. Without You, there is only death and destruction.

Therefore, I am not ashamed of telling the world: "*Yeshua* is the way, the truth and the life. No one will enter into the kingdom of heaven unless they proclaim *Yeshua* as Lord of all!"

May we shout it from the roof tops, that salvation may come to all we know.

For it is in Christ name alone I pray. Amen.

December 24

My Offering

*Therefore **Adonai** Himself will give you a sign: Behold, the virgin will conceive. When she is giving birth to a son, she will call His name Immanuel.*
Isaiah 7:14 TLV

Adonai, how precious is Your name, my Lord. How great is the love You pour out on Your people.

You must have cried a million tears knowing the sins of the people You have given life to and the rejection they would show. Yet in Your grace, You still created us, then sent Your Son to save us! How incredible is Your love. How profound is Your mercy.

Adonai, how I praise You for answering my deepest prayer. Which was to save my soul from Satan's grasp. And then You continually answer prayers for me to show me Your love and to keep my spirits high! Lord, I offer You everything I am, every part of my soul. Show me what Your desire is for me this day.

Should I make a meal and take it to the needy? Should I buy a blanket and give it to someone on the street? Should I go to a retirement home and spend it with someone who is lonely? Show me, my Lord, let me be an answered prayer to one of these.

Give me a vision, convict my heart this day. I promise You, my Lord. I promise to obey. Let me show others a sign of Your love. Let me tell them about You and the birth of Your Son. Give me an insight of what You would have me to do. For my life is not mine. It's all about You.

Help me to be Your gift to someone else this day.

In *Yeshua's* name I pray. Amen and Amen.

December 25

The Gift

By this God's love was revealed in us, that God sent his one and only Son into the world that we might live through Him.
*1 **Yochanan**(John) 4:9 WMB*

Christ, You are the risen Son, the one and only King who was and is now and will be through all eternity. You came down from Your heavenly throne to a world so corrupt that we who are evil might live and reign with You for eternity.

How amazing is this love! How incredibly selfless this gift You have given us.

May we celebrate Your birth every day. May we seek each day to offer a special gift to You. May we look at others with love and compassion. May we give of ourselves selflessly when we see a need.

I thank You this day for my life, all the good, the difficulties, and the lessons I am learning. I praise You, Lord, that I have been given a second chance. For You have taken me, cleansed me and given me the gift of life. I thank You, my Lord, for this amazing love! I praise You, my Lord, for this Christmas gift!

It is in the Holy name of Christ I pray. Amen.

DECEMBER 26

My Refuge

The eternal God is your dwelling place. Underneath are the everlasting arms. He thrust out the enemy from before you and said, "Destroy!"
Deuteronomy 33:27 WMB

Abba, I went in yesterday, ready for battle. But was unprepared for what I encountered. For I was prepared for battle on the ground, but totally unprepared for the air strikes that happened.

But Lord, You were there for me and threw a rope down to pull me off the cliffs. For even though I may have gotten cuts caused by the jagged rocks, You my *Jehovah Rapha* will heal each wound.

I thank You that I had prayed before I entered into battle, for I did not use my tongue to strike down those in my way. I pray now, my King, that You, knowing all, will put Your everlasting arms around me and keep my heart close to Yours each day.

Let me fight for what is right. To show justice where it is needed. May I have mercy for those who have hurt me because You have given grace in abundance to me.

Let all things, both good and bad work for the good to those who believe. And for those who choose to not follow You, well, my Lord, I lay them at Your feet.

I thank You that I am not their judge. I pray they shall soon see everything through Your eyes, my Lord. For only You my a Lord are King!

In *Yeshua's* name. Amen.

December 27

Unfailing Love

But let all who take refuge in You rejoice! Let them always shout for joy! You will shelter them and they exult—those who love Your Name. For You bless the righteous, **Adonai.** *You surround him with favor as a shield.*
Psalms 5: 12–13 TLV

    Abba, You are so good to me. How can I ever repay You for Your kindness?

    For I have tried to love my enemies and I have failed. I have given when I don't have and yet grumbled about it. I have gotten angry with my brother for not understanding my needs. I have failed You in every way possible, my Lord, and yet You still embrace me in Your arms. How good You are, my King! How faithful and true is Your love.

    So, my *Adonai,* since I am weak and unable to do this on my own, and I tend to call on Your name then act in my own flesh, help me to be totally submissive to You! Help me to act and love according to Your *Ruach* that lives within me.

    For I want nothing more than to please You, my Lord…. So, Satan, get behind me! For You, my Lord, and I are going to walk hand in hand throughout this day!

    I trust You with all I am and I give it all to You this day.

    In *Yeshua's* name I pray. Amen.

December 28

Grasp Of Your Hand

Fear not for I am with you, be not dismayed, for I am your God. I will strengthen you. Surely I will help you. I will uphold you with My righteous right hand.   Isaiah 41:10 TLV

Abba, how these words bring peace to my soul. My heart rejoices in Your love. For nothing and no one can take me from the grasp of Your hand.

No matter the circumstances, I will trust You. No matter the mountains I must climb or downhill streams I must travel, I know You will be there. If there is anything or anyone in my life Lord that tries to hurt me, You will always be there to comfort me and shield me with Your mighty right hand.

Abba, You have directed and allowed circumstances in my life to grow me, to strengthen me and to show me what a loving, Holy, and just God You are. May You continue to let the north winds blow if this brings me closer to You.

I love You, my Lord. And I trust You and praise You, that in all things, You will turn them to good for me. May I come into Your throne room of grace today and bask in Your presence forever.

In *Yeshua's* Holy name. Amen.

December 29

Buried Treasure

For this reason also, ever since we heard about you, we have not stopped praying for you. We keep asking God that you might be filled with the knowledge of His will in all wisdom and spiritual understanding— to walk in a manner worthy of the Lord, to please Him in all respects, bearing fruit in every good work and growing in the knowledge of God. We pray that you may be strengthened with all the power that comes from His glorious might, for you to have all kinds of patience and steadfast.
Colossians 1:9–11 TLV

Abba, I pray that myself and others do not cease to grow in the love and knowledge of Your word. That we search for You as buried treasure and adorn ourselves with Your jewels. That we give unto others as You have given to us. That we never stop sharing the love that Christ shared as He suffered and died that we might have eternal life!

Abba, I praise You from the depths of my soul for another day. One in which I can share this love, that I can serve and honor You. May I love in truth and in giving, bearing good fruit in all that I do.

Build up my endurance. For this walk is long and the road is not easy. Build me up in knowledge and wisdom that I don't act or say things that are not of Your truths. Let my name, when spoken, be one that makes people say, "She is a child of the most high God." Let this be what is remembered about me.

On the day when You call me home, may You stand there with arms wide open. And as I run into Your arms, may You say "Well done, You have finished the race. Come sit at the my table and enjoy the wedding supper of the Lamb."

Then as I grasp the palm of Your hand, I shall know that I am forever home in Your presence. Amen.

December 30

Still Waters

Remain in me, and I in you. As the branch can't bear fruit by itself unless it remains in the vine, so neither can you, unless you remain in me.
Yochanan (John) 15:4 WMB

Abba, lead me down the stream of still waters. Let this journey I am on be smooth. For I can see in the not so far distance there will be some mountains I need to climb. So may I have time to build up my strength in You.

I am grateful, my Lord, for the changes You have made in me. For I am not the same person I was many years ago. Continue to mold me and shape me into a pillar of strength, but let my heart be as soft as the petal of a rose.

May I bear the sweetest of fruits so that others might partake. May my branches be big and strong. May the roots of my tree grow deep and wide, so they can work through the soil to find only the water that comes from You!

You are the God of hope, the God of love and truth. Envelope me today my love. Let me walk only in the strength that is given from You.

In *Yeshua's* name I pray. Amen.

December 31

Taking Me Places

*But the Helper, the **Ruach ha-Kodesh** who the Father will send in My name, will teach you everything and remind you of everything that I said to you.*   John 14:26 TLV*

Abba, this is the last day of another year. And I would like to thank You for all the trials and tribulations, and for all the lessons that I have learned. For You have taken me places where I did not want to go, but I have come out changed. For I am stronger and more dependent on You because of these things.

I would like to ask You, my Lord, for a few simple things for this next year to come. That in all things, I never lose sight of You. That each day I awake, I praise You for every breath. That I take time to help others. That I am a better steward of the things You have given me. That I am careful with my words and actions so I edify and do not hurt those around me.

Lord each day You give is a new beginning, another chance to do what is right. A new day to search for You and to find a new wondrous opportunity awaiting us around the corner. Please, my Lord, may You remind me of this every day!

I love You, my *Adonai*. Teach me through Your *Rauch*. Build me up in You this day, that I may grow to be the creation You designed me to be.

For it is in *Yeshua's* name I pray. Amen.

About the Author

Nita Schnitzer is an author, speaker, entrepreneur, spiritual director, and chaplain. She was born in Houston, Texas and has two adult children and two grandchildren. From 1996–2016, she owned and operated a Christian preschool as a ministry to her staff and families. Her passion was to teach them about Jesus and minister to their educational, financial, emotional, and spiritual needs.

In April of 2016, Nita was called to become ordained through Hunter Ministries. She sold her preschool to focus on a new full-time service-based ministry she founded called Gifted to Grace Ministries. Gifted to Grace, or G2G, is a mission-driven organization that lends a hand to firefighters, EMS responders, and their families in their times of need. She is also currently serving as the Corps Commander for the

Houston Chaplain Corps through the International Fellowship of Chaplains, is a Chaplain for Billy Graham's Rapid Response Team and works as a Hospital Chaplain.

In 2013, God put the desire in Nita's heart to write prayers and share them with her friends. This has grown into a ministry of its own. These prayers have been complied in this book, *Before His Throne,* and are reaching believers and non-believers with the message of Jesus Christ, showing that His desire is to have an intimate relationship with us, His bride, as we walk each day in total dependence of Him.

Are you a fan of this book?
Help us spread the word about
Before His Throne
by:

- Posting a positive review on Amazon
- Tweeting about it
- Sharing the book with friends through social media
- Asking the local bookstore to carry copies
- Ordering extra copies to give away to friends

INVITE NITA TO SPEAK AT YOUR NEXT EVENT

Nita's heartfelt presentation is like having a conversation with a friend. She loves sharing about:

God's Grace
Time alone with Christ
Moving forward in hard times
What do you do when a family member hurts you
Being a godly parent
Praying over your child
Praying before His throne
How to start a prayer-life
Train up a child in the way they should go

To book Nita, please contact her at: <u>Nita@G2GMinistries.org</u>

G2G Ministries is a non-profit organization that helps Firefighters and EMS responders in their time of crisis. We assist in meeting the financial, emotional, and spiritual needs of our heroes as they rise.

On our website, you are able to donate a one time gift or become one of our monthly partners. All the proceeds from the donations are used strictly for this ministry. We also have affiliates that you can buy from on our website, such as Amazon, Target, Home Depot, and more. A portion of these purchases will be given to help a firefighter in need. It is people like you who keep this ministry able to serve our heroes in their times of crisis.

If you would like more information about volunteering or know a Firefighter or EMS responder in need, please visit us online at G2GMinistries.org or contact me at nita@g2gministires.org.

God bless you, and shalom!
Nita Schnitzer, Founder and Senior Ordained Chaplain

References:

Unless noted, all words in Hebrew were taken from the Messianic Jewish Family Bible: Tree of Life Version (TLV) Copyright © 2015 by the Messianic Jewish Family Bible Society.

Dates:

January 4:	Shekinah @ Wikipedia.org
January 20:	El malei Rachamim @ hebrew4christians.com
January 31:	El Roi @ hebrew4christians.com
February 5:	Jehovah Jireh, Names of God by Marilyn Hickey 2009
February 12:	Yeshua ha-Mashiach @ hebrew4christians.com
February 17:	Yeshua ha-Mashiach @ hebrew4christians.com
March 8:	Jehovah Rapha @ Biblehub.org
March 7:	Yeshua ha-Mashiach @ hebrew4christians.com
March 9:	El Olam @ hebrew4christians.com
	Yahweh @ Biblehub.org
March 11:	Yahweh @ Biblehub.org
March 15:	Yeshua ha-Mashiach @ hebrew4christians.com
March 17:	Elohim Yachal @ harvestnet.org
March 22:	Hey @ hebrew4christians.com
March 24:	Yeshua ha-Mashiach @ hebrew4christians.com
	Jehovah Jireh, Names of God by Marilyn Hickey 2009
March 28:	Yeshua ha-Mashiach @ hebrew4christians.com
April 2:	Jehovah Rapha @ Biblehub.org
April 4:	Rhema @ Wikipedia.org
April 20:	Yeshua ha-Mashiach @ hebrew4christians.com
April 25:	Rhema @ Wikipedia.org

May 3:	El Roi @ hebrew4christians.com
	Jehovah Shammah, Names of God by Marilyn Hickey 2009
	Jehovah Jireh, Names of God by Marilyn Hickey 2009
May 6:	Yeshua ha-Mashiach @ hebrew4christians.com
May 13:	Jehovah Jireh, Names of God by Marilyn Hickey, 2009
May 30:	Yeshua ha-Mashiach @ hebrew4christians.com
June 2:	Jehovah Rapha, Names of God by Marilyn Hickey 2009
June 6:	Yeshua ha-Mashiach @ hebrew4christians.com
June 8:	Yeshua ha-Mashiach @ hebrew4christians.com
June 13:	El Olam @ hebrews4christians.com
June 29:	Jehovah Rapha, Names of God by Marilyn Hickey 2009
July 2:	Jehovah Shammah, Names of God by Marilyn Hickey 2009
July 8:	Jehovah Rapha, Names of God by Marilyn Hickey 2009
July 13:	Jehovah Machaseh @ Biblehub.org
	Jehovah Rapha, Names of God by Marilyn Hickey 2009
	Jehovah Shammah, Names of God by Marilyn Hickey 2009
August 14:	Yeshua ha Mashiach @ hebrew4christians.com
August 15:	Hey @ hebrew4christians.com
	Jehovah Jireh, Names of God by Marilyn Hickey 2009
	Jehovah Rapha, Names of God by Marilyn Hickey 2009
	Yahweh @ Biblehub.org
August 22:	Yeshua ha Mashiach @ hebrew4christians.com
August 31:	Yeshua ha Mashiach @ hebrew4christians.com
September 3:	Yahweh @ knowingthebible.net

September 13:	Jehovah Rapha @ Biblehub.org
September 14:	Jehovah Rohi, Names of God by Marilyn Hickey 2009
September 26:	Rhema @ Wikipedia.org
October 3:	Jehovah Nissi, Names of God by Marilyn Hickey 2009 Tizrah @ Wikipedia.org
November 3:	Jehovah M'Kaddesh, Names of God by Marilyn Hickey 2009
November 23:	Yeshua ha-Mashiach @ hebrew4christians.com
November 25:	Yeshua ha-Mashiach @ hebrew4christians.com
November 28:	Jehovah Rohi, Names of God by Marilyn Hickey 2009
December 8:	Jehovah Jireh, Names of God by Marilyn Hickey 2009 Jehovah Yatsar @biblehub.org Jehovah Shammah, Names of God by Marilyn Hickey 2009
December 9:	Jehovah Yatsar @biblehub.org
December 10:	Jehovah Nissi, Names of God by Marilyn Hickey 2009
December 14:	Jehovah Jireh, Names of God by Marilyn Hickey 2009
December 26:	Jehovah Rapha, Names of God by Marilyn Hickey 2009

Lightning Source UK Ltd.
Milton Keynes UK
UKHW021458060622
404004UK00009B/2031